CONSERVATIVE SOLUTION

CONSERVATIVE SOLUTION

THE WORLDVIEW

OF A SPORTS

FANATIC FROM

WISCONSIN

PAUL M. GALLAGHER

Conservative Solution © 2024 by Paul M. Gallagher.

All rights reserved. No portion of this book may be reproduced, stored in a retrieval system, or transmitted in any form or by any means, except for brief quotations in printed reviews, without prior permission from the author. Requests for information should be addressed to the author.

Contact author at paul@conservativesolution.com

ISBN: 978-1-7352823-2-9 *(paperback)*
      978-1-7352823-3-6 *(epub)*

All Scripture quotations, unless otherwise indicated, are taken from the Holy Bible, New International Version®, NIV® Copyright © 1973, 1978, 1984, 2011 by Biblica, Inc.® Used by permission. All rights reserved worldwide.

Scripture quotations marked "KJV" are taken from the King James Version. Public domain.

Contents

Preface — 7

1. State of the Union 2022 — 15
2. Political Parties — 23
3. Liberalism — 43
4. Overview of the Issues — 52
5. Political Correctness — 62
6. Equality and Entitlement — 86
7. Feminism — 99
8. Sustainability — 113
9. Rewind: Our Nation's Leaders — 134
10. Terrorism — 157
11. Illegal Immigration and Drug Violence — 179
12. Homosexuality and the Gay Agenda — 186

13. Same-Sex "Marriage"	222
14. Abortion	237
15. Racism and All Lives Matter	242
16. False Teachers	245
17. Mental Illness	266
18. Firearms: Our Second Amendment Rights	271
19. Crime and Law Enforcement	296
20. Public Education	307
21. Christianity	315
Conclusion	357
God's "Epilogue: Invitation and Warning"	361
Recommended Resources	365
Endnotes	369
Bibliography	381

Preface

I'm a lifelong sport fanatic (understatement) and from 1986, age twelve, an avid follower of world, national, and local news and current events. This book "fields" both passions. (See what I did there?) Bear with me as I primarily discuss world events from 2012–2022 as we head into the 2024 presidential election. (Go Donald J. Trump!) There's a lot of ground to cover as I share how I came to form my worldview.

Three events stand out in my memory from year (1986): The Iran Contra Affair, the Space Shuttle Challenger's tragic explosion, and the New York Mets winning the World Series.

> *Side Note:* I'd much rather see the New York Mets win a World Series than the Chicago Cubs (which unfortunately happened in 2016)! Not holding my breath that the Milwaukee Brewers will win a World Series in my lifetime. But I have seen the Green Bay Packers win championships (1997 and 2011) and the Milwaukee Bucks (2021). I'm thankful for that.

My news gathering is from every angle: conservative, liberal, and everything in between. I daily visit Fox News, MSN, *Milwaukee Journal Sentinel*, and *The Vail Daily*, and from every mode: print, radio, television, internet, and from conversations with people in my life. I read the greatest victories to the worst of human behaviors. The worst includes trade-offs people make and the trends people follow that consume their true identities and warp their true purposes. There is truth in this world.

Conservative Solution examines

- the issues that are accelerating the decline of our nation's and people's political, moral, mental, emotional, and spiritual sanctity,

- the underlying erosion of values and principles that once supported the founding of our nation, and

- the ever-expanding chasm dividing our citizens into two fiercely opposing teams, formerly united as one league of patriots (not the New England team).

The foundation and framework of this book are the themes of my 2012 to 2016 blog posts. *Conservative Solution* is the springboard from those posts, showing evidence of our nation's and citizen's further spiraling demise (2023). This world truly is insane and getting worse by the day. Just look at the daily news headlines and social media. However, there is good news (the gospel) that I'll share throughout this book.

The original blog title was "The Ogg Blogg," which holds a funny backstory. In high school, early 1990s, I was a lanky white kid playing JV basketball and averaging two points and rebounds per game (not exaggerating), much like a gentleman by the name of Alan Ogg (University of Alabama-Birmingham) in his NBA run. My JV teammate Mike liked to hang posters of college basketball players in his gym locker, and nicknamed me "Ogg," which stuck. Thirty-plus years since, most of my classmates still call me Ogg. The nickname has stuck for all these years. I like it.

Years later, I became friends with another Mike. We met through the Wisconsin Jaycees organization. He liked and supported my views on US foreign policy and jokingly named me "The Solution." Six months into my blogging, I changed the blog title to "Conservative Solution." The title is fitting. I firmly believe in the singular solution, which this book shares. The one solution is the only solution that can reverse America's fatal condition and trajectory. The only solution that can restore and reunite our citizens as one team.

Our youth, based on my extensive baseball and softball coaching for years, are by far the most impacted by the issues that now rage more loudly and threateningly of our freedoms and our national and individual stability and clarity. The line between right and wrong is grossly blurred, and in some areas totally erased. What remains of that line emits the overpowering stench of indifference and self-entitlement that persistently tantrums, *My way! Me first! I deserve whatever I want.* That mindset is now referred to as "woke entitlement." We've become a woke nation—not good. As they say, "Go woke, go broke!"

Because I'm a firm, diehard sports enthusiast, I peppered (sport term) this book's content with a bit of sports commentary. The snapshot of *Conservative Solution* can be viewed as a baseball team of increasingly combative players (US citizens). They do not get along. The team members chose sides and drew a line (and then more lines, which became ditches) down centerfield, and an ugly war of countless arguments ensued. Will we one day have another civil war? I'm starting to wonder, with all the hatred and bickering in this country.

What's at stake? What's been at stake since our founding freedom on July 4, 1776? America's defining values and principles we once stood strong on, deeply rooted in, and pledged our united alliance as "one nation under God, indivisible [inseparable] with liberty and justice for all."[1] Now we see gods—political parties, environmental wackos—being worshiped, liberty under attack, and minimal justice.

Since that date in 1776, we've fought and won wars and battles against opposing nations and lost countless loved ones across the now 247 years. Why? To preserve the one viewpoint that had initially united us and had grown us into the most formidable and blessed team [nation] on Earth.

Conservative Solution addresses many issues that began and continue to divide us. I often think of five major league players that are the greatest threats to our protection and well-being as a country of communities, marriages, families, and individuals:

- abortion
- Islam
- the gay agenda
- persistent attacks against our Second Amendment—the right to bear arms

- unsecured southern border

These topics can be summed up as follows:

- Abortion is murder.
- Islam is evil.
- The gay agenda is perverted.
- An unsecured southern border is costly and dangerous.
- The Second Amendment is a blessing.

Conservative Solution is inlaid with facts and resources that reiterate the fallibility of human viewpoints. If I were to list a #6 above, it would be "election integrity." Many of us continue to believe we know more than the head coach in this game. Our varying perspectives of "what we should do" can only, by human nature, divide and destroy unity from the top down:

adult individuals
marriages (1 man + 1 woman)
children
communities
local and state leaders and government
national leaders and federal government

The pages of this book concisely present the divided human viewpoints alongside the one and only perspective that holds the power to fully guard, realign, and reunite mankind and thereby fulfill our purpose for existence.

I'm grateful—so thankful—there's a proven solution. A conservative solution.

It's not too late; we're not yet completely self-destroyed, though we're looking grim and now unrecognizable, and many still offer themselves in service to our greatest enemy (Satan).

Conservative Solution consistently points to another book. A playbook. The only playbook of rules, principles, and strategies that guarantees unity and consistent wins, authored by the head coach of all coaches. The playbook's purpose is to fully unite us, ready us, and maintain our readiness under the head coach to win the ultimate and most important game of all: eternal life.

"We the people" must daily practice the details of that playbook in every circumstance and consistently consult with and follow the head coach: God. This plan is the only solution that will reunite us and sustain our power to defeat the shrewdest of all opponents in every circumstance. An opponent whose singular mission is to pull every person in the world to his side of the field (hell)—at all costs.

Every day is game day, and every moment is practice in staying fit to win.

Thank you for joining me in this locker room, where we'll rewind the film from 2012 forward and revisit the winning playbook. You will see soon how my worldview was formed.

PART 1

THE CORNERSTONES

CHAPTER 1

State of the Union 2022

Politics is an ugly game. We daily see proof of this on the news in the form of politicians colluding, criticizing, and complaining. Our federal government is more concerned with political correctness than defeating terrorists, securing the border, and defending the USA.

A prime example is Russian fighter jets flying near US naval ships. Why don't we shoot them down? Our weak military, also in crisis, is afraid to engage. The Heritage Foundation's 2022 year-end index indicates our military is "at significant risk of not being able to meet the demands of a single major regional conflict."[2] Contributing factors are our military presence spread across various engagements, a "recruitment crisis,"[3]—and the Biden administration's low budget for our military, "below the rate of inflation . . . a loss of \$59 billion in funding between 2018 and 2023."[4] The report summarizes the crisis as an "erosion of capacity, capability, and readiness"[5] that are especially significant in our

Navy and Air Force. We need a strong military to play defense. As they say in sports, defense wins championships.

Our military is no longer as feared as it once was. Our weak, liberal, immoral leaders from the highest level and down the chain of command are leading our country further down the road of decay and indistinction. Such administrations are void of what had set America apart as the greatest country in the world. Looking ahead, my vote for 2024 is on re-electing Donald J. Trump. The other candidates, in my opinion, are wasting their time in these presidential debates. Democrats want to imprison their political opponents, and that is not okay. This is the stuff of socialism. I pray for Mr. Trump.

The family of a Wisconsin friend, fearful about the direction our country is taking, has prepared to flee, if need be. I understand that fear in light of the state of our country's union—or rather disunion. Presidents Obama and Biden failed this country's four cornerstones, originally cemented to function truthfully and faithfully "in God We Trust," which would render us fruitful economically, militarily, socially, and morally. Tragically, our nation is continuing in the opposite direction of fruitful.

Economically, our deficit is now in excess of $33 trillion.[6] For perspective, consider the following numbers from just five years ago, 2018: $25 trillion.[7]

The projected 2023 net interest alone is an added $10.5 trillion![8]

During then-Sen. Barack Obama's 2008 campaign, he explained in a speech his challenge toward winning the votes of Pennsylvania's economically frustrated working-class people:

It's not surprising then that they get bitter, they cling to guns or religion or antipathy to people who aren't like them or anti-immigrant sentiment or anti-trade sentiment as a way to explain their frustrations.

Well, Mr. Obama, there's the Second Amendment to the US Constitution that states, "the right of the people to keep and bear Arms, shall not be infringed." I will continue to cling to my guns and Bible.

Without protecting and exercising our Second Amendment rights, how can we possibly defend our First Amendment rights?

I look forward to attending Colorado's gun shows with like-minded individuals. The persistence of Colorado and other liberal states' politicians' attacking the Second Amendment may result in gun shows soon becoming a thing of the past. We must protect the Second Amendment!

Militarily, we now allow gays to serve, which as a soldier friend of mine put it, "damages the morale of our troops." We are drastically cutting defense spending and playing games with Iran as they attempt to build a nuclear weapon. (Hint: sanctions do not work!) We are now more concerned about pronouns than safety. Please stop making the military a social experiment.

Socially, Obama hailed the US Supreme Courts' 2015 ruling that gay "marriage" is a legal right across the US and stated, "This ruling will strengthen all of our communities."[9] How do you strengthen communities by promoting sin? Biden took the issue a step further at the end of 2022 when he signed into law the same-sex marriage bill.[10] Where are the morals our country was founded on? What happened to our strong traditional families and values? Obama was a political opportunist and extremist and I believe he's pulling the strings behind the Biden administration. The backbone of society is the traditional family. A child needs a nurturing mother and a stern, protective, loving father. We owe that to our nation's youth.

Morally, beginning with the Clinton administration, our country took a nosedive. Our current administration (Biden) is intent on honoring, supporting, and promoting the gay agenda and the now "all-inclusive" immoral lifestyles represented by the ever-expending acronym that's currently "LGTBQIA2S+."

I miss the days of *Leave it to Beaver*. I understand that feminists won't like that comment. However, the husband should lead, provide, and protect his family. Dad Lives Matter.

Considering our nation's four cornerstones—economy, military, society, and morality—I don't blame my Wisconsin friend for prepping for the future. Occasionally, I watch *Doomsday Preppers*, a National Geographic series. The network's video ad synopsis for the show reads: "Follow a group of people as they obsessively prepare for apocalypse, each expecting the world to end in a different way, for a different reason, at a different time. ... From bunkers to fortified off-the-grid homesteads, see how these Doomsday Preppers go to extremes to make sure they are ready for just about anything."[11]

Preppers have constructed underground bunkers, stockpiled firearms, excess food supplies, and other essentials in the event of a natural disaster or civil unrest. And I cannot blame them.

In the past, I may have thought such prepping was out of paranoia. Now, not only do I understand their concerns but I'm considering doing some prepping. We each must be wise to take the safeguards we believe are necessary—not from a basis of fear of the future but of logic. For safe living in a continually declining society exercising God's gift of free will, He also gifted us with the ability to think and strategize logically. Have you prepped for the future we're headed toward? Stock up on water, canned goods, and other necessities, because our world has gone mad and is headed for doom. Globalists and Democrats cannot be trusted. A lot of the chaos we see today is intentional. They care about themselves, not the average American. It's about power, control, money.

I realize my liberal friends would call me paranoid and an extremist, but they cannot guarantee my future safety, nor are they responsible to do so. Consider the effect on daily survival brought about by World War I and II. Now is the time to prep.

Preparing for the practicalities of living through extraordinarily tough times is wise.

I believe in individual sufficiency, not government protection. We cannot trust the government anymore. It has turned against the American people, especially under the Biden administration.

Not only will we have dooming circumstances ahead but the other truth is that this life is temporary. In the end, the most critical "prepping" needed is for our eternal life and eternal home.

What the Bible says about fear, logic, wisdom, and the future:

Fear:

- "Do not worry about tomorrow, for tomorrow will worry about itself. Each day has enough trouble of its own" (Matthew 6:34).

- "Do not be anxious about anything, but in every situation, by prayer and petition, with thanksgiving, present your requests to God. And the peace of God, which transcends all understanding, will guard your hearts and your minds in Christ Jesus" (Philippians 4:6–7).

- "The Spirit God gave us does not make us timid, but gives us power, love and self-discipline" (2 Timothy 1:7).

Logic:

- "Whoever obeys his command will come to no harm, and the wise heart will know the proper time and procedure" (Ecclesiastes 8:5).

- "Do not conform to the pattern of this world, but be transformed by the renewing of your mind. Then you will be able to test and approve what God's will is—his good, pleasing and perfect will" (Romans 12:2).

- "Do your best to present yourself to God as one approved, a worker who does not need to be ashamed and who correctly handles the word of truth" (2 Timothy 2:15).

Wisdom:

- "Everyone who hears these words of mine and puts them into practice is like a wise man who built his house on the rock" (Matthew 7:24).

- "If any of you lacks wisdom, you should ask God, who gives generously to all without finding fault, and it will be given to you. But when you ask, you must believe and not doubt, because the one who doubts is like a wave of the sea, blown and tossed by the wind. That person should not expect to receive anything from the Lord. Such a person is double-minded and unstable in all they do" (James 1:5–8).

- "Be very careful, then, how you live—not as unwise but as wise, making the most of every opportunity, because the days are evil. Therefore do not be foolish, but understand what the Lord's will is" (Ephesians 5:15–17).

Future:

- "Do not let your hearts be troubled. You believe in God; believe also in me. My Father's house has many rooms; if that were not so, would I have told you that I am going there to prepare a place for you? And if I go and prepare a place for you, I will come back and take you to be with me that you also may be where I am. You know the way to the place where I am going" (John 14:1–4).

- "I have told you these things, so that in me you may have peace. In this world you will have trouble. But take heart! I have overcome the world" (John 16:33).

- "'What no eye has seen, what no ear has heard, and what no human mind has conceived'—the things God has prepared for those who love him" (1 Corinthians 2:9).

CHAPTER 2

Political Parties

Republican Party (GOP: Grand Old Party)

I no longer consider myself a Republican. I'm a conservative Christian independent. Both the Republican and Democratic parties continue to have their share of corruption. That being said, I do like what the GOP platform stands for:

> The Republican Party has always stood for freedom, prosperity, and opportunity. Today, as those principles come under attack from the far-left, we are engaged in a national effort to fight for our proven agenda, take our message to every American, grow the party, promote election integrity, and elect Republicans up and down the ballot. The principles of the Republican Party recognize the God-given liberties while promoting opportunity for every American.[12]

Gov. Andrew Cuomo of New York said about conservatives:

> Their problem is not me and Democrats, their problem is themselves. Who are they? Are they these extreme conservatives, who are right-to-life, pro-assault-weapon, anti-gay, is that who they are? Because if that is who they are, and if they are the extreme conservatives, they have no place in the state of New York. Because that is not who New Yorkers are.[13]

His comment shows what we're up against as conservatives. If you believe in the truth, the sanctity of life, the Second Amendment, and you oppose the gay agenda (which is an *agenda*), you'll be labeled "extreme" by liberals, which yet again reveals the hypocrisy. Leftists' bumper stickers are such messages as Coexist and Love Your Mother (Earth), and verbally they claim to be loving, tolerant, and inclusive, but demonstrate the opposite when their stance on cornerstone issues is challenged. In other words, leftists speak out of both sides of their mouths, showing that they only truly love and respect those who agree with their sinful, nonsensical viewpoints. Their worldview is warped, and if you disagree with their view, you'll be called names.

At the dawn of 2022, Gallup cited a nine-point "shift" in party preferences, stating "more US adults identifying as Democrats or leaning Democratic."[14] Pew Research's 2022 survey following the Supreme Court's overturn of Roe vs. Wade indicates that 62 percent of US adults believe that abortion should be legal.[15] Clearly, a majority of our nation has turned against their Maker and the truths of His Word that we are to live by. I do not understand how anyone can support the Democratic Party.

If you are living as a liberal and supporting liberalism, the urgent message of this book is for you to see all the ways Satan is deceiving you. You can see this when you compare the Word of God (shared throughout this book) to the issues shared throughout this book. Satan's sole mission is to "steal, kill, and destroy" (John 10:10)—by any and every means possible, which includes masking the eyes and ears of those who do not yet know Christ. God's Word to mankind is very clear (many passages) about the issues bringing down our nation, and the consequences of turning against Him and continuing to live in sin and promote issues that go directly against God's instructions and plans for mankind. This world is fallen.

Likewise, God's Word makes clear His instructions for how we all should be living and the eternal and present rewards for those who have faith in Him and abide by His Word.

I urge everyone to read the Bible references peppered throughout this book, which are only several of many. My hope is that the Bible references will help you to begin immersing your mind and heart in knowing God and His Word.

Believers, among God's instructions to us is to share the gospel of Jesus Christ (Mark 16:15), make disciples (Matthew 28:19), pray (Ephesians 16:18), and love our enemies and all people (Matthew 5:43–48).

Be diligent to pray for those who are deceived by Satan (liberals, progressives, Democrats). Pray that they will seek God and His Word and accept Jesus as their Savior. Time is running out. As related to sports, we're in the fourth quarter (football), the second half (basketball), the third period (hockey), and the late innings (baseball).

A tool used effectively by Satan is getting people to think they have plenty of time left in the game. The game is almost over, folks. I guess you could say it's time for the seventh-inning stretch!

Spiritual warfare is real and constantly at work.

The gospel message of Jesus Christ to all of mankind:

> Gospel is "the new goods" in three parts:
>
> (1) **God's design** of the universe to bring Him glory,
>
> (2) **our brokenness (sin)** in need of a Savior, and
>
> (3) **the solution**: His son, Jesus Christ who died as the penalty for our sins.

Democratic Party

The following excerpts from the "2020 Democratic Party Platform" document, highlight just a few of the numerous agendas "approved by the Democratic National Convention on August 18, 2020." As of this writing, the download can be found on their website.

Stated under "Civil Rights":

> Democrats are committed to ending discrimination on the basis of race, ethnicity, national origin, religion, language, gender, age, sexual orientation, gender identity, or disability status. We will appoint US Supreme Court justices and federal judges who look like America, are committed to the rule of law, will uphold individual civil

> rights and civil liberties as essential components of a free and democratic society, and will respect and enforce foundational precedents, including Brown v. Board of Education and Roe v. Wade.[16]

Under "Protecting Women's Rights":

> Like the majority of Americans, Democrats believe every woman should be able to access high-quality reproductive health care services, including safe and legal abortion. We oppose and will fight to overturn federal and state laws that create barriers to women's reproductive health and rights, including by repealing the Hyde Amendment and protecting and codifying the right to reproductive freedom.[17]

Since when was it a "constitutional right" (per the liberal populace) to mass-murder babies? Thankfully, the US Supreme Court overturned Roe v. Wade (June 24, 2022)—a stunning victory for the sanctity of life!

Abortion is murder.

We should protect life at every stage, from birth to natural death, from precious babies through old age.

Under "Supporting Faith and Service":

> Democrats celebrate America's history of religious pluralism and tolerance, and recognize the countless acts of service of our faith communities, as well as the paramount importance of maintaining the separation between church and state enshrined in our Constitution.[18]

First, there is nothing in our Constitution about the separation of church and state. That idea, phrase is a misnomer. The John Birch Society does a great job of sharing the Constitution, Bill of Rights, and Declaration of Independence.

Secondly, under that mythical separation of church and state, liberals want religion kept from politics and want their politics in our religion. But, apparently, their door only opens one way. The liberal view once again shows hypocrisy! Look at what happened with the Covid-19 outbreak; our government meddled in church affairs under the guise of "health concerns." Government: get out of the church!

Under "Democracy and Human Rights":

> Democrats believe that the United States has an urgent, moral obligation and strategic interest to help alleviate suffering around the globe.[19]

Democrats know nothing about "moral obligations." How many unborn babies have suffered during the course of abortion? According to the Guttmacher Institute's and Pew Research's latest reporting (2020), the number of abortions performed in the US was 930,160 in 2020,[20] an increase of 1.5 percent in only a one-year period![21] A 2023 report by World Population Review shows Washington D.C. with the highest percentage of abortion, followed by New York, New Jersey, and Maryland.[22] Thankfully, the US Supreme Court overturned Roe vs. Wade in 2022; however, the number of daily murders of children remains astronomical. This is not moral or acceptable. We should not promote death.

Abortion is murder.

The Democratic party's statement of "moral obligation" is yet another example of blatant hypocrisy as members of the party support pro-"choice"—which is actually pro-death—and pro-gay "marriage." These are immoral acts!

Stated under "Ending the Epidemic of Gun Violence":

> Gun violence is a public health crisis in the United States. ... We can and will make gun violence a thing of the past. ... Democrats will also ensure the Centers for Disease Control and Prevention have sufficient resources to study gun violence as a public health issue, including the ongoing health care, mental health, economic, and social costs that can affect survivors and their families for years.
>
> We will close the "Charleston loophole" and prevent individuals who have been convicted of hate crimes from possessing firearms. Democrats will ban the manufacture and sale of assault weapons and high capacity magazines. ... We will pass legislation requiring that guns be safely stored in homes. [23]

The liberal catch phrase is "gun violence," which you will find eight times in the platform document. The catch phrase is their efforts to seize our right to bear arms by pushing strict gun control. Liberals put way too much trust in government to protect us in times of uncertainty and trouble.

Gun control is people control.

You could confiscate every firearm in the world and still there will be evil acts. There are still knives, machetes, cars, and a host of other ways to commit evil acts—countless ways to harm another human being. The singular "gun problem" in America and our world sits in the human heart, which by nature of free will is "wicked" (Jeremiah 17:9).

Stated under "Combating The Climate Crisis and Pursuing Environmental Justice":

> Climate change is a global emergency. We have no time to waste in taking action to protect Americans' lives and futures. Like so many crises facing the United States, the impacts of climate change are not evenly distributed in our society or our economy. Communities of color, low-income families, and Indigenous communities have long suffered disproportionate and cumulative harm from air pollution, water pollution, and toxic sites.

An October 2022 article by *Time* magazine reported again on former US Secretary of State John Kerry's long-held liberal view that the US has "a moral obligation"[24] to act on climate change. So murder babies while recycling? Makes sense to me!

"Mother Earth" was created by God and will remain in His sovereign care until He alone makes change to Earth as He declared in Revelation 21. Just as He alone instantaneously spoke the earth and its elements into existence as He desired and designed.

The only climate to worry about is the climate in hell.

In my view, "climate change," is complete nonsense. Liberals use this terminology as a scare tactic to profit from and gain more political power. Power, money, control.

Just when I thought I could not be further astounded by the direction our country is headed, I watched the video of political commentator Thom Hartmann expressing his view that "climate change deniers" should be "in jail."[25] This reflects back to liberals' disdain for President Trump. They want to imprison their political opponents. Get ready for what is coming: imprisonment of political opponents (conservatives) and the persecution of Christians.

Conservatives have indeed been jailed for adhering to their beliefs rather than folding to "political correctness." Kentucky county clerk Kim Davis was jailed in 2015 for "refusing to issue same-sex marriage licenses to gay couples."[26] I had to remind myself that God is sovereign. Until Christ returns and defeats evil, such lunacy will happen. Democrats again want to imprison those with opposing views (Kim Davis, Donald J. Trump, J6 individuals, Christians). Is this Venezuela or the US?

God is faithful to carry out the good work He began in believers! (Philippians 1:6).

When we give into our own human thinking—as opposed to following God's plan—we quickly see the destructive results. Liberal thinking is human thinking that is void of God's Word, which results in a lack of common sense, flawed thinking, and sordid, destructive, evil thinking and acts.

Picture what I refer to as Liberal Land: men having sexual relations with other men; women aborting their babies; sexually transmitted diseases (e.g. monkeypox, HIV, AIDS) spreading among the population. Below are staggering numbers from 2020 published by the World Health Organization (not exactly an organization I trust) on sexually transmitted infections—and these are just the numbers that have been reported!

- More than 1 million sexually transmitted infections (STIs) are acquired every day worldwide.

- Each year there are an estimated 374 million new infections with 1 of 4 curable.

- More than 500 million people 15–49 years are estimated to have a genital infection.[27]

Yet, conservatives are mocked and imprisoned. Liberal Land is a death sentence—not "sustainable"—a term liberals love to spout. Their agenda is a deadly agenda.

Tea Party and Libertarian Party

The Tea Party are those who possess a strong belief in the Judeo-Christian values embedded in our great founding documents. We believe the responsibility of our beloved nation is etched upon the hearts of true Patriots from every race, religion, national origin, and walk of life sharing a common belief in the values which made and keep our beloved nation great. This belief led to the creation of the modern-day Tea Party.

We stand by the Constitution as inherently conservative.

We serve as a beacon to the masses that have lost their way, a light illuminating the path to the original intentions of our Founding Fathers.[28]

I've come to realize I'm much more Tea Party-aligned than Libertarian-aligned. I once had a conversation with a gentleman at work who told me he is a Libertarian and did not fully support or agree with the Tea Party, and in particular Ted Cruz. The Tea Party is viewed by liberals as extremist, simply because the Tea Party believes in conservatism and our US Constitution. It's unreal how our world is turning immorality into normalcy and categorizing what is moral and decent as hateful and bigoted. I really like the Tea Party platform. Conservatism and the US Constitution are good—morally, ethically, and logically sound.

The conversation with my coworker started because I had seen in the local newspaper a picture of him with Rep. Ron Paul (R-TX) at a fundraiser. Out of curiosity, I had asked him about his political and social views. He had some valid points about the economy, but on some of his social views, I took issue. One thing he shared stands out in my mind as total nonsense: "My truth may be my truth, but it may not be your truth."

Truth is truth as fact is fact.

Ron Paul also shared that while he believes abortion is wrong, he believes that the differing view may be someone else's truth. The truth is that abortion is wrong. Abortion is murder. That is *the* Word of God truth.

Such divided thinking is known as *moral relativism*—"the idea that there are no absolute rules to determine whether something is right or wrong."[29]

Who better to know right from wrong than the Creator Himself? God is truth incarnate—"the way, and the truth, and the life" (John 14:16). He is undivided and unchanging (Hebrews 13:8). His "do not" list is not long but very clear and purposed for our utmost protection and provision. Why? Because of His great love for us, the love that sacrificed His only Son for the forgiveness of sin.

Wrong is wrong as determined by God.

I'm guilty of many wrongs (a long list!), and that's where repentance and faith come in. I'm so grateful to God for His love and His Son, Jesus Christ, and the hope we have, by faith, in Him. What hope do unbelievers have?

To know what is wrong and right, simply read His Word, the Bible. His Word is direct and includes examples (and some crazy but true stories, e.g. Jonah) that make very clear what is wrong and what is right.

After the conversation with the coworker, I read the Libertarian platform. The excerpts below are among the many that cause me concern.

- Consenting adults should be free to choose their own sexual practices and personal relationships. Until such time as the government stops its illegitimate practice of marriage licensing, such licenses must be granted to all consenting adults who apply.[30]

In other words, God's directives mean nothing and I can have whatever I want—for example, a male and a female spouse can simultaneously date others and have sex with others? Live and let live? Whatever I want in life is what I should get? Not according to God's directives meant to protect us and honor Him in holiness. He has given us absolute directives of morality in His Word that He expects us to follow because He loves us and wants His utmost best for us. (Speaking of "utmost," I recommend the book *My Utmost for His Highest* by Oswald Chambers.)

> The Libertarian Party supports the decriminalization of prostitution. We assert the right of consenting adults to provide sexual services to clients for compensation, and the right of clients to purchase sexual services from consenting sex workers."[31]

Immoral! Sex was created and sanctioned by God as a holy union between husband and wife (1 Corinthians 6:15–18), and God defined the human body as His "temple" of dwelling in us and that we are to "honor God with our bodies" (1 Corinthians 6:19–20), "holy and pleasing to God—this is your true and proper worship" (Romans 12:2).

> "Each person is the presumptive owner of his or her own body."[32]

To promote and legalize prostitution is disgusting.

While the Libertarian platform makes no direct mention of abortion, their statement above implies the right to choose abortion. What about unborn babies' right to *continue* living as a human being? Abortion is murder and the Bible states that murder is a sin. For the same reason, we are not to take our own lives (suicide). God, not us, has predetermined the number of our days as individuals (Psalm 139:16; Job 14:5). I pray for those who are suicidal.

Conversely, here's the Tea Party's definition and purpose:

> The Tea Party is a grassroots movement calling awareness to any issue which challenges the security, sovereignty, or domestic tranquility of our beloved nation, the United States of America.

Conservative Solution

As a national effort we have a choir of voices declaring America must stand on the values which made us great, only then will the politically blind see and deaf hear![33] The issues I feel most strongly about, I've underlined:

- <u>Illegal aliens are here illegally</u>.
- Pro-domestic employment is indispensable.
- <u>A strong military is essential</u>.
- Special interests must be eliminated.
- <u>Gun ownership is sacred</u>.
- <u>Government must be downsized</u>.
- <u>The national budget must be balanced</u>.
- Deficit spending must end.
- Bailout and stimulus plans are illegal.
- <u>Reducing personal income taxes is a must</u>.
- Reducing business income taxes is mandatory.
- Political offices must be available to average citizens.
- Intrusive government must be stopped.
- <u>English as our core language is required</u>.
- <u>Traditional family values are encouraged</u>.[34]
- I agree with Judeo-Christian values, our nation's founding documents, our Constitution as inherently conservative, a strong military, gun ownership as sacred,

balancing the national budget, traditional family values, and English as our native, ongoing core language. These are good things!

I put little faith in people, and especially politicians. People will lie and live lives of greed and corruption, cheating and stealing to "get ahead" in life. By nature, we are all sinful. Out of God's great love for us, "not wanting anyone to perish, but everyone to come to repentance" (2 Peter 3:9), He sent His sinless Son, Jesus, to Earth to pay the penalty of death for all sin, for all people, for all time, that "whoever believes in him shall not perish but have eternal life" (John 3:16). Jesus rose from death to new life, showing His unmatched power while demonstrating that those who accept God's gift of salvation by faith alone are spiritually raised to new life in Him. That new life is not only eternal life but new life in the way we choose to live out the rest of our days on this Earth. To be made new in Christ is to have the desire to please God by living "righteously"—right living—according to God's Word. Of course we continue to sin as human beings, but once saved by faith, believers are to "continue to work out your salvation" (Philippians 2:12) by ongoing obedience to God's Word. We cannot be perfect but we can be obedient to God in right living.

Jesus is the conservative solution, defining the point of this book.

Once this nation is humbled and repents of sin, the *right* (righteous) political leaders will be voted into office and we may then see other victories—as we saw with the overturned Roe vs. Wade. We know, though, from the Bible's final book, Revelation, that this world will grow worse in every regard; however, we can choose to help our country by honoring God: upholding the Second Amendment, returning to traditional family values as the only moral model, firmly unaccepting gay "marriage" and murdering unborn babies. We can pay our debts and get economically back on track while also restoring the strength of our military to protect our nation.

I urge you to read the Bible daily to know God, His great love, mercies, and justice, and His purpose and plan for mankind and how to carry out His plan.

I encourage you to become knowledgeable of other political parties, including the Constitution Party, Conservative Party, Socialist Party (but aren't Democrats essentially socialists?), and Reform Party (think Ross Perot, 1992 and 1996). It's important to be informed.

Regardless of where you stand politically, please do your research to know the issues and candidates rather than blindly following what you hear from the media. The media is *not* trustworthy. You will not find truth from mainstream media (CNN, MSNBC, Fox News, etc.) or social media (Twitter, Facebook, etc.). Such outlets have fixed agendas.

Why do we have only Democrat and Republican presidential debates?

Regardless of your political party or position, the bottom line is unchanging and the most important: the greatest authority over all things, all of mankind, all of life and eternity is God our Creator, the King of Kings who speaks to us on all issues.

What the Bible says about affiliations:

- "Do not be misled: 'Bad company corrupts good character'" (1 Corinthians 15:33).

- "Do not be yoked together with unbelievers. For what do righteousness and wickedness have in common? Or what fellowship can light have with darkness?" (2 Corinthians 6:14).

- "Walk with the wise and become wise, for a companion of fools suffers harm" (Proverbs 13:20).

- "You must not associate with anyone who claims to be a brother or sister but is sexually immoral or greedy, an idolater or slanderer, a drunkard or swindler. Do not even eat with such people" (1Corinthians 5:11).

PART 2

LIBERAL AGENDA

CHAPTER 3

Liberalism

Are you familiar with Occupy Wall Street (OWS)? The protest movement to "fight back against the richest 1% of people that are writing the rules of an unfair global economy" began on Wall Street, quickly gained momentum around the world but survived for only fifty-nine days. As of this writing, the website still stands, from which I pulled the following excerpt:

> Occupy Wall Street is a people-powered movement that began on September 17, 2011 in Liberty Square in Manhattan's Financial District, and has spread to over 100 cities in the United States and actions in over 1,500 cities globally. #ows is fighting back against the corrosive power of major banks and multinational corporations over the democratic process, and the role of Wall Street in creating an economic collapse that has caused the greatest recession in generations. The movement is inspired by popular uprisings in Egypt and Tunisia, and aims to fight back against the richest 1% of people that are writing the

rules of an unfair global economy that is foreclosing on our future.[35]

OWS wanted an economic collapse. They wanted socialism rather than capitalism. The real eye-opener for me was learning that OWS was associated with the Arab Spring (anti-government protests) in Egypt and Tunisia. Always look into the fine print of who's associating with whom.

While I was okay with Muammar Gaddafi no longer serving as Libya's dictator, those who captured and killed him were Islamic extremists. OWS was a threat to the region, along with the still-active Muslim Brotherhood, Egypt's oldest and largest Islamist organization who remains a threat to the region, a threat to the state of Israel, and a threat to the security of the United States.

Wake up to the dangers of Islam, the *Qur'an*, and Sharia Law.

Advocates for Islam and *political correctness* claim that Islam is a religion of peace but in truth is everything opposite of peace. Islam seeks world domination through manipulation and violence. Please read the website Understanding the Threat.

OWS's reference to "the richest 1% of people" is the typical class warfare schpiel (Yiddish). To OWSers and others who feel entitled: Maybe the wealthy one percent got where they are by hard work and entrepreneurship. For people who inherit their wealth, I would rather their inheritance be protected from government taxation by cronies like President Biden and former House Speaker Nancy Pelosi. Wealth is a good thing. It creates jobs and opportunities.

When an individual works hard in a moral and ethical field, by such means they're entitled to enjoy the money and success they earned that placed them in that one percent. Such opportunities to work hard and become successful are strong, fundamental threads of America's founding fabric. High earners have earned their high pay. They deserve what they work hard to earn. One of our nation's founding principles that has made our country the greatest on Earth is freedom of enterprise—"free enterprise"—to pursue our best and highest potentials as unique individuals. Work is a good thing!

> *Side Note:* If it weren't for the one percent, I most likely would not have a job here in Colorado. Wealthy consumers pay my salary because they desire services my employer provides. Thank you, one-percenters! Free enterprise creates jobs! Celebrate the rich!

As you probably know, Mr. Obama, in contrast to the fundamentals of free enterprise, was a community organizer who had connections with ACORN, a union-loving, capitalism-hating radical group pushing for liberal economic and social policies, focused on organizing protests and supporting socialist ballot initiatives. They disbanded in 2010 due to accusations of voter fraud and condoning illegal behaviors![36] I recommend you read about the late Saul Alinsky, referred to as "the father of community organizing." His book *Rules for Radicals* is dedicated to Lucifer! Read it to become further educated about people who salivate for power and thereby won't play nice: Mr. Obama, the Clintons, the Bidens, and their socialist cronies (George Soros, Bill Gates, Klaus Schwab) rooted in their left-wing ideology. Do your research on these people. They have ill intentions.

Evidence proves there truly is good versus evil at work in this world.

Likeminded were the misplaced radicals and socialists of the Occupy movement. Instead of protesting hard-working Americans, they needed to return to their homes and become valuable members of society by getting jobs and paying taxes. These protesters really need to get a life. And a job.

Those who do not like true freedom, opportunity, and hard work should visit socialist countries to experience the tragic ramifications of failing socialist societies. Just look at Venezuela, for example.

> *Side Note to Liberals:* I've heard that Canada offers universal health care, and Mexico offers great employment opportunities. I wouldn't move to Mexico even if I landed a job paying $500,000 a year. There's corruption, drug violence, and poverty. The police are corrupt in Mexico and the drug cartels run the country.

I encourage you to read the article "City of Madison Thanks the Occupy Movement" by Christian Schneider.[37]

Take a look at all the Democrats who supported the OWS movement, including President Obama! The Democratic Party opposes efforts to give additional tax cuts to the wealthiest Americans. This opposition is at the expense of our middle class because the wealthy provide high-paying jobs by investing in new technologies and projects, thereby investing in our nation's future. Unfortunately, a majority of the American people gave Obama a second term (2012). I was upset when he won in 2012.

Liberalism

A Presbyterian minister here in Colorado posted a weekly current events article in the *Vail Daily*. I often responded by email to him. In an early 2012 article, he agreed with President Obama's State of the Union Address regarding "fairness" between the rich and poor. My viewpoint was that the then-president was asking the rich to give to the poor. While I agree with that view in principle, and would like to see the wealthy give more to the poor, I do not agree that the wealthy are *obligated* to do so. They earned their money and have every right to manage their expenditures as they desire.

The Presbyterian minister's column implied that he believed in social justice from a liberal worldview. He's what I consider a "liberal Christian"—a phrase that, in my view, is an oxymoron. A true Christian cannot believe in liberal causes, such as so-called "social justice" that's moving our nation's freedom into the prison of socialism, and the liberal causes of gay "marriage" and abortion. Therefore, a minister who *claims* Christianity as their faith but promotes liberal causes is what the Bible calls a false teacher—apostate. This gentleman was an apostate.

Apostates must be called out on their false, deceptive teachings. Such teachings are anything that goes against the written Word of God. Speaking out to false teachers against their teaching, by stating Scripture, is part of God's commission to believers.

> Elders who are sinning you [believers] are to reprove before everyone, so that the others may take warning. (1 Timothy 5:20)

We need pastors, business leaders, politicians (don't laugh!), and others to stand strong for truth. If teaching doesn't align with

God's Word—according to your own reading and studying the Word rather than simply believing what you hear—that's false teaching. Two of many false teachers are Rob Bell and Joel Osteen.

Socialists who are in the public eye, like Pope Francis and Bernie Sanders (I would roll my eyes when I heard "Feel the Bern" during his 2020 presidential run), support taking from the wealthy to give to the poor. What then is the motivation for people to work, to be innovative in creating products, and to establish independent businesses that benefit society? When socialism reigns, motivation, innovation, and individualism are lost. Considering how many young Americans prefer socialism is scary. You would in fact "Feel the Bern" if we elected a socialist as president. You'd "Feel the Bern" right in your pocketbook! I believe that our liberal public education system, especially at the college level, is a tremendous influence over our young people. Considering that our up-and-coming generation will become the leaders—from parenting to political, social, and educational leadership—is frightening for the future of our nation. We must ground our children and students in the conservation solution.

A look at income tax: I believe in a flat ten percent tax. If an individual earns $1 million for the year, he pays a $100 thousand tax. If an individual makes $100 thousand for the year, he pays a $10 thousand tax. And so forth. That's fair across the board for all Americans—rich, poor, and everyone in-between.

This current fiscal mess was brought on by those who are supposedly trying to keep our country from going off the cliff. Barney Frank, where are you?

Our nation is in deep trouble: homosexuality running rampant; ISIS on the move in the Middle East; the traditional family under attack; and our Second Amendment rights perpetually targeted. No politician or party is going to save us. There's only one solution—the conservative solution. As much as I want Donald J. Trump to win in 2024, he can only help the country, not save it.

Liberals appear blind to the destruction of our society as they gain victory in getting their perverted and politically-correct way. As this downward direction continues, it's not improbable to imagine ISIS coming into America and throwing homosexuals off rooftops—as they have in the Middle East. Our 2015 and 2016 news was a firehose of headlines reporting ISIS throwing Middle Eastern homosexuals off rooftops. This has happened! They're still holding strong to that means as their solution to make an impact against homosexuality. A May 8, 2023, article reporting Saudi Tourism Authority welcoming LGBTQ visitors into their country also stated:

> Jihadis and opposition figures have taken the opportunity to condemn the rulers of Saudi Arabia for promoting immorality, while supporters of the Islamic State (ISIS) suggested that execution of homosexuals by throwing them off high buildings was the practice to follow.[38]

Once our nation is prohibited by law from our right to bear arms, ISIS will have more impunity to harm our citizens! There will be nobody to stop ISIS! Oh, the irony of liberalism. ISIS coming to our shores, targeting areas where homosexuality is approved, encouraged, and legalized, like California and in particular San Francisco, is not unimaginable. Coexisting around the globe are liberals, communists, socialists, and Islamists with agendas to end democracy, and in insatiable greed for power and wealth by any immoral and unethical means, wanting to destroy America as the greatest nation, wanting to destroy freedom to pursue the American dream, entrepreneurship, and the right to openly serve God. Their end goal is strictly to gain the power of money and the reign of politics to dictate, which begins with establishing socialism—the next step toward communism.

As an American, conservative Christian, I believe we must stand immovable and fight for a strong democracy, strong military, strong economy, and strong traditional families, and fully return to "in God we trust." The Liberal agenda has proven to be against these. The mindset is anti-Christian, anti-military, anti-capitalism, and anti-traditional family. Liberalism doesn't work.

What the Bible says about standing firm, overcoming, and persevering:

Standing firm:

- "My dear brothers and sisters, stand firm. Let nothing move you. Always give yourselves fully to the work of the Lord, because you know that your labor in the Lord is not in vain" (**1 Corinthians 15:58).**

Overcoming:

- "Everyone born of God overcomes the world. This is the victory that has overcome the world, even our faith. Who is it that overcomes the world? Only the one who believes that Jesus is the Son of God" (John 5:4–5).

Persevering:

- "Since we are surrounded by such a great cloud of witnesses, let us throw off everything that hinders and the sin that so easily entangles. And let us run with perseverance the race marked out for us" (Hebrews 12:1).

CHAPTER 4

Overview of the Issues

America was made great due to our individual, commercial, religious, and societal freedoms, founded and fought for since the Mayflower ported in Plymouth Bay, Massachusetts in 1620. We became known as "the land of opportunity"—not handouts. Issues threatening to extinguish all that made America the greatest land are found in the *liberal political agenda.*

Abortion is murder, whether on-demand or not. Liberal individuals declare that abortion is a right, yet a number of those individuals oppose the death penalty. To oppose one's own beliefs is nonsensical.

> **To take a life is to take a life, regardless of the means and purpose!**

Taking a life is only warranted in hostile circumstances of law enforcement, self-defense, and war against evil (like ISIS, al-Qaeda, etc.).

Overview of the Issues

The Affordable Care Act (Obamacare) is by name a lie. The act is neither affordable nor sustainable. Many businesses are irrefutably crippled (some irreparably) by the act's mandate and threat of penalties! What does this say about "free" commerce?!

> The Affordable Care Act requires employers with 50 or more full-time equivalent employees to provide health coverage to at least 95% of full-time employees and sets a minimum baseline of coverage and affordability. Employers who do not comply face annual penalties if any of their employees end up qualifying for premium tax credits (subsidies) in the marketplace.[39]

Government involvement in health care is one of the many hammers abolishing our freedoms. Stay out of the private sector!

Through research, I learned that despite Mr. Obama's promise (as president) that rates would go down, health care premiums increased significantly. Like wage setting belongs to the private sector—the people—so do our health care coverage decisions. For the government to push otherwise is to push socialism onto our democratic nation.

A federal tax increase is not the answer to our country's current $33-plus trillion and compounding debt. There is no sign of reduction. A tax increase is unacceptable. The solution is to cut waste, fraud, and other economic abuses that will *save* taxpayers trillions of dollars. Our debt is irresponsible.

We need *common sense* economic reform, which starts with our willingness to stand against entitlements. No more handouts. Force people to work.

I believe that a majority of people receiving food stamps, for example, are capable of working and should be working rather than relying on, and taking advantage of, hard-working, tax-paying citizens to support them. The lazy rely on the hard-working. This isn't right.

Same-sex "marriage" is not marriage, it is perversion. In same-sex marriage, who is the husband and who is the wife? Neither. Who is the father and who is the mother? Neither. How do they conceive children naturally? They cannot. This disobedience to God must end.

> **Marriage is the union of one man and one woman and is the backbone of a strong society.**

Common Core, like all other education plans, should solely be the decision of school boards with parents' informed input, as it was when American public education was the envy of the world. Originally, forty-six states adopted Common Core. Surprisingly but thankfully, many of those educators came to see the absurdity of the methodology, and at this writing, sixteen states are repealing or have successfully repealed the standards.[40]

We need more conservatives on school boards and in our classrooms protecting our youth—our nation's future—from ideologies and methodologies that brainwash. We must return to

- *common sense* over common core,
- accurate history, including creation facts rather than nonsensical evolution theories,
- God and prayers central in our schools,

- American patriotism—our nation as the greatest on earth,
- allegiance to our flag,
- our Constitution,
- our Bill of Rights,
- teaching truth about the liberal agenda, environmentalism, Islam, and all other issues that twist and abandon God's Word and His divinity and holiness as the Creator of all things
- the fundamentals of math, science, social studies, English, physical education, and practical life skills such as laundry, cooking, budgeting, job interviewing, and computer basics.

If schools are to survive, much less thrive, vouchers are necessary to motivate schools to succeed.

Homeschooling is in rapid rise due to school failure by the following:

- government involvement, insisting schools teach and encourage ungodly world views that have now successfully erased fundamental boundaries— examples: a male is still a male and a female is still a female; we don't get to choose "what" we are—God does; evolution and the rewriting of history in favor of lies based on living "politically correct,"
- banning the mention of God and the practice of prayer in favor of inviting and sanctioning evil ideology that's at the core of liberalism, and

- parents ill-equipped to teach formal school and feeling forced to take on that added responsibility to protect their children physically, mentally, emotionally, and spiritually.

> **A nation is in crisis when parents feel they must protect their children from schools!**

National Defense

Our government's role is not to *dictate* but to *defend*.

An essential role of government is to keep us safe militarily rather than pouring our money and time into handouts, unlimited unemployment benefits, and food stamps to people who are fully capable of working.

1. **US Foreign Policy**

    The solution to US foreign policy issues is

    - securing our borders,
    - peace through strength,
    - eliminating threats overseas by reattaining our superior air power,
    - supporting Israel,
    - limiting monetary foreign assistance (Ukraine funding must end)—we need those funds to support our military and pay against our insanely huge deficit, and

- defunding the U.N.

2. **Amnesty for illegal aliens** should be discouraged because "illegal" still fundamentally means "illegal"—against the law. Yet liberal federal administrations are bent on turning a blind eye to law. Immigrants who do not go through our US due process for citizenship are law-breakers.

- I respect foreigners who take the lawful route, work, pay taxes, and learn the English language. Props to them and welcome to the United States!

- Every time our government grants amnesty to lawbreakers is a slap in the face to every immigrant who lawfully obtained citizenship, often at great expense.

We must prosecute criminals to the full extent of the law. Liberal prosecutors fail to protect society. George Soros-appointed DAs are a threat to our safety.

3. **The Iran nuclear deal** was a dangerous agreement, threatening not just our national security but Israel's. Iran has close ties to Syria, Russia, and terrorist organizations like Hamas and Hezbollah. Fortunately, in 2018, then-president Donald Trump withdrew the US from the deal and imposed harsh sanctions that are still in effect at this writing.

- **No nukes for terrorists.**

Planned Parenthood—As of January 19, 2023, we saw greater strides toward defunding this mass murderer. Why should our tax dollars partake in funding murder?! They should not! The mass murder of unborn children can be viewed as history's longest-running pandemic—far more extensive and evil than any virus pandemic. Thank God for the conservatives who are continuing to fight this evil. We are seeing victories, as with the 2022 overturn of Roe vs. Wade and the 2017 law signed by then-President Donald Trump that states could defund Planned Parenthood.

Don't get comfortable; we are still very much at war to preserve the sanctity of life!

USA TODAY referenced in 2020 an article in which Planned Parenthood founder, the late Margaret Sanger, purportedly wrote,

> Given Birth Control, the unfit will voluntarily eliminate their kind.
>
> Birth Control does not mean contraception [is] indiscriminately practiced[;] . . . It means the release and cultivation of the better elements in our society."[41]

From 1966 to 2015, Planned Parenthood gave their "highest award" to individuals who "recognize leadership, excellence, and outstanding contributions to the reproductive health and rights movement"[42]—the Margaret Sanger Award. The award demonstrates that Planned Parenthood has not shunned her views, despite their claims to the contrary. Since 2016, the organization has attempted to quietly distance themselves from the founder yet continue to honor their chosen recipients with the award. Shouldn't the organization be called Planned Slaughter?

> Planned Parenthood's introduction for their list of "Campaigns": Planned Parenthood is the nation's leading provider and advocate of high-quality, affordable health care for women, men, and young people, as well as the US's largest provider of sex education. On campuses and online, in schools and community settings, in health centers, and in the media, Planned Parenthood is a visible and reliable source of expert reproductive and sexual health care, education, and information. We do this work because we're passionate about helping people lead healthier lives.[43]

Their primary purpose is to murder babies while concealing from the mothers what abortion really does, opposite of Planned Parenthood's claims. A mother's health is at risk while allowing her baby to be murdered in utero. One of many examples is the claim by former employee-turned-whistleblower, Mayra Rodriguez, who worked in Arizona's Planned Parenthood clinics across the state for fifteen years:

> She uncovered a disturbing trend of shoddy abortion patient care that was putting women's lives at risk. While what she found shocked her, it will come as no surprise to those who are well-acquainted with the duplicity behind Planned Parenthood's carefully crafted public façade.[44]

The funding of murder by abortion must stop! With Roe vs. Wade overturned, we now need to strengthen the Second Amendment and overturn rulings supporting gay "marriage" by appointing conservative justices to the SCOTUS. What a blessing that would be! Conservatives need to go on the offensive instead of always being on the defense. Another great sports analogy there!

The First Amendment Defense Act is common sense. After all, it's the First Amendment, which states:

> Congress shall make no law respecting an establishment of religion, or prohibiting the free exercise thereof; or abridging the freedom of speech, or of the press; or the right of the people peaceably to assemble, and to petition the Government for a redress of grievances.[45]

The First Amendment guarantees our freedoms concerning religion, expression, assembly, and the right to petition the government. It forbids Congress from promoting one religion over another and restricting individuals' religious practices. It guarantees freedom of expression by prohibiting Congress from restricting the press and individuals to speak freely. The amendment also guarantees the right of citizens to assemble peaceably and to petition their government with their grievances.

Please visit the website Faith & Freedom Coalition.

What the Bible says about murder, life, and freedom:

Murder:

- "You shall not murder" (Exodus 20:13).

Life:

- "I have come that they may have life, and have it to the full" (John 10:10).
- "I am the light of the world. Whoever follows me will never walk in darkness, but will have the light of life" (John 8:12).

- "Whoever heeds discipline shows the way to life, but whoever ignores correction leads others astray" (Proverbs 10:17).

- "His divine power has given us everything we need for a godly life through our knowledge of him who called us by his own glory and goodness" (2 Peter 1:3).

Freedom:

- "It is for freedom that Christ has set us free" (Galatians 5:1).

- "You, my brothers and sisters, were called to be free. But do not use your freedom to indulge the flesh; rather, serve one another humbly in love" (Galatians 5:13).

- "Live as free people, but do not use your freedom as a cover-up for evil; live as God's slaves" (1 Peter 2:16).

- "They promise them freedom, while they themselves are slaves of depravity—for 'people are slaves to whatever has mastered them'" (2 Peter 2:19).

CHAPTER 5

Political Correctness

There's no shortage of stories on political correctness. Before I share a few of mine, I'll define the term:

> Political Correctness is a doctrine, fostered by a delusional, illogical, liberal minority and rabidly promoted by an unscrupulous mainstream media, which holds forth the proposition that it is entirely possible to pick up a turd by the clean end. (Unknown)

> (That's too good to not include in this book!)

A niece of mine played basketball for one of our two middle schools in Colorado. Each school had a boys' team and a girls' team. The team name imprinted on the boys' jerseys at one school was "Wolves" and the other school's was "Pirates." Both administrations insisted on mirroring those names for the girls' teams, with a distinction: "Lady Wolves" and "Lady Pirates." Why was that distinction not forced for the boys' teams as "Men

Wolves" and "Men Pirates?" I didn't get it. How about disregarding gender, and all uniforms simply read "Wolves" and "Pirates?"

A friend and I have the same sense of humor and share the same beliefs as Christian conservatives. We really enjoy making fun of political correctness. In that vein of sarcasm, I told him his child (a boy) was very cute, but instead of specifying the child's gender, I said, "'Ze' is cute." In a cynical show of tolerance, we agreed that his child should decide his gender on his eighteenth birthday.

"Maybe the 'boy' will want to be a 'girl' or vice versa!" we joked.

"We're not willing to label human beings as male or female," one of us then responded. "If a baby is born with a wiener, let's not discriminate and label him as a 'boy.' Let 'it' decide 'their' sex."

Oh, the foolishness. Kids are pawns in today's perverted society.

Another friend was there, and during the rhetoric he shared a story and used the term "businessman." I was quick to correct him: "businessperson." We had a good laugh.

I once noticed at work the title on an owner's manual for a bicycle: Worksman Bike Manual. Shouldn't that read "Worksperson?" The manual stated: "Your bicycle has been handmade in the USA by our American craftspeople." Is it just me or does "craftspeople" sound silly? Craftsmen!

I find it interesting that our US Air Force continues to call all Air Force members (male and female) "airmen." I love our military! Don't go woke, military brass. You have an important job to do in keeping the American people safe. If you're unfamiliar with the term "woke," Merriam-Webster defines the political definition as "aware of and actively attentive to important facts and issues especially of racial and social injustice."[46] In other words, awoken to, aware of the insidiousness consuming nearly half of American thinking.

I heard a "politically correct" story on the radio station K-Love: a Peter Pan play featuring a female Peter Pan. Well then, let's have men play the female characters in the television show *Golden Girls*. Why bother to have women play female roles? Isn't that discriminatory? We have lost our minds in this country. How did this happen? It happened bit by bit over time. It's now full speed ahead!

Our local high school hosted a Diversity Week that included a Tie Dye Day sponsored by the Gay-Straight Alliance. I wonder if the decision-makers ever gave thought to hosting a Heterosexual Day? I highly doubt it as that would be "too controversial" and "offensive" to those who are not heterosexual. This world is upside down.

By the way, to my knowledge, there was only one gay student in the entire senior class! He was catered to and the majority was punished. What a backward country we live in and what a backward world our young people are growing up in. Not only do kids have to deal with broken homes and split families by broken marriages, social media, peer pressure, athletics, and academics, but now sexual identity and gender identity "options." These poor kids are the true victims in a woke world.

Anytime you see the word *diversity* (should be "perversity"), I urge you to pause and ask yourself, *What views are they trying to force on me?*

Political Correctness

Often the term *diversity* is used in connection with homosexuality, transgenderism, globalism, and other liberal issues. Diversity essentially means *unbiblical.*

When I worked for a politically left-leaning hotel, the employees were subjected to a presentation on diversity. The word makes me cringe. Diversity, as termed and overused by the left, represents perversion and immorality. The hotel's general manager, referring to gay guests, said to us, "Those who have an issue with diversity, get over yourself." I wanted to respond, "Get over your perversion, sir." Why would a hotel subject their guests, and especially children, to the perverted ways of homosexuality? I no longer wanted to work there. Just let the guests be guests. If they're gay, who cares? No need to discuss it. There should be no mention of sexual preference. A guest is a guest!

Morality is not bigotry. Don't let perversion convince you that "love is love." Take a stand for conservatism, and more importantly a stand for Jesus Christ. Jesus is love, and He set the rules.

Political correctness is a pandemic in my Colorado county. For example, in the Young Adult Nonfiction section at my local library are highly visible titles that blatantly promote liberal agendas, like global warming, and immorality, like homosexuality. Where are the books that draw young minds into a deeper understanding of God and His Word and purity? You may be hard-pressed to find Christian books for young adults in your local library. Look the next time you go. I'd love to donate books on Christianity and firearms, but that would be "too extreme."

Other examples of political correctness have to do with my election to serve as a Republican Party precinct committeeman (er, my bad, "committee*person*") and with being a sports fanatic. In 1994, the Marquette Warriors (my alma mater) became the politically correct "Golden Eagles." I often received donation requests from Marquette University. *Maybe I'll donate once you tell me why there's an undergraduate program on Social Welfare and Justice. Perhaps I'll then send a dollar your way and hope it's tax deductible!* I am not giving my money to a university for them, in turn, to use that money to push a liberal worldview.

The growing undergraduate programs pushing liberalism concerns me. These once-prestigious colleges and universities are now pushing an agenda. I also have an agenda, and that agenda is to share the truth.

A lot of talk began in 2013 about the Washington Redskins possibly changing their name. The name "Red Tails" was thrown in as a possibility, which is still—ten years later—on the table. The longevity of this battle shows the persistence of both sides. Anything to not offend people!

The Redskins became the Commanders in 2022. When I hear "Washington Commanders," I instinctively roll my eyes. The same goes for the Washington Wizards (NBA team formerly known as the Bullets) and the Cleveland Guardians (MLB team formerly known as the Indians).

The left is okay with aborting precious babies, but a team nickname offends them? This is unbelievable to me. So let me get this straight: murder is okay, but you cross a line with certain words (Warriors, Redskins, Bullets, Indians).

If I were a fan of these organizations, I would find another team to support. Hopefully the Packers, Bucks, and Brewers are not seen as offensive.

My favorite team names include Washington Redskins, Marquette Warriors, and Cleveland Indians. The left wants to claim that the team name "Indians" is insensitive to American Indian tribes. In my view, the team name is manly, tough, and honoring. Can we please stop being woke?

The Indians are now known as the Guardians.

What if I decide these new names are offensive to me? What if my feelings are hurt?

"Tolerance" is a one-way street to the left.

I watch a *lot* of sports coverage on ESPN. In fact, while writing a post in 2012 about political correctness, I had one eye and ear tuned to the UNC vs. Duke men's basketball game. Sadly, ESPN has adhered to political correctness for decades by broadcasting sports of lesser interest on their primary channel, as opposed to their related channels, like ESPN2 and ESPNU. The network continues to be more dedicated to political correctness than to majority-interest sports. ESPN highlights women's basketball on their primary channel, though, truth be told, most ESPN viewers are not interested in women's basketball. Even fewer care about the Women's National Basketball Association (WNBA), which is likely still afloat (financially) because they maintain political correctness. In other words, ESPN and the NBA appear willing to lose money to be seen as politically correct—inclusive, diverse, and tolerant. Let me be clear: I'm not anti-woman sports; for three years I coached a girls' softball team and I enjoy watching the annual Women's College Softball World Series. It's a great event! What I am is anti-political correctness and anti-bowing to political correctness.

While we're on the subject of sports broadcasts, let's note that poker is not a sport and shouldn't be televised on a sports channel—much like NASCAR doesn't have athletes, they have skilled drivers.

ESPN and the NBA are far more "diverse" than they were in the 1980s and 90s. They're now a mix of sports, politics, and liberal agenda. I'm no longer a big fan of either. They've become way too political for me. I still enjoy and follow the Milwaukee Bucks (2021 NBA champions), but overall, pertaining to the league, I was done by 2012. The NBA was running anti-gun commercials sponsored by Everytown for Gun Safety USA (a Michael Bloomberg gun control group) and pro-gay ads featuring Jason Collins, the first NBA player to come out as gay. Any advertisers that support immorality are unacceptable to me and the many other people who support conservative, traditional, moral values. I would ask Mr. Adam Silver (NBA Commissioner): What is the logic in alienating your prime customers by being involved in the political game?

I recall the NBA moving the 2017 All-Star game from Charlotte, North Carolina, because of a bathroom law preventing men from using women's restrooms, locker rooms, and shower facilities.

To the NBA and other sports organizations and athletes supporting all-inclusive bathrooms: Whatever happened to decency, values, and protecting women and children?

Athletes: We pay to watch you play sports, not carry on about your liberal worldviews (LeBron James), which are all warped and immoral. Just play the game you're passionate about and highly compensated for and let the public decide for themselves which political candidates to support and how we deem best to handle social issues. Sports used to be an outlet for everyday life. Now it's political and trapping rather than relaxing and a time of freedom from the escalating issues of this world.

There was an NBA commercial featuring Grant Hill of the Phoenix Suns, encouraging people to not use the word "gay" when describing something other than homosexuality. The commercial had political correctness written all over it. Apparently, the NBA had become a partner in policing word usage with organizations like GLSEN. How about we encourage people to *stop* using God's name in vain? No wonder NBA ratings tanked: a poor product, marketing individual players and big-market teams instead of promoting all teams in the league. I like the Milwaukee Bucks (they just signed Damian Lillard), but the NBA (like ESPN) bothers me at times. It isn't what it used to be. Just look up videos of Detroit Pistons versus Boston Celtics in the late 1980's and see how it has changed.

In the early 1970s, homosexuality began to openly infiltrate America's mainstream senses—seeing and hearing homosexual men flaunt their unnatural, ungodly sexual activities including acting like, talking like, and dressing like women. The movement mushroomed darkly over America like the massive cloud of a nuclear explosion and has proven to be just as lethal to mankind. We learned of AIDs and then its infiltration into mainstream society as liberalism plundered our nation's morality and birthed "political correctness."

Among the pilfering was the hijacking of a 600-year-old word: *gay*.

Since its first known use in the fourteenth century, the definition of *gay* was "full of joy, merry; light-hearted, carefree," derived from the Old French *gai* meaning "joyful, happy; pleasant, agreeably charming."[47] As with everything Satan touches in his mission to "steal and to kill and to destroy," the term *gay* was stripped of its purity.

The next hijacking was far greater than stealing a human word. The target was directed straight at God's glory—the rainbow—hijacked by the gay community and other liberals to be the premier symbol of their "pride"—their glory. The true meaning of the rainbow is God's promise to never again flood the earth as He had in the time of Noah.

But, what's the big deal about liberals using the rainbow? How do we know the rainbow is part of God's visual glory?

The first reference of "rainbow" appears in Genesis 5 when God placed it in the sky following the great flood. In that passage of Scripture, God defined that stunning display of color as "my rainbow" and said that it was "the sign of the covenant [binding promise] between me and the earth."

The fourth mention of the *rainbow* in the Old Testament is by the prophet Ezekiel who was permitted by God to see part of God's glory in heaven, "Like the appearance of a rainbow . . . , was the radiance around him [God]. This was the appearance of the likeness of the glory of the Lord. When I saw it, I fell facedown" (Ezekiel 1:28).

The rainbow is referenced two times in the final book of Scripture, the Book of Revelation (the end times) by the apostle John who was also permitted by God to see His glory in heaven. Speaking about God on His throne, John described "a rainbow that shone like an emerald encircled the throne" (Revelation 4:3).

The big, *big* deal about liberals choosing the rainbow (God's rainbow)—of all things—as the premier and now-flooding sign of their pride and glory is to encourage and force human beings around the globe to see human's "political correctness" (liberal ways) as equal or superior to the supremacy of God's blinding glory. "Pride goes before destruction, a haughty spirit before a fall" (Proverbs 16:18).

Of the countless things liberals could have chosen as their "inclusivity" and homosexual pride symbol, they chose the rainbow, blaspheming the glory of God. This is no coincidence; this is a hallmark strike by Satan that again shows that we are in a spiritual war that's reflective of the warfare on earth between what is right and good and what is wrong and evil.

God is the One who will win in the end. There will be a day of reckoning by God against all people whose hearts and minds are still contrary to His and against Him as God the Father, God the Creator, the One true and living God.

Political correctness has also "sissified" the American male and has contributed to the deaths of American military at home and abroad due to "inclusivity" forced upon our military. Liberalism encourages American males to be *diverse, tolerant, inclusive,* and experimental outside their natural design. Such incessant prodding leads men to act like girls, tolerate the gay lifestyle, and forget what it's like to be a man. There's nothing better than to see a man with his wife and kids, him not only being loving but also protective.

Let's bring back manhood. This country needs men to raise boys into men. Go hunting, fishing, shooting, grill out, be the breadwinners, husbands, dads who protect and provide for their families. This is what men were created to do.

"Tolerant" is another liberal term that's been twisted by the code of "political correctness." *Tolerant* has long been known as Godly "patience" with one another but liberals have changed the meaning to encourage people to take "liberties" to do pretty much anything they want and without the expectation of consequences for immoral and unethical actions. *Tolerant* has been changed to the progressive view meaning "my way," in opposition to God's way—anti-God, anti-Christian, anti-male and female, and anti-family, free to decide "what" we're going to "identify as." At work, we once had a lady come in to discuss inclusiveness. In such group circumstances, taking turns sharing your name is common, but we were asked to share our pronouns. I said, "I am a dude, a man. That's all I got." Coworkers chuckled because we all knew how silly it was to state our sexual orientations.

Again, I strongly disagree with the ungodliness of liberalism.

A growing number of women are pursuing male activities in an effort to prove the lie that males and females are the same. They're not! A couple of examples are weightlifting, pursuing playing on male football teams, and have infiltrated our military, vying for combat roles! A vast number of females are simply looking ridiculous, and males are looking like wussies! We need men in the military and preferably in law enforcement. Men protect. Women nurture.

Likewise, the hot issue today (2023) is men "identifying" as women to play women's sports, and defeating the rightful female winners in female sports (look up Lia Thomas). Why? Because men and women were created different! They were not created the same—to carry out the same roles—because that was not God's divine plan. Yet liberalism is out to deny God's supremacy in every regard. Liberalism has blurred all the lines across the board, not reinforcing for children and young people the boundaries that will provide clarity and protection but presenting them with a free-for-all that's a freefall to instability, irrationality, and destruction—as we've seen again and again.

Seeing the demise and destruction of "my way all the way," from the beginning of time, why give away, exchange, or try to undo the supreme work of our Creator that makes all things right and working?

Another example of destruction that liberalism created: Had US Army superiors not been so politically correct, the 2009 Fort Hood shooting in Texas could have been prevented. They allowed US Maj. Nidal Hasan, a Muslim, to radicalize as an Islamic extremist. Army officials refused to take action for fear of upsetting Muslims in our military in terms of appearing intolerant of Islam. Instead of doing the right thing, based on military intelligence, we allowed Hasan, for the sake of the Army's appearance as politically correct, to continue talking against America's war on terrorism and plotting to *kill fellow soldiers*! I remember listening to Michael

Savage (a conservative author, political commentor, and activist) talk about this very upsetting story.

And guess what? Where troops had gathered for immunizations, *Hasan shot and killed in rapid succession* thirteen people and wounded thirty. Unbelievable! This was preventable.

We must return to keeping the safety of our citizens and military members above "politically correct" ideology!

On my drive to work, I occasionally listen to either K-Love (Christian music) or NPR radio (a liberal news station). Important to me is staying aware of current events and foreign policy, what's happening in and to our nation, and around the world, from both viewpoints—conservative and liberal.

What I often hear on NPR is liberals playing cutesy with world affairs. *Political correctness* popped into my head when an announcer said (2013) an advertiser "has Muslim art and history ties." My second thought was, *I suppose Christianity is too extreme for NPR broadcasters to support.* Funny how they're willing to accept advertising dollars from Muslims, but if a Christian or conservative advertiser were to ask for air time, I can almost guarantee NPR would not allow it. Ironic and unnerving is how the truth is scorned and ignored while lies (Islam) are given public favor.

Ten years later, as of now (2023), liberalism is so sickening, I can no longer stomach listening to NPR. Life is too short to spend time listening to that rhetoric, though I do continue by other means to stay in the know about local, national, and world news and the divided perspectives of our once-united states. There aren't many news sources I trust.

In 2013, on the twelfth anniversary of 9/11, I was visiting my home state, Wisconsin. I looked into going to a Muslim prayer service and learned that I needed a reservation to attend. Since when do churches require a reservation? Perhaps the mosque had something to hide? Other churches, that I knew of, did not require a reservation. The various churches I'd attended through the years had an open-door welcome: "Come as you are, grab a coffee, and enjoy the church service." Apparently not in the Muslim world. The Islamic Society of Milwaukee left me feeling suspicious of them. Why a reservation?

As political correctness has applied to our national leaders are the following examples. When so-called Republican Chris Christie was governor of New Jersey, he appointed an Asian and a homosexual to the state supreme court, in order to be seen as *diverse*. Sickening. I liked when he had taken on the unions, but having read more news reports, I was disappointed in his motive behind the nominations.

To be clear: If two nominees are the most qualified to serve at the supreme court level, I support those nominations, regardless of race or sexual preference. However, if more qualified justices are overlooked in the name of *political correctness*, that is a grave disservice to citizens and society. Hire the best and most qualified candidates! That goes for any and all jobs.

As governor, Chris Christie showed why he was a RINO (Republican in Name Only)—not a true conservative. He gave in to gay "marriage" in New Jersey. The GOP gave us weak presidential candidates in 2008 and 2012. Approaching 2016, I foresaw the GOP giving us the not-so-conservative Christie and saw that socialized medicine (a.k.a. Obamacare or rather the *un*Affordable

Care Act), was off to a rough start. Many problems were reported on the exchanges.

Whenever government is involved in private sector issues, problems will occur.

Health care and the United States Postal Service are just two leading examples! Government: stay out of health care and mail delivery, please. Neither experiment has gone well and will not turn for the better, as we've witnessed for years. Turn these over to the private sector. They will get it done.

On the continuum of political correctness, I think of the 2016 presidential election—frightening that Hillary Clinton and Chris Christie were the leading contenders for their respective parties. Those choices didn't bode well for our future, Hillary being a socialist and Chris a RINO known for being pro-Islam and pro-Sharia Law. I would have liked to have seen the GOP nominate a Rick Santorum-Rand Paul ticket, but knowing the GOP, I had suspected they'd give us more moderates, like a combination of Chris Christie, Mitt Romney, and John McCain. They are not conservatives. They are moderates.

We must not put our faith and trust in mankind; we'll only be thoroughly disappointed.

Christie was a dangerous man. He was supposed to represent the US conservative political party. However, he was pro-Islam and pro-gay agenda. These so-called conservatives are selling out the Republican Party, which is supposed to stand for a free-market economy, a strong national defense, individual freedom, energy independence, and traditional values.

Republicans like Christie, Romney, and McCain were bringing down the Republican Party. Such moderate Republicans have no backbone. They're willing to cave on vital issues like Obamacare and Islam.

The solution for our nation is to keep weak, left-leaning Republicans and all Democrats out of office and vote in true conservatives.

The 2016 GOP nominee ended up being the greatest president of all time. Thank you, Donald J. Trump. May you win again in 2024, perhaps with Ron DeSantis as VP. No man can save this country, but they can help this country. I have said this before because it's true.

Political correctness in our judiciary system: The gay "marriage" debate headed to the US Supreme Court in April 2014. The justices, in all their "intelligence and wisdom," decided on October 6, 2014, that same-sex marriage (in the states presented) would stand as legal. What a tragic day for our country as this precedent was set by our highest court for other states to follow. Perversion was permitted to reign at the federal level, further un-uniting our once "united states."

Our justices can debate all they want, but God's truth never changes and every test against His nature and commands has failed. The following is noteworthy about our Supreme Court and our need for vigilant prayer over our justices:

- 1962, the court took prayer out of public schools
- 1963, the court took the Bible out of classrooms
- 1980, the court ended the teaching of creation in schools

How has that turned out? It has been a disaster. Until overturning Roe vs. Wade in 2022—a historical turn—the court had continued to refuse to intervene in important rulings supporting our nation's founding conservative views.

We've seen that prayer works. Bring it back.

Our justices who continue to favor political correctness and formidable issues of liberalism, like the gay agenda, will ultimately pay the price when they stand before the greatest judge, the King of kings. Pray that their hearts will be humble, repentant, and turned to Christ before they meet their Maker. Those who continue to openly oppose and mock God and His Word will have to face the ultimate Judge, and His Word tells us that His verdict will render eternal separation from Him. Though God's great love and greatest desire is *not* "wanting anyone to perish, but everyone to come to repentance" (2 Peter 3:9), the fact of eternal separation from God should bring each and every person to our knees in repentance to Him and faith in Jesus Christ. The very real battle between good and evil—God and Satan—eternal life and damnation is won humbly on knees through prayer in submission to God's will.

Pray for those struggling with homosexuality and gender confusion. They, like every person, need the gospel of Jesus Christ. It's not too late for unbelievers to be saved from eternal separation from God. But one day it will be too late. Why risk the most important, defining issue of all time and eternity—salvation? The time to repent is now. The gospel is literally the solution to every problem: drug abuse, sexual immorality, adultery, murder, etc. The list is long, but the memory of God is short, if there is repentance (Jeremiah 31:34).

Likewise, pray for all Muslims to leave Islam and experience the freedom and truth found in Jesus Christ.

Terminology, as we've seen, is a fundamental aspect of political correctness, from gender-based words (like changing "mankind" to "humankind") to political issues, giving new meanings to terms I've earlier touched on and the following, giving them new meanings.

- "Social justice" is simply another way of saying "wealth redistribution"—the wealthy giving to the poor by mandate rather than by philanthropy (by desire).

- "Sustainable" now represents the seventeen goals of the United Nations. For example, Agenda 21, the "comprehensive plan of action to be taken globally, nationally and locally by organizations of the United Nations System, Governments, and Major Groups in every area in which human impacts on the environment."[48]

- "Tolerant" now means not only accepting all lifestyles and choices but approving of and encouraging all lifestyles and choices.

- "Diversity" from the left perspective places emphasis on all workplaces representing various demographics—such as race, ethnicity, and gender identities (for example)—as opposed to skill, experience, and knowledge base (for example).

- "Coexist" encourages people to live in harmony without regard to beliefs, practices, and people who pose military, moral, or unethical threats. For example, believing and living as though Islam is a peaceful religion.

The political correctness police have influenced many people who are unaware of the liberal agenda to buy into that worldview. Your worldview matters!

Liberals and socialists (aren't they pretty much the same thing?) love the term "social justice." They think that regardless of education or work ethic, we should all live in the same-sized homes, drive eco-friendly electric vehicles (EVs), work in the green jobs market while worshiping Mother Earth (pagan spirituality), and ignore biblical truth. This sect of thinkers are the same blinded people who drive around with Love Your Mother (Earth) bumper stickers. Who made the Earth? God did.

The bumper sticker I despise most reads Coexist. How many new-age followers know these facts: they're prompting and desiring to coexist with Islamists who would not blink at beheading them and their loved ones, simply because they (new-age followers) are Americans, Westerners, Christians, Jews, or because they don't submit to Islam and Sharia Law?

While swimming and tubing in a Colorado river, I realized just how powerful Mother Nature is. She's a strong mother, not one to mess with. She should be feared, yes; not *worshiped*. Let's worship the Creator of Mother Earth—God. He is who should be thanked and worshiped for the beautiful, powerful Earth He designed for us to marvel at and enjoy—and be reminded that it is His glory that Mother Earth reflects.

Political correctness also includes the terms *climate change* and *global warming*, and our government has made the following distinction between the two:

> "Global warming" refers to the rise in global temperatures due mainly to the increasing concentrations of greenhouse gases in the atmosphere.

> "Climate change" refers to the increasing changes in the measures of climate over a long period of time – including precipitation, temperature, and wind patterns.[49]

What a waste of time and a scare tactic. As ridiculous as these trumped-up "issues" are, advocates for the environment have taken the rhetoric to a whole new low. There are many ludicrous examples, like this one: Talk show radio host Thom Hartmann, along with a few concerned others have spoken their concerns that cow farts are a problem contributing to global warming. They're out in the open fields. Let them fart away!

I cannot make this stuff up.

Liberals and progressives have a very flawed ideology, to put it kindly. Their worldviews—all under the umbrella of political correctness—meaning their ideology on any issue is to be seen as "correct," are warped. They put their faith in mankind and in nature.

With all the sin, evil, and disparity in this world, should we really be concerned with a human-formed ideology about global warming and cow fart effects? The only "warming" to be feared is hell and the eternal separation from God our Maker. I joked about this with my sister, though it's no laughing matter! Eternity is at stake.

> Woe to those who quarrel with their Maker, those who are nothing but potsherds among the potsherds on the ground. Does the clay say to the potter, "What are you making?" Does your work say, "The potter has no hands"? (Isaiah 45:9)

I live in a small town in the Colorado mountains. Years ago, when my niece was a freshman in high school, the school had an assembly seminar on global warming, climate change, and our carbon footprint. It was *so* over the top; my sister and I (in attendance) were outraged.

The earth is fine, it is not warming, and God the Creator is in control. End of story.

The school had brought in a group from the Alliance for Climate Education (ACE) who led the seminar pushing radical environmentalism. My sister and I sat through this for almost an hour, listening to the foolishness. They exampled the lack of snow in Colorado as due to global warming, along with glaciers melting across the globe, polar bears disappearing and becoming extinct, and yes, even how cow farts contribute to the climate change "problem." Among their solutions were that we all should walk or bike when one's destination is less than five miles away, that we should buy local or farmers' market produce, emphasized the importance of recycling, and that doomsday is approaching unless human beings take immediate action. Let it be known that the 2023 ski season saw record snowfall here in Colorado! But, but . . . global warming!

In other words, they were saying we all need to get on board with them and drink the Kool-Aid. The fact that they were pouring their poisonous Kool-Aid into our vulnerable young people was the actual *highly* concerning issue—not global warming. I'll say it again: they have an agenda.

Schools should be teaching history, math, and science (according to fact), and physical education rather than gender as a choice and this environmental foolishness.

Guess what? Ten years later and we're still here, there are still harsh winters—in fact, the ski industry is booming (2022–2023), we've had record snowfall, and there's still plentiful glaciers and polar bears! I thought we had to take "immediate action?" Back in 2014–2015? Let's stop buying into the fear tactics of the left, whether it be global warming or Covid-19.

There is, however, an accelerating concern that's metaphorical to cow-farting changing the environment: the increased stench of aversive nonsense that's radically, adversely changing the heart and mind environment of our young people, adults, and the trajectory of our nation that is, indeed, in peril. There are so many lies out there.

ACE brought with them two professional X Game skiers to speak to our impressionable youth. Yet, ironically, the video shown was of the two skiers being flown by helicopter to the top of a snow-packed mountain where they jumped out and skied down. My question was: *What is the carbon footprint of that helicopter?* Do they honestly care about carbon footprints and the environment? No, they care about being seen as saviors and about gaining power, money, and control.

There is only one Savior and one solution: Jesus Christ.

At the end of the ACE assembly, the kids were asked to come onstage if they had an interest in starting a "climate change" group at school. About two-thirds of the school's population—yes, two-thirds!—trooped onstage: the brainwashing, scare tactics, lies, and peer pressure, I'd say, made them feel obligated to take a place onstage.

The high schoolers likely left the presentation afraid.

- afraid of the future
- afraid and hesitant to buy material goods
- afraid they're adding to waste dumps
- afraid of contributing to the world's pollution
- afraid they're leaving a bigger carbon footprint
- afraid to one day have kids of their own

I say buy whatever goods are needed to live!

One of my missions throughout this book is to inform readers of such groups as ACE who are infiltrating our high schools and junior high schools and handing out gallons of poisonous Kool-Aid that's turning our children—our future leaders and parents—from God.

Politically correct is opposite of biblically correct.

For the truth on climate change, and additional reading, please visit the website American Policy Center. Also, read the book *Global Warming: And The Creator's Plan* by Dr. William M. Curtis and Jay A. Auxt.

What the Bible says about fearing others and God:

- "Fear of man will prove to be a snare, but whoever trusts in the Lord is kept safe" (Proverbs 29:25).

- "Even if you should suffer for what is right, you are blessed. Do not fear their threats; do not be frightened'" (1 Peter 3:14).

- "The fear of the Lord is the beginning of wisdom; all who follow his precepts have good understanding. To him belongs eternal praise" (Psalm 111:10).

CHAPTER 6

Equality and Entitlement

Liberals want "equality," correct? Again, their bumper sticker, Coexist, is primarily written in symbols and their thoughts on marriage "equality."

The coexist bumper sticker prompted a question in my mind about the push for "equality," and took my thoughts on a journey illustrating equal rights. Is it my right to go back to grade school to sit with the children and relearn subjects if I want? I'll go to my local grade school and register as a student, and if I'm not allowed access, I'll bring a lawsuit against the school, stating that my constitutional rights are being violated. After all, we all have equal rights, right? So, it's only fair that I be allowed in the grade school classroom—also because I should get to live exactly as I want, right? What does it matter that I'm a grown man if we're all equal and we get to do whatever we desire?

Perhaps I'll want to sing in the fifth grade Christmas concert with the students of St. Alphonsus Grade School in my hometown

Equality and Entitlement

of Greendale, Wisconsin. I don't care that I'll be on stage with kids a fraction of my age; I just care about the equality I want and will demand.

Or maybe at my local church here in Colorado, I'll want to be a student in the children's ministry class of three- to five-year-olds and want my own little chair, my own carton of chocolate milk and a juice box, because—dang it—we are all equal in rights, right? No matter our age, size, gender, etc.

In other words, I could "identify as" a grade school student, because it's also my right to identify as whatever I want, right? Like the children who are identifying as "furries." Students and teachers are expected to accept what furries want and treat furries (those who identify as animals with human characteristics) as though they are literally animals with human characteristics instead of as human beings. I was told that a local high school here in Colorado now has students in hallways purring like cats and that other students must go along with this silliness and pet the "cats" if approached.

I ask you, has our world gone nuts?

In my home state, Wisconsin, Channel 5 (an affiliate of CBS) reported on their news website a local talk show host who had received an email about the Waunakee School District's expectations of students regarding the treatment of "furries" in the classrooms. The article included the email and reported that the talk show host Vicki McKenna had received several subsequent emails on the issue. Below is the email (verbatim as it appears on the channel's news website). I bolded the issues that are highly concerning regarding the behavior of *adult leaders*:

> I have grandchildren in the Waunakee School District. They have been instructed to not take pictures of, make fun of, stare at or in any way call out the behavior of their classmates who are Furrys. The **Furries can choose whether they want to speak in class or not**.
>
> The Furrys are allowed to dress in their choice of furry costumes. The Furries **can choose not to run in gym class but instead sit at the feet of their teacher and lick their paws. Barking, hissing and similar animal noises are common place in the hallways at the schools**.
>
> The children have been told that **they must treat these children normally** and the **school administration and teachers have normalized the behavior** of the Furries in their schools.
>
> I am appalled!!![50]

Appalling indeed. The school board and teachers abandoned their sanity along with their roles and responsibilities as mature adults tasked with raising, teaching, and guiding our young people.

When I come to your door selling cookies in my Girl Scout uniform, because I want to be a Girl Scout (in this illustration) and we're all equal to be and do as we want, please don't laugh or giggle at me, because that would be intolerant of you. After all, what's wrong with a grown man doing what he wants in a Girl Scout uniform? Nothing to see here.

Stop being intolerant—of behaviors that are outside of God's design!

Leftwing persona: Are you a bigot? Are you intolerant? Come on, society is evolving so get with the program!

Welcome to the liberal mindset. Clearly, it's not logical or natural; it simply doesn't work and the only aspect that's "sustainable" is the underlying evil, until Jesus returns and puts an end to all things that do not honor Him. Good news: This all comes to an end one day.

Entitlement Mentality

The big problems wrapped in the entitlement mentality, leading our country into further fiscal collapse, include unions, Medicaid, food stamps, and other such privilege handouts.

> **Stop depending on the government to provide for your every need! That's socialism—the doorway into Communism. Get a job and work! Provide for yourself!**

Don't we want to retain our freedoms?

Indications are that nearly half of our US adult citizens have conveniently forgotten, or aren't educated, that our country was founded for freedom and opportunity—not taxation and handouts! We must take on the unions and balance the budget! Example: Former Congressman Paul Ryan (R) of Wisconsin had a common sense budget plan that was criticized by the left. What's not to like about a commonsense budget? Being $33 trillion in debt is not "sustainable." Nor is it responsible.

I had wanted a Walker-Ryan GOP ticket in 2016, but he (Ryan) was exposed as a RINO and I'm no longer a fan. I'm very thankful

Conservative Solution

for Donald J. Trump and the outspoken Ron DeSantis of Florida. (Trump/DeSantis 2024—if they can play nice).

Here in Colorado, Amendment 66 (tax increase for education) was soundly defeated. It would have been the largest tax increase in state history (to date). Who would have benefited from the income tax raise? Not students, but teachers, teacher unions, and illegal immigrants. Well done, Colorado. However, mark my words: Unions will keep coming back with plans until their agendas are met. I'm sick of paying taxes to further agendas that support liberal views! We're headed for socialism.

Off the freeway exit near my home, I often saw a gentleman holding a sign: Homeless Vet. Please Help. I'm an avid supporter of our military veterans, but panhandlers' rampant deception has me skeptical about beggars. I was suspicious of that supposed vet because he was wearing very nice steel-toed boots and nice jeans, he was clean-shaven, and overall didn't have the look of the hungry or desperate. Of course I didn't know the facts of his circumstances. If there had been a way to learn the facts of his circumstance, and those proved him truly in need, I would have loved to help him. However, the simple truth is that I have no faith in mankind. Man will lie, cheat, and steal.

Other than by sight, it's hard to know who is really in need and who's a swindler and freeloader. Even more difficult to know is whether a man holding a sign on a street corner is legitimately a veteran. Any person can make any sign. What has been proven true is the great number of people who simply don't want to work, other than the hours they spend coaxing people to feel sorry for them, the swindlers, and who will spend the dollars on drugs and alcohol.

Equality and Entitlement

Among the yearly surveys publicly reported on the U.S. Bureau of Labor Statistics' website is the number of "Persons Not in the Labor Force by Desire and Availability for Work, . . ." Here are tidbits, a small piece of the bigger pie of laziness:

> "Labor Force Statistics from the Current Population Survey" state an increase from 100,110 people to 100,222 people "not in the labor force" from April 2022 to April 2023. Among those was an increase from 94,398 people to 95,077 people who "do not want a job now."[51]
>
> Put simply, of 100,222 people not working, 95,077 don't want a job! That's 94.86 percent! Nearly 18,000 were in the 16 to 24 age bracket and over 21,000 were in the 25 to 54 age bracket—prime ages for working!

Utterly despicable.

Certainly, there are individuals in our nation who are truly unable to work and legitimately need our assistance. But what's astonishing about the labor force survey is that *under 200* of those were not working due to being in school, training, illness, or disability!

Logical conclusion?

A large percentage of capable people are milking the taxpayers.

They should be ashamed of themselves. Stop being lazy! Earn your way by getting a job! Be productive, pay your taxes, save for your future, and be the independent individual our country was founded for—not a government- and tax-payer-dependent people.

For all I know, the beggar gentleman I spoke of earlier could have been making more money—tax-free—than the average forty-hour a week, tax-paying worker in a legitimate job by not doing a darn thing. Any money the man received from passersby was tax-free dollars. Not a bad gig.

A March 2023 abstract reported that panhandlers make on average up to minimum wage and $200–$500 per month. And that income is not being reported nor taxed, unlike those of us reporting tax-payers who are working legitimate jobs.

If a person can stand for hours with a sign in hand—in the heat of summer and cold of winter—they can stand on their feet in better conditions indoors and work for at least an hourly wage. At the very least, the man holding the sign near my home likely qualified for food stamps and unemployment insurance—is he truly a veteran?—but then again, he may have been in a higher tax bracket by way of a scam he may have been running. Dude, go work at Walmart. Push carts. Pick up trash.

Rather than taking the chance of adding my taxed earnings to the pockets of those who "do not want a job now," I should ask those panhandling for my earnings to hop in my car and head to the local factories and stores for job applications. Costco, Walmart, and Home Depot are often hiring.

While grocery shopping at a local mom-and-pop store, I saw a man in a wheelchair—working! He was stocking shelves. I give him all the credit in the world for doing so. If disabled men and women can work despite their challenges, it sure makes me think of the outrageous number of Americans who can work but are choosing instead to live as though "entitled"—living on our governments' handouts (welfare, food stamps, Medicaid, government housing, etc.) and private sector charities (shelters, food pantries), all supported by taxpayers.

> **People: Get a job! Get a Bible! Get a gym membership! Working is a good thing.**

The wheelchair-bound employee got me thinking again about the Occupy Wall Street movement. It appeared that their motto and philosophy was entitlement. Putting that mindset into words could sound like this:

> "I want what you have because it's not "fair" for you to live better than me. If you want to work, save, and take out loans to go to school and build your business, that's your choice, but that's not my choice, which is my right. Just like it's my right to live a lifestyle equal to those who have more than me. Besides, it's the government's responsibility to make sure we all have equal slices of the pie because we're all *equally "deserving."* So, until we all have equal portions by redistribution of wealth from the rich to the poor, I'm protesting!"

This sect of thinkers, growing larger each day, is America's "entitlement society." We need only to visit the website Federal Safety Net for a list of the federal government's "entitlement programs,"[52] which include Medicaid, Medicare, Social Security, Unemployment, and welfare. Recently added to that list is President Biden's student loan forgiveness program.

A February 2023 report by the FDA on SNAP (US food stamps) showed a total payout—only for that month—of $10.6 billion from taxpayers' hard-earned incomes to the over 42 million enrolled in the entitlement program.[53] That same month, Medicaid.gov reported an enrollment of 93.3 million combined enrolled in the Medicaid and CHIP entitlements,[54] a reported increase of 21.6 million people! from three years prior, February 2020.[55] Take, take, take.

Do you see the insanity? The irony of a hard-working, handicapped employee and other hardworking US taxpayers mandated by the Federal government to financially support the multi-millions of US citizens living off of entitlement programs? This isn't right.

As we've seen, government dependency is at an all-time high and America is losing its entrepreneurial advantage. The practical, logical conservative solution?

1. Cut entitlements (previously known as "food stamps"). We need economic common sense.

2. Limit unemployment compensation to a maximum of six months. If needed, sell your home and stop going out to eat. Have an emergency savings account set up to fund these unforeseen emergencies.

3. There's always a job to be had. There's no shame in working at McDonalds or The Home Depot. Work is work.

4. Make a budget and live within your means. If need be, get an additional job. It won't be forever, especially if you're applying the highly successful get-out-of-debt plan by Dave Ramsey: Financial Peace University—a truly worthwhile investment of your time and money. The program will radically change your life for the better.

Equality and Entitlement

Visit Dave Ramsey's website. (See "Recommended Resources" at the back of this book)

5. Give to God and experience the wealth of His promise:

    - Honor the Lord with your wealth, with the firstfruits of all your crops; then your barns will be filled to overflowing, and your vats will brim over with new wine. (Proverbs 3:9–10)

    This is called tithing, which is biblical. He even invites us to test His promise:

    - "Bring the whole tithe into the storehouse, that there may be food in my house. Test me in this," says the Lord Almighty, "and see if I will not throw open the floodgates of heaven and pour out so much blessing that there will not be room enough to store it." (Malachi 3:10)

6. Promote job growth by encouraging small businesses to grow and hire—which means being a patron of small businesses. Shop local, as they say.

7. Vote for conservatives who will stop heavy regulations and taxation on small businesses.

8. Vote for conservatives who will end wars. We won't and cannot force the Afghanis or any other nation to accept democracy. Instead, we can bring our troops home to secure our northern and southern borders. Build the wall.

9. Vote for conservatives who will increase financial appropriations for our military!

10. Vote for conservatives who will monetarily strengthen our nation.

A businessman from New Orleans, visiting Vail Valley regarding the department I work for, chatted with me. In the course of our conversation, he said, "You wouldn't believe the waste and fraud happening in my home city with federal money, in the aftermath of Hurricane Katrina [2005] and the BP oil spill [2010] that grossly affected our city.

I assured him, "I can believe it!"

He'd been encouraged to apply for federal funds and he said he did so "for the heck of it." A few weeks later, he received a check for $30,000 and couldn't believe it. I could. Waste, fraud, abuse.

That payout was so wrong; money coming out of our—*my*—tax dollars. Part of me wanted to tell him, "Return it. Federal money is not free money!" The other part of me thought, *The government has no clue how to spend money wisely and responsibly.* It doesn't grow on trees.

Liberal political leaders act as though our country is in a financial surplus and turns a blind eye for the sake of padding their own pockets! This is a serious problem, which reminded me of a local freeway project here in Eagle County, Colorado. The Colorado DOT replaced rusted guardrails with brand new shiny ones, which in my view was not necessary. The old ones, despite some rust and age, were still perfectly sturdy for the intended job. Such examples (there are countless) are why our nation's debt is currently over

$33 trillion and rising. This country is in danger economically, politically, and socially, and we can thank Democrats *and* Republicans for this mess. Both parties are to blame.

Affordable Care Act a.k.a. Obamacare

I was very disappointed to hear a Republican-appointed Supreme Court nominee Chief Justice John Roberts side with Democrats when in 2012 he voted to uphold the constitutionality of so-called Obamacare (enacted March 2010). In my opinion, the Affordable Care Act goes against our Constitution. The example of Roberts sidling up is why I put little faith and trust in justices and politicians. Many have been proven corrupt, greedy, and bought off. Money talks, people listen.

> **Rather than blindly following an individual or group labeled conservatives and Republicans, learn the truth about each to make informed decisions.**

Obamacare consists of "death panels" as explained by former 2008 vice presidential running Sarah Palin:

> The America I know and love is not one in which my parents or my baby with Down Syndrome will have to stand in front of Obama's "death panel" so his bureaucrats can decide, based on a subjective judgment of their "level of productivity in society," whether they are worthy of health care. Such a system is downright evil.[56]

Anyone who calls you insane for believing this, ignore them; they're naive.

How can we judge the value of one life over another? Whether the individual in question is in the womb, middle age, or ninety-seven. God decides who is given life, who lives, and when one's life is to end. Human beings are the *created*, not equal to the Creator, God, and to make decisions that belong to Him alone is sin against Him. That's why I also struggle with capital punishment. The role of government is to reward the righteous and to punish the wicked.

We must protect the sanctity of human life.

I'm still holding out hope that our Supreme Court will ultimately overturn Obamacare as they did Roe vs. Wade. Both show the importance and consequences of elections.

What the Bible says about work:

- "The Lord God took the man and put him in the Garden of Eden to work it and take care of it" (Genesis 2:15).

- "Warn those who are idle" (1 Thessalonians 5:14).

- "The one who is unwilling to work shall not eat" (2 Thessalonians 3:10).

- "The craving of a sluggard will be the death of him, because his hands refuse to work" (Proverbs 21:25).

- "All hard work brings a profit, but mere talk leads only to poverty" (Proverbs 14:23).

- "Whatever you do, work at it with all your heart, as working for the Lord, not for human masters, since you know that you will receive an inheritance from the Lord as a reward. It is the Lord Christ you are serving" (Colossians 3:23–24).

CHAPTER 7

Feminism

First, I have absolutely nothing against women, only against feminism. As a heterosexual man, I find women to be a beautiful creation of God.

As I've read the Bible and followed the news, I've come to the truth that feminism is anti-God, thereby anti-Christian. Print and protests through the decades since 1848—the public onset of the women's liberal movement—have often indicated that feminism carries a disdain for men and motherhood.

Feminism is selfish, rooted in dislike of the fact that men and women are designed differently.

Men are not women, and women are not men. They are different.

Does "different" mean better or worse? No, just different. Does different mean men or women are more valuable than the other? No, just different. Does different mean men or women are more capable human beings than the other? No, just different. Does different mean the roles of men or women are greater than the other? No, just different.

As I've read the Bible, I've found obvious that God designed men and women differently in order to fulfill differing roles that together become the complete picture and purpose, which is a good thing! Just read the book of Ruth, for one! That's a great story on womanhood.

Before I further expound on feminism, I credit women with having the most difficult task in the world: child-rearing. I can't imagine giving birth. Where would we all be without the patience and love of attentive mothers? My grandmother and mother made a big impact on my life and I'm thankful for them. My fondest memories are of spending time in Merrill, WI with Grandma Lorraine. She passed away in 2016 at age one hundred. That's a good, long life.

What I oppose is not women but the caustic views of feminism that twist and want to eradicate God's design and plan for men and women, marriage between one man and one woman, pregnancy, and the values of the traditional family. I cringe when I hear a mother referred to as a "birthing person."

I pray that all who do not know Christ will turn to Him for truth and no longer "conform to the pattern of this world, but be transformed by the renewing of your mind. Then you will be able to test and approve what God's will is—his good, pleasing and perfect will" (Romans 12:2). This is probably my favorite Bible verse, as the mind, in my opinion, is the most powerful thing in this world. The mind must be renewed!

I pray that men and women will focus on fulfilling their God-given purposes rather than self-assigned duties. Our responsibilities have already been assigned by God. And I write this commentary from a heart of love, though many on the left would claim that my thoughts are "hate speech." Far from it. Wanting people to end up in heaven after this life is not hate, it's love. There is no place called purgatory. You're going to one of two places when you die: heaven or hell. A sports analogy would be "There is no on-deck circle."

I don't oppose equal pay for equal work, but that's just one branch of feminism. Feminists want men to reverse their God-given purposes and traits. For example, men being the primary caregiver of the children while women become the primary breadwinners. This view works to abolish God's design of men and women as different for specific purposes. God makes clear that He designed men to lead with love (not rule), to provide with love (not prohibit), and to protect with love (not wield power over women). Getting back to "equal pay for equal work", do women playing professional basketball (WNBA) or soccer (USWNT) bring in the ratings that men do? No.

Feminists want men to be effeminate, which declares that activities like cross-dressing is okay and normal for men. It's not okay or normal for men to behave like women and for women to behave like men. Gender-crossing and gender-diminishing behaviors, whether male or female, are opposite of God's design and plan for mankind, which dishonors Him and mocks Him. For whatever reason, feminists want weak men. The country needs strong men to serve in the military and law enforcement. We need men to keep the country and our communities safe.

In Brannon Howse's book *Grave Influence*, he wrote:

> Feminism has accomplished its goals—the destruction of the American family through the destruction of the father and the resulting rise of the welfare state. . . . The bottom line is that feminism has been a tool of the humanists to destroy the family. . . . Leading humanist Paul Kurtz said, 'Humanism and feminism are inextricably interwoven.' Humanists and Communists have sought the destruction of the American family because they know that, for America, the family has been the instrument for passing on Christian values and a Biblical worldview-the source and foundation of our freedoms and Constitutional Republic.[57]

(*Grave Influence* is an excellent book for those who enjoy current events and biblical truth.)

The following paragraphs are examples of our nation's radical changes, many the result of the feminist movement. Most issues I address in the following pages are in direct opposition to God's design. The first two examples are cautionary, as they reek of the "politically correct" definition of inclusivity, encouraged by the feminist movement if not spurred in large by the movement:

- Was Shanna Easton, first-ever female official of a pre-season NFL game, hired because she was the most competent candidate for the role? If so, great! I wish her well. I felt awkward because this change appeared to be the NFL forcing inclusivity as the priority.

- A bumper sticker I saw in Colorado read: "Silly boys, trucks are for girls." I suppose then that there's a bumper sticker out there in our backward country that reads:

Feminism

"Silly girls, Barbies are for boys." I'll say it again: males and females are different!

The more serious issues of feminism are terrifying. Although the term "woke" is recent, our military became "woke" with the June 2008 Defense Directive 1304.26, "Don't Ask, Don't Tell," 1993–2011. Our now all-inclusive military is not only an institution allowing homosexuals to serve but allowing women in combat. As of 2016, women became eligible for every combat role. Such alterations should not be made to the institution challenged and charged with defending our nation and ensuring our country's safety. Such allowances create more and greater challenges that weaken our defense—the primary role of the US military to keep America safe—due to the distinct differences between males and females. Feminism doesn't deal with reality. There's a video on YouTube of a male Marine wrestling a female Marine. I'll give you one guess who won that match. It was over in about five seconds. Testosterone matters.

As seen in the example above, women are simply not as strong as men; women lack the level of testosterone produced in the male-created body. This lack alone weakens our troops' effectiveness and places our warriors and soldiers in greater peril. For example, I once attended a dodgeball event at a local middle school where the teams were a mix of both genders. By the end of the event, the game had turned to males versus females, no longer working together but against each other. The outcome was predictable, as nature dictates. Males are naturally much more aggressive and dominant, so naturally the male team members cleared the other side within minutes. Again, reality.

The scorekeeper, recognizing that the outcome wasn't looking so good for the gals, *changed the rules to accommodate the women* by preventing the males from going to mid-court! The guys had to stay between their wall and the free-throw line, not permitted to go beyond that point. Yet, the females were allowed to pass mid-court and go all the way to the males' free-throw line. How can that possibly be "equality?"

Guess what happened? The males still dominated the match despite the huge advantage given to the females. People oppose reality.

The distinct God-created differences between males and females doesn't mean that one is non-competitively better than the other—just different.

There's now a growing uprise in our nation due to homosexual men identifying as women and being allowed to compete in women's high-ranking sports for national and Olympic titles. Again and again we see the titles stolen by female-posing males because that's their so-called "right." Females who have dedicated their entire lives to excelling in women's sports are rightly taking a stand against this unjust inequality while many are also still demanding to participate in male sports. Just as men are now competing in women's sports, women are boxing and fighting in mixed martial arts. Look up the story of Lia Thomas, the dude swimmer that identifies as a woman.

What's wrong with this picture?! What is this world coming to?! It's so wrong.

As a man myself, I don't find attractive women who are wearing mouthguards, or throwing jabs and roundhouse punches at other women. Likewise, it's insulting to see men pretending to be women and hijacking women's sports. Thankfully, we have women like Riley Gaines speaking up and standing up for women. She's bold and courageous.

God created male and female to function differently to fulfill different purposes.

We need only to look at the wholeness and balance of creation as our example and proof of God's design and intentions. The differences between males and females are like two puzzle pieces—unique, different, and perfectly fitting to create God's complete picture and purpose for creation, including mankind.

What continues is liberal males and females attempting to defy the Creator's perfect design by forcing roles that destroy the master picture and purpose while mocking God. "Do not be deceived: God cannot be mocked. A man reaps what he sows" (Galatians 6:7).

The forced philosophy of political correctness that's invaded our military is extremely dangerous. The work of protecting our nation is not a scoreboard or title at stake. Our national security, military members, and citizens are rapidly moving deeper into grave danger! Stop playing games with our national security! Only males should be on the front lines, fighting in combat, because protecting is part of God's divine design for men. The physiological nature of men produces the aggression and dominance needed to win in combat. Men have testosterone, which is a good thing.

Political correctness on any level and platform (military, gender, sports, parenting, government) is not to our citizen's and nation's advantage but to our destruction.

This brings me to the reverse role of men staying home to raise the children while women work to provide for the family. Backwards. The terminology includes house dad, stay-at-home dad, and caregiver. This role reversal brings its own unique challenges that weaken and destroy individuals, families, societies, and nations. When dads assume the role as their children's primary caregivers, there are fundamental nurturing needs not being met in the children. By nature, men do not possess the nurturing capabilities necessary to grow the wholeness and inner balance in children. The father and mother roles in partnership create the stability, balance, and strength to fulfill God's supreme purposes for mankind.

Without inner wholeness and balance, the thoughts and actions of children work against them, against community, against society, against their futures as adults, and against future generations.

In all of creation, we see that male creatures protect the family while female creatures nurture the family. We've seen this *natural* design work perfectly effectively since the beginning of time. Why? Because God's design is perfect and meant for creation's utmost well-being across the board, from environmental nature to creatures to mankind. We see the perfection of wholeness and balance by God and destruction by mankind. We destroy what He gifted.

Does God's design differences between men and women mean that one sex is better than the other? No! Simply different to best fulfill—together—God's divine purposes. Men protect. Women nurture.

The distinctive roles of mothers and fathers are equally important roles. God designed "equality" of men and women, without favor for one over the other but as "one" in the union of marriage between one male and one female and "one" with Christ in the fellowship of believers, the church. Christ is the groom. The church is the bride.

Absolutely, single and childless women have every reason to have jobs and careers, and earn good money. Go for it! But when a woman becomes a mother and a man a father, their lives must be dedicated to their roles and purposes as *parents*. Every child needs their mother in the mothering role and their father in the fathering role—male and female united as "one," creating wholeness and balance that's modeled to and invested in their children.

There's a rapidly-growing role reversal of the sexes that's become a pandemic. Girls trying to be boys and boys trying to be girls, mocking God as Creator by thinking we have the power and right to change His divine work. Johnny, go play with your Legos and Matchbox cars while Jill plays with Barbie.

Girls and boys: Females and males were made differently for the vital reasons and purposes addressed above.

> **Girls:** I urge you to return to dressing and behaving as a girl, enjoying activities that are natural female tendencies, such as playing with dolls and make-up, preparing you for your future role as a woman, wife, and mother.
>
> **Boys:** I urge you to return to dressing and behaving as boys. Enjoying activities that are natural male tendencies, such as warring with boxing gloves and climbing trees as

watch towers, preparing you for your future role as a man, husband, and father.

Feminists: If you want to be tough and be seen as tough, take back the extraordinarily tough, challenging, hard-work role God specifically designed for women: birthing, nurturing, caring for, and raising our children. Womanhood is not a curse; it's a blessing and enormous responsibility! Thank God for mothers. I mentioned earlier how big a role my grandmother and mother played in my life.

I recalled an article in *USA TODAY*, "celebrating" the 50th anniversary of *The Feminist Mystique* by well-known feminist Betty Friedan.[58] Looking at what she believed and pushed for, I have issues with this statement from her book: "We can no longer ignore that voice within women that says: 'I want something more than my husband and my children and my home.'"[59]

That's a picture of the epitome of selfishness, ingratitude, and lack of appreciation for one of the highest and holiest roles bestowed on women. Your husband and children matter a lot!

These character flaws are prominent in women who insist on not "merely" being or "just" being a stay-at-home mother, as though the role is somehow the lowest of low. Lies. Deception. Like many liberal thoughts, our society has been saturated with both to the immense dilution of truth about the reverence of motherhood: raising human beings, the next generations. Kids need their mother!

In chapter three of Friedan's book, she shares her decision to leave her doctorate studies in psychology after she'd won a graduate fellowship.

> During the congratulations, ... I felt a strange uneasiness. ...
> "Is this really what I want to be?"
>
> I married, had children, lived according to the feminine mystique as a suburban housewife. But still the question haunted me. I could sense no purpose in my life.[60]

It's tragic when a mother and wife is blinded, oppressed, and shackled by the devastating lie of Satan that she holds "no purpose" in those roles. It's tragic to miss this truth: motherhood shapes lives far greater, deeper, and lasting than a career in psychology. I'll say it again: We need mothers!

Kids need their mothers—present and involved, along with fathers. Nurturing, shaping, guiding, and preparing their hearts and minds to become all that God created them to be—women and men of God in the highest positions of responsibility and honor! I think I have made it clear that it all starts in the home with loving parents.

- Not all are meant to be married or to become parents, as was the case of the apostle Paul, and for Saul's daughter Michal. Here is what God says about children:

- Children are a heritage from the Lord, offspring a reward from him. (Psalm 127:3)

- Children's children are a crown to the aged, and parents are the pride of their children. (Proverbs 17:6)

A home without a parental presence is like a garden without the essential tending that results in thriving, whole, healthy produce—the "fruit of the spirit" of God. Parents impact the future of the world. Instead of being present and tending to the family, our society has reduced child-raising to a sport, a competition, a scoreboard, even a fad, and also a "mistake" one must thereafter tolerate.

A future of thriving is dependent on the family behaving according to the decrees and promises of God that produce that greatest honor and recognition—God's, for all of eternity.

The family should

- read together,
- eat together,
- pray together,
- attend enriching activities together,
- worship God together,
- practice and example values, principles, and morals together,

Children are often left to essentially nurture themselves with the aid of sitters, school teachers, and coaches who are otherwise divided by the fact that they have their own lives, not responsible for the child outside their hours of duty. Children who lack their parents' active involvement and demonstrated love will suffer mental, emotional, and spiritual damage. Neglect is not okay.

Marriage and parenting are vital to creating and maintaining a strong society, country, and world, Yet, Ms. Freidan assessed those two high callings as over-rated and insignificant.

Feminism

Other reasons this country is headed down a dangerous path includes: (1) redefined and undermined marriages and (2) parents not taking their elite positions of responsibility fully and seriously.

Discussing one of Ms. Freidan's quotes, a blog writer wrote, "women were not satisfied with their role in society anymore and wanted more in life. Women had a new life plan . . . ; not trying to find total fulfillment through marriage and motherhood alone."[61]

My response? Thank God for dedicated wives and mothers! All others and feminists, stop chasing things of this world and start embracing your God-given roles.

What the Bible says about marriage and parenting:

- "He who finds a wife finds what is good and receives favor from the Lord" (Proverbs 18:22).

- [Jesus] "'Haven't you read,' he replied, 'that at the beginning the Creator "made them male and female," and said, "For this reason a man will leave his father and mother and be united to his wife, and the two will become one flesh"? So they are no longer two, but one flesh. Therefore what God has joined together, let no one separate'" (Matthew 19:4–6).

- "Start children off on the way they should go, and even when they are old they will not turn from it" (Proverbs 22:6).

- "In everything set them an example by doing what is good. In your teaching show integrity, seriousness" (Titus 2:7).

- "As a father has compassion on his children, so the Lord has compassion on those who fear him" (Psalm 103:13).

- *[Mothers]* "She speaks with wisdom, and faithful instruction is on her tongue. She watches over the affairs of her household and does not eat the bread of idleness. Her children arise and call her blessed; her husband also, and he praises her" *(*Proverbs 31:26–28).

CHAPTER 8

Sustainability

Years ago, I watched a CNN Town Hall featuring Green Party presidential candidate (2016) Jill Stein and her running mate. I was more afraid of their views than I was of Bernie Sanders'! Jill Stein was less than impressive. She spent considerable time discussing the environment and our military. She's another example of a politician who will expose us to grave danger. Such influencers are not qualified to serve as our commander-in-chief.

Ms. Stein wanted a "green new deal, by transitioning to 100% clean renewable energy by 2030, and investing in public transit, sustainable agriculture, and conservation."[62] Red flag!

Not realistic. Sorry to be the bearer of bad news, but we need fossil fuels. As for public transit, I'd rather not be one of the three people on the bus. You have all that room, but one loses their personal freedom to drive. No, thank you. I'll keep driving my fuel-injected car. And sustainable agriculture? What does that even mean?

We need coal plants to continue operating because coal is abundant, inexpensive, produces electricity, can safely be stored, isn't dependent on the weather, like wind, or solar power, is easy to transport, and reduces our dependence on foreign oil.

Ms. Stein examples the left who wants to demonize fossil fuels to "save Mother Earth." Let's use the natural resources we have, which also provide jobs to local economies. Fire up the coal plants! Coal is what's needed to power electric vehicles, by the way. Coal is cool in my book. Literally, in my book!

Candidates who are pro-earth ("averting climate catastrophe") and anti-US armed forces, should prompt in us a red flag of warning. Ms. Stein was this candidate. Much like a cow fart, she's gone with the wind, thankfully. And by the way, that wind cannot power a town or city!

Visit Ms. Stein's website (Jillstein.org), to read her "Power of the People Plan," which also includes

- health care as a right;
- $15 an hour federal minimum wage;
- a global treaty to halt climate change;
- ending police brutality;
- expanding women's rights and protecting the LGBTQ community;
- legalizing marijuana and hemp;
- closing Guantanamo;
- ending wars and drone attacks;

Sustainability

- cutting military spending by at least 50%; and
- closing the 700+ foreign military bases[63]

A "right" is something you have that doesn't cost someone else anything. Health care isn't a right but part of what the American workforce works to gain.

Health care packages are offered by most employers. If an individual cannot get coverage through their employer, there are alternatives for a monthly premium. The purpose of health insurance is to help cover you financially when you have unexpected medical expenses. Please don't falsely assume, believe, or state that health care is a right. Health care is a gain for those who work for it. There's that word again: work. Those who are able to work but refuse to do so should not be given handouts of any sort, such as free health care and food stamps that working people are forced by our government to pay through taxation. End the food stamps!

Minimum wage of $15 an hour may sound great, but private sector wage is not a matter that any level of government should be meddling in. Wage, job title, job requirements, job education, and job responsibilities are the free-enterprise rights of employers, just as determining what constitutes an entry level versus a high-skill position is an employer's right. The federal and state governments are not in a position to determine how minimum wage will affect the profitability of a company. That's the right of employers, including determining wage based on employee experience, education, needs of the company, and other such good-business factors. Government should not be meddling in the private sector, whether it be minimum wage or health insurance.

On so-called climate change, scientists (mortal beings who often have a political agenda) tell us there's an urgent need to address this subject that they and others have turned into a "critical issue." The human race has survived (and thrived) for approximately 6,000 years, and we are still here, along with God's designed four seasons. He is in control of whatever climate and earth changes He deems—as exampled by the downpour on Pharoah's kingdom, "the worst hailstorm that has ever fallen on Egypt, from the day it was founded till now" (Exodus 9:18). In the king's wicked, arrogant, greedy, and persecuting ways, he had refused to release God's people from captivity. God controls the weather.

The least of our concerns is environmental changes, such as global warming and climate change. We have far greater, pressing needs we have control over, such as fighting terrorism, the daily mass murdering of babies (abortion), the persecution of Christians throughout the world, our US economy in shambles and under the on-growing weight of debt, which is currently at $33 trillion. As I finished writing this book, Roe v. Wade was overturned. What a blessing for those precious babies! The sanctity of human life wins! Life wins!

On the issue of police brutality, this does occasionally happen. I get it. Every profession has good and bad employees because employees are people and people have a sinful nature and free will to make good and bad choices. I believe the vast majority of police officers are ethical, professional, and truly serve to protect the public. Law enforcement should not be vilified. We should instead thank officers of the law for their public service and willingness to place themselves in harm's way every time they put on their uniforms. In light of our radical, unhinged nation, where would we be as citizens without protection by law enforcement? They are, in fact, "the thin blue line." I pray for their safety. They are local heroes and should be thanked. Buy them a coffee or a meal when you see them at restaurants. It's the right thing to do out of gratitude.

Regarding women and those who have chosen alternative lifestyles, they have the right to work, vote, bear arms, and serve in the military. In most states, they now have the right to "marry" same-sex individuals. So, what additional rights are needed? They are Americans. Therefore, they have rights.

But to say homosexuality should parallel heterosexuality is not okay. The backbone of our society is the traditional family. I love seeing families out together, at ballgames, restaurants, church, etc. There's just something special about traditional families spending time together, even if they're just on a walk in the neighborhood.

The continued moral decline of America also includes legalizing marijuana and hemp, a Schedule I drug. Marijuana, like any medically-controlled substance, is reported to cause impaired mental functioning, anxiety and panic, hallucinations, flashbacks, and depression. Yet, we should legalize this drug? Should we then legalize other Schedule I drugs, such as heroin and LSD? In 2022, Colorado legalized mushrooms in a ballot measure. This world does not need more people on drugs.

Some people feel that the war on drugs is a waste of resources. But do we really want a country where drugs are legalized, leading to more crime and other dysfunction? We have enough of both as it is. We need district attorneys, who are tough on crime, to sentence criminals to lengthy prison sentences when needed to protect society. I'm big on ensuring safe communities, just as I am on the right to bear arms—our Second Amendment. Towns and cities should focus on creating jobs, fighting crime, and overall cleanliness. If I was a mayor, I'd want people to work and be safe, and we would keep the city clean. Just a random thought.

Law-abiding citizens have every right to protect themselves.

On the subject of closing Guantanamo Bay (Gitmo)—a detention center where terrorists are held by our military to help keep Americans safe—why would politicians want this military base closed? Answer: political correctness. Maybe we hurt the feelings of the terrorists. We need such a place to keep evil individuals locked up. We need intelligence agencies that work to keep us safe. If safety against terrorists means keeping Gitmo open, so be it, as with allowing intelligence interrogation tactics like waterboarding. (I once attempted to buy a T-shirt that read, "I'd rather be waterboarding." It got lost in the mail. Good job, USPS).

Evil is not nice or soft and does not respond to nice or soft but instead seizes nice and soft opportunities.

We cannot coddle terrorists and other criminals. Lock them up. Throw away the key.

ISIS and other radical Islamic extremists want to kill Americans. They are still plotting and taking action to do so, and will continue. Where evil people are committing evil acts, wars and war tactics, like drone attacks, will continue to be necessary. This is reality. Thus, we need to *increase* military spending and keep our foreign military bases well-equipped and trained. We need a strong military to protect us. Protect the borders and protect Americans.

Sustainability

On environmental issues:

- Recycling will not save one soul. Much of our refuse ends up at landfills anyway. We have plenty of land in this country to throw things away. When people ask "What's the environmental impact?" I just roll my eyes. Have you ever flown and seen how much land we have? Plenty of room for garbage.

- Climate change (Greenpeace, sustainability, etc.): We are to worship the Creator, not creation. He made everything. Should we really spend money to decrease the earth's temperature by one degree? No, we should not. Follow the money, because someone is profiting from this scare tactic.

Earth Day, celebrated annually on April 22 since 1970, is, in my view, a day worshipped by pagans, liberals, and humanists, marked to remind us of their faith and hope in Mother Earth. Instead of worshipping God, the Creator of all things, they worship Mother Earth. I pray for these people.

> In the beginning God created the heavens and the earth. (Genesis 1:1)

On Earth Day, we hear in over-abundance the terms climate change and sustainability. Here's a thought: we, believers in Jesus Christ, should turn Earth Day celebrations around, to worship the Creator. How about a Creator Day?

Our local school administration encouraged students to "go green." Liberal brainwashing of children continues on a daily basis. Parents and school boards need to step up and say enough! We must hold school boards accountable for what they're allowing to be taught in every grade. Unfortunately, liberal teachings include the lies of evolution, environmentalism, sustainability, and others. Worse is the teaching that God does not exist. They will find out one day that He does, in fact, exist. Every knee will bow.

I have a friend in Milwaukee whose family member attended the University of Wisconsin–Madison. On the first day of class, the individual was told, "The Bible isn't real." Welcome to college!

If this country doesn't repent and turn back to God, soon, it will be doomed.

On "Going Green," I once came across an *Alvin and the Chipmunks* episode when channel surfing. With nothing else entertaining to watch, I settled on the cartoon and, to my astonishment, found the episode was about "Going Green" and the carbon footprint of the Chipmunks. *What in the world?!* I googled the episode and found the following excerpt from the synopsis:

> The Chipmunks and the Chipettes are excited to be participating in a Going Green contest in which the winner earns a trip to Hawaii. Jeanette, who's more concerned with spreading awareness, brings news that she told a competitive eco-friendly classmate, Pamela, about the competition so other families can participate and lower their carbon footprint.[64]

How would the contest winner get to Hawaii? Via an airplane! Maybe the competition winner should swim to Hawaii!? We have airplanes. Use them. Fly them. Enjoy them.

Sustainability

Very disturbing is leftist propaganda in cartoons, further saturating the minds of our children. Who, other than children, primarily, is watching cartoons? Children are being brainwashed into adopting a liberal mindset—even when they're watching cartoons! They're pushed to think they must recycle and do as little damage as possible to the planet. In truth, the planet is just fine—it's under God's control. Now, kids, go outside and play. Climb trees, play sports, play kick the can.

Green Week has been celebrated by the NBA since 2009. Millionaire athletes star in commercials that encourage people to recycle. They probably care as much about recycling as Mr. Obama cared about your health. In reality, the participating NBA players are likely driving gas-guzzling vehicles. I'm reminded of the following idiom with a twist: Do as we say, not as we do! I'm reminded of Al Gore regarding his carbon emission credits. I smell hypocrisy. Such political elites care only about gaining power, money, and control—not the good of the people. There is so much hypocrisy—do as they say, not as they do!

At this writing, the school's still-standing position echoes throughout various areas of their site, as does their Earth Day celebration, Earthstock.[65] I have an issue and concern with the second paragraph of their "sustainability movement" and "reducing our carbon footprint." The rest is fine and dandy—go ahead and recycle, use recycled materials, and promote alternative fuels for transportation—whatever they believe. However, we have resources and it's okay if we use them. These resources provide energy and also jobs.

Sustainability. Simply put, people need to be aware that the term was coined by the UN in their desire to establish a one-world government. Many communities in the US are complying with this UN effort. What's truly behind UN initiatives is global power and politics! It's about power, money and control. Likewise, the "*plan*demic" (Covid-19) was another attempt toward establishing a one-world government. The virus was manufactured in a Wuhan, China lab. Our own government was in on it.

Be aware of what's going on in the world.

I was especially concerned about the 2012 Earth Summit held in Rio de Janeiro, Brazil. The summit involved a lot of global goals, UN desires, and sustainability talk. Be aware of those who are behind all the socialist agendas. Such people believe that man is in control, not God. They want manmade laws while ignoring God's laws and truth. Pay special attention to Agenda 21.

> *Side Note:* Tom DeWeese, founder and president of The American Policy Center does an excellent job explaining Agenda 21. People need to know the basics of this agenda because it's a knife, actively carving out America's future. Educate yourself. Visit the website The American Policy Center, one of the other trustworthy resources included in back of this book, and get involved locally. We can stop this madness.

I think of a small town in Colorado that, like many towns and cities, made recycling mandatory. How can the government possibly enforce such a law? Will town officials rummage through garbage in search of violators? If so, what exactly might be the punishment for not recycling? "Mandatory" recycling might go over about as smoothly as Obamacare. Since the beginning of time, many government officials have had their eyes and hearts set on power, which returns us to the subject of worshiping ourselves and the things of this world. People cannot worship God while worshipping money. One must choose between money and the Creator.

> "No one can serve two masters. Either you will hate the one and love the other, or you will be devoted to the one and despise the other. You cannot serve both God and money." (Matthew 6:24)

I used to recycle. Actually, I was obsessive about it, feeling guilt and shame about not recycling. Now, I think recycling is just a show of self-righteousness (like wearing a mask during the Covid-19 "*plan*demic"). I don't use an eco-friendly grocery bag. In my view, they look too much like a purse and, I prefer plastic and paper bags. Plastic bags come in handy when I'm walking a dog. With plastic bag bans, it's ridiculous to see people loading their groceries into a shopping cart with no bags. Just provide bags already! Environmentalism has gone way too far. It is nonsense and inconvenient.

People are concerned about what all goes into a landfill. Well, as I've mentioned previously, we have plenty of land for garbage in this country. As I fly to various places, I look out the window and realize again how much land we have for waste disposal. If I was the governor of Montana or Wyoming, I'd try to profit from it! God created the earth to meet all our needs, including refuse. What if we build holes for trash and after decades of use, we simply lay soil and plant grass to cover it up? Like it never existed! Genius.

I have recycled aluminum cans, mainly to donate to the Boy Scouts, and recycled newspapers and plastics. But, no longer.

Recycling isn't a bad thing, but like other leftist issues, the hype has gone overboard. What if we were all as concerned about the state of our families and our eternities? Recycling and focusing on the earth and such pale in comparison. Some local youth went on a recycling binge by making their prom dresses out of newspapers. God bless them for their efforts, but the dresses looked ridiculous—as though the girls were wearing shaming, cardboard signs like criminals are forced to wear in lineups. Come on, people. Just buy a dress.

Locally, there was an event called "Save the Planet." Like many awareness issues, "Save the Planet" platformers are pulling people into extremes at the cost of far greater crises like sex trafficking (estimated 2,100 victims per day[66]), and child abuse (untold thousands of children are suffering). Watch the movie *Sound of Freedom* to see what's happening in the world of sex trafficking. People, please stop trying to save the planet! I'm not saying we should abandon the responsibilities God gave to us to care for the created gifts He's blessed us with. Be a good steward, yes. But God created and controls the earth, so who are we to play savior of the planet? There are far greater issues at stake. Environmentalism is now a religion and Satan is the senior pastor.

Those marching for the cause that our world should address global warming (a.k.a. climate change) is yet another example that distracts people from the gravest issues. At the 2014 march in New York City, Al Gore wanted you to do as he said, not as he did. How about these activists spend quality time with their families?

My buddy and I often joked about liberal activists who want to save planet earth. The truth, though, is far from funny: Earth will pass away but human souls will either spend eternity with God or apart from Him in perpetual darkness, misery of every aspect, and eternal hopelessness and despair, regretting that they dismissed their Creator, many not believing there is a God, and took their own way through life. There will be "weeping and gnashing of teeth" (Matthew 8:12) where they go.

We, believers, will be held accountable too. We all must give an account. And as a sinner, that scares me!

We will stand before God and give an account of how we used our time here on earth. Are we using this time to fulfill His purposes for us? Are we sharing the gospel?

Unlike planting trees and recycling cardboard (temporary things), the Bible and our choices to follow God or dismiss Him will have eternal consequences.

Have you pondered the term *eternal*?

Forever is a concept that's hard for human beings to grasp. We all function within the element of timeframes. I want to be certain that my forever and others' forever will be forever in the glory of God.

Here in Eagle County, earth worshippers are among those who attend the local Yoga Fest. They take pictures of their friends recycling various items, post them on social media, and also send photocopies to our local paper. They are so absorbed in this world that most, if not all, are blinded to our Creator, God.

> **Our purpose as Christians is to not only glorify God in our daily lives but also to be bold to lead others to the truth found in Jesus Christ.**

A social media friend posted that he'd like every person who reads his post to pick up one piece of garbage the following day. I have a better idea: read one Scripture verse a day! Encourage people to read the gospel. People will just continue to litter. This life is temporary.

Think about it: picking up a piece of garbage is a matter of maturity and common sense. Again, be a good steward. Those who leave garbage strewn around have apparently not yet achieved either. While picking up someone else's garbage may temporarily make the person feel better about themselves, that good deed has no eternal value. Leading someone to the gospel leads them to eternal life!

While I am against littering, obviously, I believe people need to be taught instead of postered, platformed, and catered to. One day, all the garbage (literally and figuratively) will be destroyed by God when He destroys this earth.

This life is short. We need to reevaluate our highest priority, which should be the gospel. Pick up something that carries eternal value. Pick up a Bible—the living Word of God.

United Nations and Agenda 21

When I lived in Wisconsin, the Hales Corners Public Library raised the UN flag to fly alongside the US flag. Perhaps the library thought nobody would notice or care. They were wrong. I noticed and cared. I found the display disturbing, especially because our community had plans to build a Veterans memorial just a few yards from the flagpole. Our Veterans fought and died for the American flag and all that it represents as a republic—not for the

United Nations! I have long disliked the United Nations. It is a threat to American sovereignty.

Displaying the UN flag disturbed me to the point that I asked the library staff why a UN flag was flying at the library. The staff member seemed confused or played dumb, or maybe they truly didn't know the answer. The conversation went nowhere.

Wanting to see to it that the UN flag came down (and considering pulling it down myself if it came to that), I emailed Mark Belling, a Milwaukee conservative radio talk show host, and made him aware of the situation. Within a week, the UN flag was down. While I'd like to take credit for that victory, Mark Belling may have made a call to the librarian that flying the UN flag was unacceptable, and if it wasn't taken down soon, he'd use the concern as a topic on his radio show. Speak up when you see a wrong!

Conservatives must unite in defeating liberal agendas.

Send an e-mail to your congressman, make a phone call, write an op-ed and send it to the local newspaper. There are a number of things we can do as individuals. If enough people speak up, they will listen. There is power in numbers, and I truly believe this great country has a lot more conservatives than liberals.

Before moving to Colorado, I drove by the library and noticed that the UN flag was still no longer displayed. Let's keep it that way. Please be aware of what's displayed in your community and the leaders who try to pull such stunts. Hold people accountable for their actions. The Town of Avon, Colorado (near my town) is on board with the UN agenda. Pay attention to what your local government is up to. A good starting place is to visit your local government's website. Stay informed and, again, watch for talk about "sustainability." That's a red flag.

When I think of the UN, I think of the name Kofi Annan, and "corruption" comes to mind when I pair the two (much like I think of Illinois when I hear the term "corruption"). Mr. Annan was a corrupt leader, evidenced by his oil-for-food debacle. While I'm by no means a UN expert, I have concerns about the organization. The Council on Foreign Affairs reported:

> In 2023, the United Nations assessed the United States' share of the regular budget at 22 percent and its share of the peacekeeping budget at 27 percent.[67]

The US is the most prominent contributor! That's ludicrous, especially in our current US economy. Our money would be better spent securing our borders, especially in light of the ongoing drug war violence and cartels, and better spent paying off our $33-trillion national debt and creating jobs.

An article on the website Heritage Foundation included this statement:

> The scandal surrounding the U.N.-administered Oil-for-Food Program has also done immense damage to the world organization's already shaky credibility. The Oil-for-Food scandal is undoubtedly the biggest financial scandal in the history of the United Nations and probably the largest fraud of modern times. It shattered the liberal illusion that the UN is an arbiter of moral authority in the international sphere.[68]

Sustainability

The Oil-for-Food Program was subverted and manipulated by Saddam Hussein's regime, with the complicity of UN officials, to help prop up the Iraqi dictator. Saddam's dictatorship siphoned billions of dollars from the program through oil smuggling and systematic thievery by demanding illegal payments from companies buying Iraqi oil and through kickbacks from those selling goods to Iraq-all under UN noses. Bureaucrats.

Despite widespread criticism, Kofi Annan never took responsibility for the scandal that irreparably damaged the UN's reputation. A vast cloud remains over the UN Secretary-General concerning his meetings with senior officials from the Octenal, Swiss Oil-for-Food contractor that employed his son, Kojo, from 1995 to 1997 and continued to pay him through 2004.[69]

Regarding "sustainable development," here we are today (2023) with the UN's Agenda 21 targeted for 2030. According to *Worldview Weekend Broadcast Network*, the term was first introduced in the document "UN Sustainable Development Agenda 21" at the 1992 Earth Summit as the official UN policy. Today the policy is simply referred to as Agenda 21. The following quote is how proponents of Agenda 21 define *sustainable development*:

> Agenda 21 proposes an array of actions which are intended to be implemented by EVERY person on Earth. It calls for specific changes in the activities of ALL people. Effective execution of Agenda 21 will REQUIRE a profound re-orientation of ALL humans, unlike anything the world has ever experienced.[70]

At the summit, President George H.W. Bush signed American acceptance of the Agenda 21 plan. The next year, in compliance with Agenda 21, President Bill Clinton signed Executive Order 12852, establishing the President's Council on Sustainable Development[71] "in order to 'harmonize' US development policy with UN directives as outlined in Agenda 21. The EO directed all agencies of the Federal Government to work with state and local community governments in a joint effort to 'reinvent' government using the guidelines outlined in Agenda 21."[72]

What are these guidelines and policies, and do we see them in action today? Agenda 21 calls for a reduction of energy and water use in order to:

- enforce alternative energy use, specifically wind and solar,

- control real-estate development, specifically the creation of mixed-use neighborhoods that contain high-density housing units (high-rise or tiny lots) along with office space, stores, and open space that will eliminate the use of cars, and

- develop public transportation, including high-speed light rail trains, etc.

These policies are rooted in the unfounded theory that man is creating "global warming." This charge is now in great disrepute throughout the world, yet proponents continue to press these policies. Though the Bush family is Republican, make no mistake, they are globalists.

Literally, everything related to sustainable policy leads to higher prices and a shortage of goods, and calls for sacrifice by citizens from planners. Consider the terminology used:

Sustainability

- "alternative energy" (Solyndra, anyone?)
- "controls over development" (I think of eminent domain and individual property rights.)
- "eliminating the use of cars" (Every progressive's dream. Car ownership = freedom.)
- "public transportation" (Bus ridership in Milwaukee County and Eagle County is mostly a waste—all that fuel for a handful of riders)
- "high-speed rail" (Being from Wisconsin, then Governor Scott Walker knew (thankfully) to turn down this "free" money, meaning federal taxpayer dollars.)
- "global warming" (makes ongoing appearances)
- "sustainable" (A term beat like a dead horse here in Colorado.)

On the UN's war on guns, particularly regarding our Second Amendment right to bear arms, the UN General Assembly adopted the Arms Trade Treaty (ATT). In 2011, The New American website stated that the UN "continues to promote its 'Small Arms Treaty.'... The most recent attack against the treaty was launched by Larry Bell.... According to Bell, the treaty... would force the United States to do the following:

- Confiscate and destroy all "unauthorized" civilian firearms...
- Ban the trade, sale, and private ownership of all semi-automatic weapons...

- Create an international gun registry, clearly setting the stage for full-scale gun confiscation.[73]

- I encourage you to read the article. We keep the government in check with gun ownership.

The UN also took authority on parental versus child rights. A source claims the UN's stance is that parental rights are abusive. Although numerous medical researchers corroborate that "the rational part of a teen's brain [prefrontal cortex] isn't fully developed and won't be until age 25,"[74] the UN advocates that children have the right to make their own decisions. Sex changes, anyone?

Liberals serving on the high court (especially former Supreme Court Justice Ruth Bader Ginsburg, and Supreme Court Justices Elena Kagan and Sonia Sotomayor) are frightening. I consider them a danger to this country as their agendas prove they believe the Constitution is a living, breathing document and they use this theory for political gain. Interpret the Constitution, not your agenda.

On the website of Supreme Court Justice Thurgood Marshall is the following statement from his May 6, 1987, bicentennial speech (this isn't good):

> I plan to celebrate the bicentennial of the Constitution as a living document, including the Bill of Rights and the other amendments protecting individual freedoms and human rights.[75]

What the Bible says about the earth and mankind:

- "God said, 'Let us make mankind in our image, in our likeness, so that they may rule over the fish in the sea and the birds in the sky, over the livestock and all the wild animals, and over all the creatures that move along the ground'" (Genesis 1:26).

- "God blessed them and said to them, 'Be fruitful and increase in number; fill the earth and subdue it. Rule over the fish in the sea and the birds in the sky and over every living creature that moves on the ground'" (Genesis 1:28).

- "You alone are the Lord. You made the heavens, even the highest heavens, and all their starry host, the earth and all that is on it, the seas and all that is in them. You give life to everything, and the multitudes of heaven worship you" (Nehemiah 9:6).

CHAPTER 9

Rewind: Our Nation's Leaders

Joe Biden (D)

US President, 2021–present

Our current president, Joe Biden, and his administration are intentionally destroying our country and what it stands for by (1) opening borders, (2) contributing to a failing economy, (3) promoting globalism, and (4) attacking the Second Amendment. Our nation is in shambles due to the Federal government's intentional efforts toward a one-world government (communism). The Deep State does exist and wields a lot of power—a network of appointed government officials and institutions who influence and enact government policy. I recommend the book *Killing the Deep State* by Jerome R. Corsi, PhD. (See "Recommended Resources.")

Donald Trump (R)

US President, 2017–2021

In the 2016 GOP presidential election, I was a fan of Scott Walker, Bobby Jindal, and Rick Santorum. These men had no chance of winning the GOP nomination. Instead, Donald J. Trump was nominated and voted in. When I thought of Trump as the GOP front-runner, I considered his failed marriages, casinos, and arrogance. He struck me as an angry and rude man. He claimed to be a Christian and his persona was especially interesting because he claimed he didn't need to seek forgiveness from God, which is strange since seeking God's forgiveness is a fundamental crux of Christianity.

I did like his views on illegal immigration, but overall, I was not initially a Trump fan. While I liked his bluntness and what he had to say about securing our borders and bombing ISIS, he didn't display good moral character prior to the election. How wrong I was about this man.

Having closely followed his presidency, I believe he's a true patriot and sharp businessman. Some say he is "polarizing," but in light of the grave issues our country is buried in and he's fought against, that trait pales. He got things done and took good care of the American people. We must re-elect Trump in 2024 and let him finish what he started in 2017. He won't save us, but he can greatly help us.

Donald J. Trump ended up being the greatest president of all time, in my opinion. Trump proved to be pro-military, pro-law enforcement, pro-Second Amendment, and his list of accomplishments is very impressive:

No. 1: Unprecedented growth

No. 2: Return of Manufacturing

No. 3: Record low unemployment

No. 4: Higher wages for workers

No. 5: Immigration control

No. 6: Making others pay their fair share

No. 7: Putting America first

No. 8: America at a greater state of readiness

No. 9: Decimation of the Islamic State

No. 10: Peace in the Middle East

No. 11: Reshaping the Federal Judiciary

No. 12: Establishing the Space Force

No. 13: True racial justice[76]

Barack Obama (D)

US President, 2009–2017

I wrote the following editorial to my local newspaper regarding the 2012 presidential election. I had done a lot of research prior and gathered facts and figures, primarily from the website VCY America. I recommend their radio station, WVCY, out of Milwaukee, Wisconsin—a Christian station I really like for current events and biblical truth. They do an excellent job and report truthfully on current events that mainstream media will not report. (See "Recommended Resources.")

Mainstream media is an enemy.

Rewind: Our Nation's Leaders

In 2012, I encouraged my blog readers to vote for the Romney-Ryan GOP ticket, asking (rhetorically) if we really wanted four more years of sky-rocketing federal debt, a bad-and-getting worse economy, high unemployment figures, a welfare state mentality, a weaker national defense, increased taxes, and continued administration corruption. It was obvious the Obama administration led us down the wrong path in four fundamental areas:

- **Economically:** the S&P downgraded the US credit rating from AAA to AA+; not surprising when you consider that the US government is currently borrowing approximately $50 thousand per *second*! Watch the "Real-Time Running Total" at www.usdebtclock.org. That's $180 thousand per hour, which is over $4 million per day!

- **Socially: entitlements—Biden's 2023 budget proposed over $2.6 trillion in "new entitlement program" spending.**[77]

- **Militarily**: cutting defense spending—$17.4 billion worth of programs cut[78]

- **Morally**: gay "marriage"—The U.S. Census Bureau cites 2 million same-sex couple households in the US in 2021 of which approximately 710 thousand are married, a drastic increase from 2008's .01 million.[79]

The facts show the dangers of liberal administrations. Yet, the American people spoke. How did we possibly reelect the most incompetent, corrupt, dishonest president of all time—Barack Obama? I don't get it.

When Jimmy Carter was elected (1977), I was age three. In 1980, the American people awoke to avoid a disastrous second term. That was back in the day when people had morals and exercised common sense. Case in point, we saw a true conservative in Ronald Reagan and elected him twice to office.

As you probably know, Mr. Obama was a community organizer connected with ACORN, a union-loving, capitalism-hating radical group. Again, I recommend reading about Saul Alinsky (*Rules for Radicals*).

What I saw from the Obama election was America's continued decline, both economically and morally. Apparently, a majority of U.S. citizens had either wanted incompetence, corruption, dishonesty, handouts, illegal immigration, debt, a weakened military, the promotion of homosexuality and gay "marriage," or kept their heads buried from the issues.

Keep in mind, this country will get what it deserves by our actions in voting.

Liberals would say my views are old school, archaic, out-of-touch, and that I'm a crazy Christian conservative, and so on. I simply speak my views and the truth found in the Bible. I simply read His Word and apply it to current events.

God is the source of all truth—*not Newsweek, Huffington Post*, CNN, or any other human source.

From My Blog, October 25, 2012

A friend in Milwaukee is an Independent in his political views, though I often think he's a Democrat in hiding. He's a smart man, but we often disagree on issues. However, he did have a valid point when he asked me why I wasn't supporting Andre Barnett, a conservative Independent candidate for president. That was a valid question, and my answer was, "This election is too important for me to give my vote to a candidate who doesn't stand a mathematical chance of winning the election. President Obama *must* be defeated."

We always hear how that an upcoming election is "the most important of our lifetime." This may be true in 2024 as globalists and Democrats look to steal elections—look what happened in 2020 and 2022. You cannot convince me that most Americans want corrupt and immoral people in office. These people are now stealing elections. There must be election integrity. States need to step up.

Although I wasn't a big fan of Mitt Romney, as soon as I heard that Paul Ryan was his GOP running mate, that immediately changed my view of the GOP ticket. We need a businessman in the Oval Office—a commander-in-chief who's not afraid to secure our borders and deal militarily with Iran and other threats to our national security. We don't need a political savior; we need a president who will secure our borders, protect Americans, handle foreign policy with a "peace through strength" policy, apply economic common sense, stand up for traditional values, traditional beliefs, and traditional families, a president who will defend DOMA (Defense of Marriage Act), which seeks to define and protect the institution of marriage as between one man and one woman.

President Obama failed miserably in protecting marriage, in foreign policy, gave us a failed stimulus program, and failed to secure our borders. That administration, in my view, got an F.

Our country is headed down a dangerous path morally and economically. Here are two examples among many that make my case:

1. Violence: the killing of a ten-year-old girl in Colorado by a teenager (who, by the way, dismembered the girl's body), and the recent salon shooting in Brookfield, Wisconsin. Many violent incidents have occurred recently, and a lot of the violence has been directed toward law enforcement officers. This is unacceptable.

2. When President Obama took office on January 20, 2009, we had a $10.626 trillion deficit.[80] Now (October 2023) our national debt is $33 trillion. Unacceptable, irresponsible, immoral, and dangerous.

When Governor Scott Walker (WI) won his recall election in 2012, I didn't say a thing about it to my liberal teacher friend in Milwaukee. However, as soon as Barack Obama won the reelection, the teacher texted me, gloating that his candidate had won. *Show some class, liberals. You complain and even picket at the state capitol when a politician (Mr. Walker) takes office and governs as he was elected to do, but you taunt others when your candidate wins.*

It's one thing to express political views and altogether different to complain, taunt, and trash others' views. It's great by me that my liberal friend prefers socialism over capitalism and unionism over individualism. He's an individual with choices. Sadly though, like many, he put his faith and trust in politicians. Let me know how that goes when you meet your Maker.

Obama cared little about you, but he gladly took your vote (or two. Fraud?). Obama, Biden, Trump, . . . cannot save our souls. They are mere mortal men who—like each of us—will one day die and stand before God, facing judgment. The time is near.

Presidents Obama and Biden failed when it came to foreign policy, letting the Russians go into Ukraine who, essentially, took over part of the country historically known as Crimea. Mr. Obama put sanctions on Russia at that time, much like he did with Iran. In my view, these men had no charisma or leadership skills. Obama was a smooth talker; I will give him that.

Consequently, the outside world must see America as weak. It was my hope and prayer that the next president would be strong in securing our borders, reigning in our exponential debt, controlling spending, and exercising courage when it comes to dealing with other world leadership. Not so with the present administration, President Biden. Russia, Iran, North Korea, and Islam all pose a threat to our national (and thereby personal) security, and the Obama administration made defense cuts. Funding Ukraine is not right. Something nefarious, corrupt, and evil is going on. I think it is a money-laundering scheme at the expense of the American taxpayer. This unlimited, continuous funding must be stopped. Ukraine is a money pit.

I once had a part-time job with an airline. (Free flight benefits!) I went to basic training in Denver, and during our introductions a woman said: "I'm here to pay off personal debt. Just like President

Obama said, we need to pay our bills." *Seriously? You're heeding financial advice from a socialist with no economic common sense? Do you have any idea how much debt President Obama has incurred since taking office?*

Her mindset was exactly why he was re-elected.

People are oftentimes naïve or ignorant regarding politics and what's at stake nationally and individually. I pray for all people's eyes to be opened to the truth, the conservative solution (this book's title). I am a Conservative and the Solution is the gospel of Jesus Christ. Regardless of what's happening in our nation and the world, we must keep our focus on Him. This world is passing and fleeting.

Governor Scott Walker (R)
Wisconsin 2011–2019

I voted for Mr. Walker in 2010. So, of course, I was upset by the tactics used by Wisconsin Democrats and the unions regarding the recall of 2012, especially as I wondered if our votes even mattered or were counted. And, with what happened to Donald J. Trump in the 2020 election, I'm sure the presidential election was stolen. Please watch *2000 Mules* produced by Dinesh D'Souza. Some people should be in prison! Ballot boxes and mail-in voting pose a big threat to election integrity.

In the February 20, 2012, issue of *The Weekly Standard*, I read that Governor Scott Walker (WI) faced a $3.6 billion deficit when he assumed office. I initially thought it was $6 billion. The point is, Scott Walker faced an enormous deficit and asked unions to chip in and do their part. In my mind, that was not asking too much.

He had fiscal sense, which most politicians do not. Our debt is so concerning.

Gov. Walker inherited Wisconsin's deficit from former governor (and crook) Jim Doyle and turned it into a $300 million surplus. Impressive! We need such courage and leadership at the federal level instead of automobile manufacturer bailouts and failed stimulus plans. Economic common sense!

We need to take our federal debt seriously.

The recall took place on June 5, 2012. Walker was voted in as governor by a large margin to fix a state in poor fiscal shape, thanks to his predecessor. Then, the left wanted a do-over because they didn't get their liberal way. How about first a recall of our then-President Obama? That presidency, like the present (Biden), was a big disaster. I hoped and prayed that Mitt Romney picked a conservative running mate and defeated Barack Hussein Obama in the November 2008 election. That didn't work out so well. Obama received 2 terms.

Scott Walker's then-likely election opponent was Tom Barrett. Consider the statistics from Mr. Barrett's years as Milwaukee's mayor (2004–2021):

> 1. Under Barrett, Milwaukee had one of the worst job-creation rates of any city in the US, with unemployment as high as 27%.[81]
>
> 2. Milwaukee has one of the worst graduation rates in the US.
>
> 3. Barrett raised taxes on working-class families that skyrocketed to nearly 33% by 2014![82]

Conservative Solution

I supported Scott Walker.

The only beef I had with Walker was that he didn't approve funds to improve Milwaukee's Bradley Center, home of our Milwaukee Bucks. The Bradley Center needed about $25 million in upgrades for safety and profitability. Being a passionate fan of the Bucks, I wanted to see those funds approved. The Bucks did end up getting a new arena, Fiserv Forum, in 2018 and went on to win an NBA title in 2021. Go Bucks! I believe cities that have professional sports teams should assist with funding. These teams provide economic growth and jobs. Nearby bars and restaurants do well when the city has, for example, the Green Bay Packers, Milwaukee Bucks, and the Milwaukee Brewers.

Democrat mayors and governors are usually a disaster. It seems crime increases and jobs decline when they have power. I cannot get over the unemployment rate under Mr. Barrett listed above.

I loved that Gov. Walker took on the unions with collective bargaining during his tenure. I agreed with him that teachers should assume more of the cost for their health care and pensions. After all, taxpayer dollars fund teacher's health and retirement plans. The percentages Gov. Walker asked for were very reasonable. Yes, while some workers earn more than a teacher's salary, many earn a lot less. Those who work in the private sector are not afforded the luxury of taxpayer assistance with their insurance and retirement needs.

Paul Ryan (R)

Former Speaker of the House of Representatives, 2015–2017

In August 2012, I attended my high school reunion in Milwaukee, Wisconsin and visited friends and family. During my stay, I heard that Mitt Romney selected Wisconsin Congressman Paul Ryan as his Republican running mate. I was very energized by this news as I always liked Paul Ryan for being fiscally responsible. I was enthused about the GOP presidential ticket for 2012, confident that Obama would be a one-term president. Mr. Ryan came across as intelligent, friendly, competent, clean-cut, and a good family man of faith—the complete opposite of Joe Biden. Had Romney picked Chris Christie, John McCain, Ron Paul, or any other RINO (Republican in Name Only) as his VP running mate, l would have been thoroughly disappointed and would have had to truly vote for the lesser of two evils. For the record, I have voted Republican 99 percent of the time.

> **Evidence of America's decline is clear when our only political candidate choices are evil.**

To clarify, here are my views on the three above-mentioned politicians:

- Former New Jersey governor Christie was unaware of the dangers of Islam.

- I had a tremendous amount of respect for the late Sen. McCain's military service, but he had too many moderate viewpoints. May he rest in peace.

- Former Texas congressman Ron Paul was a Libertarian at heart but weak on foreign policy.

Anticipating the 2012 VP debate between Paul Ryan and Joe Biden, I though perhaps Mr. Biden might want to stay home that night, call in sick, as Mr. Ryan was a walking, talking calculator who'd absolutely destroy Biden one-on-one. Ryan knew the budget, Medicare, Social Security, . . . The only people who didn't want to hear Ryan's facts and figures were those who feared the truth about our economy. It was and is in shambles.

Burying your head in the sand is to kick the can down the road and punish future generations.

A friend and I had decided to attend Paul Ryan's homecoming campaign rally at the Waukesha Expo Center. We'd parked a few miles away and walked to the event. The crowd was large and fired up. It was great to see, and even better (as my friend pointed out) to see all the young people in the crowd. That gave me hope that our younger generation wasn't completely fooled by our liberal media and liberal education system! But look where our youth are now—in the jaws of liberal public education. Private education and homeschooling may be the way to go.

During the event, a liberal among the crowd tried to interrupt Mr. Romney, but the liberal was quickly escorted out. Fast forward, we are used to this kind of behavior as liberals and radicals shout down conservatives. Saul Alinsky, anyone? (*Rules for Radicals*.) Read his book so you'll be further educated about people who salivate for power and thereby won't play nice. They want to shout down conservative voices.

I realize my blogs and this book sound critical. A Sunday message in church prompted me to evaluate how important it is, for many reasons, that I not to be *hypo*critical. The message stressed the importance of repenting of our sins and being obedient to Christ. So, as I take a strong stance against gay "marriage" and the gay agenda, I'm reminded to check myself. I don't want to be a hypocrite but simply a messenger of truth. Unfortunately, many people are hypocritical and I have to look in the mirror. I must obey God and not fall into sin. Easier said than done as I have 3 enemies in this life: my flesh, the world, and Satan.

The Bible says the following about hypocrisy:

- Hypocrites try to keep others from entering the kingdom of God (Matthew 23:13).

- Jesus found hypocrites repulsive (Matthew 23:27–28). Beware of hypocrisy in your life (Luke 12:1–2).

- Hypocrites try to look good though they have evil hearts (Romans 7:15–25).

- God will punish hypocrites (Luke 20:46–47). Get rid of hypocrisy in your life (1 Peter 2:1).

Judges and Justices

In the 2012 election, I was initially going to ignore the judge election section. But I realized how important it is that our judges be held accountable for their decisions on the bench. I did extensive research on the candidates and found that one judge had voted for eminent domain, and another had voted to uphold concealed carry on Colorado college campuses. Those two made my vote easy.

Eminent domain is "also called condemnation or expropriation, power of government to take private property for public use without the owner's consent."[83] Eminent domain is a threat to individual property rights. I will always support common sense and legal gun rights. A recent example of eminent domain is how the town of Vail, CO, exercised eminent domain in 2022 over Vail Resorts regarding a land dispute. The Vail Town Council took the land back from Vail Resorts because they wanted to protect the bighorn sheep that roam that area. Vail Resorts wanted to build employee housing.

Researching conservative organizations that support conservative judges, I came across Clear the Bench Colorado, a grassroots organization that holds Colorado's judicial branch (particularly, but not exclusively, our Supreme Court justices) accountable to the Colorado Constitution and the people of our state. Although our judges are not elected to office, they're subject to voter approval via retention elections. Several Colorado judges, including a majority on the Colorado Supreme Court, have betrayed the people's trust. Imposing their personal political agendas, they've neglected the proper judicial function of upholding the law. I was very glad I came across Clear the Bench Colorado because their mission helped me form an informed opinion of the balloted judges.

In Town of Telluride v. San Miguel Valley Corp., 185 P.3d 161, 171 (Colo. 2008) "Telluride Land Grab," I found the following about Judge Nathan B. Coats. The majority ruling by the town of Telluride upheld eminent domain over property outside the town limits. The ruling's upshot was that *any* municipality could exercise eminent domain *anywhere* in the state. Also, the ruling ignored a law passed by the Colorado legislature expressly limiting extraterritorial condemnations and abusive "takings."[84] This is unacceptable. Once our property rights are diminished, what's next? When the government mandates the people to buy a product (like Obamacare), what will we be "mandated" to purchase next? Only organic food and green energy? Where do mandates and conformity end? Very concerning.

Individual rights matter.

In Regents of University of Colorado v. Students of Concealed Carry on Campus, LLC (271 P.3d 496 (Colo. 2012), Judge Daniel Marc Taubman voted to overturn the CU Gun Ban. If an individual lawfully purchases a handgun and lawfully obtains their concealed carry permit through their county sheriff's office, who's to say the individual cannot have a firearm on their person?

I agree with Judge Taubman's decision. Prohibiting someone from lawfully carrying a firearm encourages criminals and those with evil intentions to target businesses, organizations, and campuses.

More guns = less crime.

The data and numbers prove that fact.

I encourage gun ownership by law-abiding citizens. The Second Amendment is constitutional, necessary, and powerful. Let's protect it.

We must protect the Second Amendment.

My vote against Judge Coats and in favor of Judge Taubman came down to two simple factors: (1) If the balloted judge votes for eminent domain, I will vote against them. (2) If the balloted judge upholds constitutional gun laws and is supportive of one's right to keep and bear arms, I will vote for them.

I hope you can see why it's so important on a local and state level to know who's running for office and where they stand on common sense, constitutional, and moral issues. Please do your homework before casting a vote. Your vote matters! All Votes Matter.

We must keep in mind that candidates are mere mortals debating against each other. They, like every human, are sinners. Although I will not put my faith in political candidates and voted-in leaders, I will pray for a moral man to lead our country—a man who is pro-life, pro-traditional values (like traditional marriage), who will strengthen our military to protect our homeland, destroy terrorists, and strengthen our economy. We need good, bold men to lead this country.

Morals matter.

Regardless of our nation's leaders, administrative entourages, and supporters, the truth is that no one man or woman can save this country. Only God can do that through people who turn their hearts and lives over to Jesus Christ, humbly repenting of their sin.

Which is the greatest concern: to save a country or save souls? The latter, of course.

Countries will one day fail to exist, but souls will live for eternity. While I believe it's important to elect leaders who best represent biblical values, we need to remember that mankind cannot save anyone on judgment day. That includes Pope Francis and those who run for president. The Pope and a president cannot save your soul.

I want a president who is faithful to God and living a life of strong, traditional, moral values, and follows through with securing our borders, especially against the evil of ISIS and other terrorist groups that now include Mexican drug cartels. I want a president who will build up our military power and capabilities, stand up for morality, unafraid to publicly proclaim that homosexuality is wrong—immoral—and unsafe, and who is pro-life, pro-business, and a strong supporter of our Second Amendment right.

On to politics and the madness we see in the GOP presidential campaign. Speaking of madness . . . .

> *Side Note:* March is my favorite month for sports (much like December is my favorite holiday month as we celebrate the birth of Christ. Nothing beats Christmas). During March Madness 2012, I looked forward to Marquette playing in the NCAA tournament and hoped for their advancement to the Sweet 16. I really liked the energy that Coach Buzz Williams brought to the game. If I was a coach, I'd be much like Buzz: energetic, animated, emotional, etc. I wouldn't be able to calmly coach a team; I'm way too competitive and passionate about sport events. I once punched a hole in my parents' wall when the Green Bay Packers lost to the Minnesota Vikings (thank you, TJ Rubley!) Funny how I sometimes allow sports to dictate my mood, whether excitement, frustration, joy, or anger. Packer fans can relate.
>
> I also liked the senior leadership of Marquette's Darius Johnson-Odom and Jae Crowder (2012). Crowder proved his future in the NBA due to his size and hustle. Today (2023), he's a member of the Milwaukee Bucks. Hoping the Bucks can win another championship in 2024! I can see him being another Joakim Noah of the Chicago Bulls. An energetic player who brings heart and hustle to the

court. Bring on March Madness! And go Marquette! I also follow the Wisconsin Badgers because my grandfather played there in the 1930s. Go Bucky!

Back to political madness, I was disappointed on Super Tuesday 2012 when Mitt Romney won six out of ten states. Rick Santorum had a fairly good night, winning Oklahoma, Tennessee, and North Dakota. If Mr. Santorum had had a smooth-running campaign and more financial backing, he'd have competed in Virginia. He wasn't even on the ballot there due to not getting the proper paperwork in on time. Had he taken Ohio, it would've been a great night for him and his supporters (including me). Mr. Santorum's campaign team failed in many aspects. If you want to become president of the United States, you need to have a competent campaign team. I didn't see that with Santorum's.

Here in Colorado, I attended a 2012 Republican caucus where a supporter for the four candidates—Romney, Santorum, Gingrich, and Paul—was to each give a five-minute presentation about why their candidate was best suited to be the GOP nominee and face Barack Obama in the November presidential election. But unfortunately, Santorum's team dropped the ball yet again; nobody was there to represent him. I felt tempted to stand before the 500 attendees and give an impromptu talk in his favor, but I had no interest in grandstanding.

The Santorum campaign also dropped the ball in Virginia where he and Newt were not even on the ballot. Very disappointing. Had Mr. Santorum won Virginia or Ohio, he'd have been on his way to the GOP nomination. Campaign staff matters! Funny side story here: I drove in Mike Pence's caravan from the Eagle County Regional Airport to his hotel in Eagle, CO back in 2016. I had

Donald J. Trump's campaign team in my SUV. It was fun and an adrenaline rush! I met some Secret Service agents and it was a cool experience. As for the hotel they stayed in, they could have done better.

I liked US senator Marco Rubio (R-FL) and US congressman Paul Ryan (R-WI) as running mates. Mr. Rubio would sway Hispanic voters to the GOP side and Mr. Ryan had common sense economically. He appeared to be pro-military, pro-prosperity, and pro-traditional family. Such candidates—strong on national defense, economic growth, and traditional values—get my vote every time.

Had Mr. Romney picked a moderate running mate, I would have been thoroughly disappointed. As it turned out, he chose Paul Ryan, though Obama defeated him in the end. God forbid if he had chosen a John McCain clone. Mr. McCain had been too old and moderate in 2008 and Sarah Palin was too divisive and unelectable, all in all giving us a very weak GOP ticket that year.

Overall, I liked Sarah Palin and her conservative idealism, but I didn't think she was electable. She and Michele Bachmann (R-MN) would have been quality cabinet members in a Republican White House. Ms. Bachmann as Secretary of State would have been a significant upgrade over Hillary Clinton. Bachmann would not have allowed a nuclear Iran, nor the Muslim Brotherhood to come into power. She was not ignorant or naive to foreign policy. She was strong.

I recommend the book, *The Blueprint: How the Democrats Won Colorado (and Why Republicans Everywhere Should Care)* by Rob Witwer and Adam Schrager. It's frightening, alarming, and frustrating how a lot of money, social media, technology, and committed donors and volunteers turned a once-strong red state into a blue state. There was no surprise that the gay agenda also played a big role in this turnaround. Read the book. (See "Recommended Resources.") I read it years ago, but it really does show the blueprint for Democrats. Every Republican involved in the GOP office should read it.

What the Bible says about authority and government:

- "All authority in heaven and on earth has been given to me" (Matthew 28:18).

- "The authorities that exist have been established by God" (Romans 13:1).

- "Let everyone be subject to the governing authorities, for there is no authority except that which God has established" (Romans 13:1).

- "Be subject to rulers and authorities" (Titus 3:1).

PART 3

SATAN'S AGENDA

CHAPTER 10

Terrorism

May 2, 2022, marked the eleven-year anniversary of the killing of Osama bin Laden. That was a great day of evil conquered in 2011. Thank you to our military for achieving this critical mission, in particular our SEAL Team Six! USA! USA! USA!

That year (2011), I made a trip "up north" to visit my grandmother in Merrill, Wisconsin. It's so peaceful and beautiful there. While there, being spoiled by the world's greatest cook, I asked Grandma about the middle-aged couple who had years before lived next door to her. The couple had lost their son in the 9/11 terrorist attacks. She told me a sad story.

I will personally never forget that day.

I was getting ready for work that morning when I heard my roommate yell, "Turn on the TV!" I quickly tuned to CNN. Initially, I was shocked at the image of a plane, American Airlines Flight 11 (we would learn), crashing into a tower, and further shocked and horrified seeing a second plane, United Airlines Flight 175, crash into the other tower. Then grief overcame me, as it did millions watching the newsfeed. We were under attack.

When the situation was confirmed as a terrorist attack, anger rose in me, joining the ring of tumultuous emotions. What an awful day in American history! Savage and evil. A severely unforgettable day for our country and countless families, friends, and coworkers who needlessly lost loved ones. This is why I stress the importance of fighting terrorism.

I went to work that day, but only for a couple of hours. I stood among crying coworkers, huddled around TVs. Of course, nobody could focus on work; our nation was seized in a sudden and dire crisis, unprecedented in our history. Our employer gave us the option to stay at work or go home. I went home; there was no way I could focus on work, I needed to watch the news. Off to my home I went.

Every 9/11 anniversary stirs emotions in me as they had that fateful day in 2001. I've pretty much recorded every televised program on this awful event. In a blog post at that time, I shared what had transpired in my personal life on 9/11. I had watched CNN and listened to the Bob & Brian radio talk show in Milwaukee, thinking right away that the first crash into the North Tower was not a terrorist attack but rather something mechanical that had gone terribly wrong. I think most Americans thought the same thing, not imagining a terrorist attack of that magnitude. I was upset that radio host Brian had jumped to that conclusion, still not believing he was correct when the second tower was hit.

Islam is evil. We must forever remember what happened on 9/11. We owe that to the victims.

We must be vigilant in praying for our country.

Islam

In Brookfield, Wisconsin near my hometown, there was a proposal to build a mosque. How unknowing were the Brookfield citizens who opened their neighborhoods to Islam—a nation hostile to the West, to Christianity, and to capitalism. The welcoming Brookfield citizens saw no issue with erecting a mosque! This news tied into one of my earlier blog posts regarding the liberal mindset on "acceptance," "tolerance," and "political correctness." Little did Brookfield residents know about the Qur'an, Muhammad, Allah, Jihad, etc. The American people need to wake up. US citizens must be made aware and cautioned to be careful what they wish for. Islam is full of extremists and the Brookfield citizens who wished to welcome Islam were, in fact, welcoming the very people who will not hesitate to kill them and their loved ones. While ignorance may be bliss, it can also be deadly. Had we so soon forgotten the destructive evil and mass murders of 9/11 that transpired at the foremost gateway into America—New York City's Northern Gateway?

> **We, the people of this great country, must wake up and stay alert to the dangers of Islam.**

The truth cannot be sugarcoated; Islam is a violent and evil religion from Satan himself. There's no convincing me otherwise. We pray for all Muslims to turn from Islam to Christianity.

Mainstream media wants us to believe that Islam is a religion of peace. It's not! And I'm not buying what liberals are selling. Fanatical extremists, Muslims, want nothing more than to destroy capitalism, America, and the Christian faith our nation was founded on. And they're in no hurry, but rather methodical toward their goal of destruction and one-world power. They do not care if their plans take ten, twenty-five, or a hundred years; they're slowly but surely making gains toward accomplishing their goals. Very scary. But, we must remember Who wins in the end!

In 2013 was news coverage of a brutal attack on a British soldier in London. The soldier was literally hacked to death by two Muslim men. Absolute evil. Yet, a growing sect of folks continue to insist that Islam is a "religion of peace." It is not. The Qur'an is full of evil.

A federal judge in Tennessee pushed for criticism of Islam to be treated as criminal. That idea alone is an attack on our freedom of speech. How about citing as criminal the daily murdering of thousands of babies through abortion? This country legalized abortion in 1973 (my birth year) and since then, we have murdered over 63 million unborn babies—truly a disturbing evil. According to Focus2023, "In 2023, abortion was authorized on request in 74 countries and in 13 countries for broad socio-economic reasons."[85] Those precious babies, full of life, seen as disposable at will. The left will scream and shout that abortion is a woman's "right to choose" and that abortion is about a woman's health. It's murder. I'm so thankful for the overturning of Roe v. Wade in 2022.

As for criticizing Islam, thank God our country still maintains freedom of speech, though that First Amendment right is constantly under attack, as demonstrated by that Tennessee federal judge. If I'm taken away by the feds, you may just find me in prison because I'd say, "Go right ahead and cuff me." Although the feds could take me physically, they couldn't touch my allegiance to

Christ and the truth of God's Word in me. "Be afraid of the One who can destroy both soul and body in hell" (Matthew 10:28).

Man can take our bodies, but they cannot touch our souls.

Anniversaries of 9/11 get me thinking again about the Islam religion and the dangers it poses worldwide. Back in 2013, I saw the movie *Lone Survivor*, which showed just how ruthless Islamic extremists can be, the Taliban in particular. They hate Americans and the values we represent. The left has no idea that these extremists would behead them in a heartbeat if given the chance. Liberals want to arm overseas extremists (Syrian rebels) while taking away our right to bear arms here in America. Who would gun-hating liberals turn to if and when things go bad? They'll turn to gun-owning conservatives and find themselves on their own. Those who want political correctness, inclusion, and diversity must know that these come at a high price. Evil does exist and Satan has power here on Earth—a biblical fact.

The following is from Usama Dakdok's website, The Straight Way of Grace:

> Muslims worship Satan by the name of Allah. For example, in Qur'an 1:1, it states that Allah is the god of the worlds. The Bible clearly teaches in 2 Cor. 4:4 that the god of the world is Satan. In Qur'an 3:54 and 8:30, Allah is known as the best deceiver. The Bible clearly teaches that the deceiver is Satan. Qur'an 35:8 says that Allah leads people astray which is a description of Satan in the Bible. Allah desires to fill hell with humans, but the Bible teaches that God desires that not one person should perish.[86]

Usama is a former Muslim who left the Muslim faith and is now a Christian. He gets it. Thanks to political correctness, Muslims have been allowed to infiltrate the United States militarily, politically, and culturally. I repeat, their goal is worldwide domination. It's tragic and scary that "We, the People," are allowing this takeover to happen, right in front of our eyes, through inclusiveness, tolerance, and political correctness. The majority of Americans, and even the majority of Muslims, fail to recognize what's in the Qur'an and what Islam's goals are. Put simply, Islam is a religion of evil, hatred, and dominance. Their women, and non-Muslims, are treated as second-class citizens. How ironic that so many liberals want to be inclusive of Islam. Is the left blinded to the fact that women are required to wear head-to-toe garb and homosexuals are put to death? Reading about Islamic (Sharia) law, I agree with one of their teachings, that homosexuality is a vile form of fornication. But they also believe that homosexuality is punishable by death, which I don't agree with. I'll speak to capital punishment later in this book. Murdering homosexuals is evil. We are to love them, while warning them that the homosexual lifestyle is a sin, share the gospel, and pray for them.

I recall watching the women from the Middle East (Qatar and Afghanistan) compete in the 2012 Summer Olympics. I was struck by the fact they had to do their running and sprinting competitions wearing full garb—a hijab and clothing that covers the entire body. The crowd cheered, essentially saying, "Yay for Islam!" I give the women credit for competing but come on. Usama Dakdok's website is one that addresses "Women in Islam":

> Hadith, Tirmzi page 300 states that [a]lso in Islam a woman cannot fast or pray during her period for she is

Terrorism

unclean during this time[.] [T]hat is why Mohammed asked them to perform more prayer, so Allah will remove them from hell.[87]

Usama Dakdok is an Egyptian-born Christian who does an excellent job explaining the Islam religion and its dangers.

We need to pray that Muslims convert to Christianity. It's a blessing when they receive Christ as their Savior and ensure their eternity with Him. It can be done. It has been done.

There is still work to be done in reaching Muslims.

If you're a current events junkie like me, you're likely aware of the attacks against Israel in the Gaza Strip by Hamas, a militant Palestinian Islamist group. After eight days of war, a "truce" was called between Israel and Hamas; but trust me, there's more warfare, violence, and death to come. Israel seems to always be playing defense. Israel is under serious threats from every direction, and I believe Bible prophecy states that Libya, Egypt, and Syria will all rise against the nation of Israel. In addition to these three countries, I can also see, and pretty much guarantee, that Hamas will again attack Israel at some point, as well as attacks by Hezbollah and Iran. I pray the US will come to Israel's aid when attacked. We cannot allow Iran and terrorist organizations (Hamas, Hezbollah) to obtain nuclear weapons. To all US military and intelligence personnel working tirelessly to keep the citizens of the United States and its allies safe, thank you! We owe you a great deal of gratitude.

I strongly support Israel and its right to defend itself against terrorism. Hamas, the militant group in the Gaza Strip is not to be felt sorry for. They use civilians as shields and seek the destruction of Israel. After raining missile after missile into Israeli cities and towns (July 8, 2014), I was happy to see Israel respond with force. Evil does exist in this world (e.g. Hitler, Stalin, 9/11, etc.), and we see a lot of evil in the Middle East in Hamas, Hezbollah, ISIS (Islamic State of Iraq and Syria), and Islamic extremism. I support Israel. It is biblical. The website Hope for Today does a good job in educating its readers about Israel.

There is so much going on in the news and current events that, in my view, are clear signs of the end times described in biblical prophecy. I recently heard that 500 of 1,000 biblical prophesies have come true. In baseball terms, God is batting .1000. And the remaining 500 prophesies will happen. It is just a matter of when. The actual number of biblical prophecies vary in research, but the point is that God is faithful and has proven Himself faithful to His Word.

> *Side Note:* Local Politics, Colorado
>
> At work, when the topic of politics came up in 2012, I mentioned I was sick and tired of all the political TV ads and that I couldn't wait until the upcoming election was over. Although a liberal coworker was okay with my thoughts, he became quite heated when the talk turned to 9/11, al-Qaeda, the Taliban, Libya, and terrorism. When the discussion turned to a terrorist attack that had transpired on the American embassy in Benghazi, Libya where four Americans were killed, my response was, "It always comes down to this: What is the truth? Who knows what, when, and if the attack could have been prevented." I'll never forget his response.

"That is such b——!"

Taken aback, I asked, "The truth is b——?"

"Yes, that is such garbage. Republicans always bring up that stuff."

Sorry the truth is inconvenient. What happened in Benghazi is unacceptable. Protect Americans!

I was stunned that he essentially said the truth was irrelevant. In response I shared, "I'm not a Republican; I'm a Christian conservative and I do tend to vote Republican because of their platform and beliefs. I cannot support a political party that's pro-choice and pro-gay 'marriage.'" My response evoked heightened emotion in him and I did my best to remain calm and cool. Emotions run high in political debates. We, Christians, must be careful to honor God with our words as we share our beliefs. It isn't easy, especially when we're verbally attacked.

Those of us in Colorado hear nonsense in spades about the so-called war on women, which roars louder during each election. Former Gov. John Hickenlooper and Sen. Mark Udall, both Democrats, were hammering the airwaves with this nonsense throughout 2014 and in the 2013 pre-election preparation. Turning on the T.V. and radio, opening a newspaper, or taking a stroll online was frustrating because of the bombardment of lies. In our country, what was once considered wrong (morally, spiritually, socially, educationally, politically, economically, militarily, . . .) is more and more postured and flaunted as what is right, and what was once considered right is being taught as wrong. Up is down, down is up, right is wrong, wrong is right. This world has gone insane.

Wrong is wrong—and we don't get to decide because God already has.

Whether the wrong be abortion, or homosexuality, all issues of wrongdoing are clearly addressed in God's Word as sin, including the sins that people have come to view as little: lying—a "little white lie" is still black sin as is stealing, cheating, gossiping, swearing, gluttony (which some of us need to look up in the dictionary and revisit the Bible to be reminded what God says about overeating). I have sworn many times, so I am guilty as charged!

Plain and simple, sin is sin and all sin is addressed in the Bible.

I look at the beautiful state of Colorado and see our nation's spiral deeper into destruction: gay "marriage," marijuana legalized (and now mushrooms in 2022), and our Second Amendment rights being eroded. Limiting gun magazine capacities won't do a thing to stop "gun violence." Will a criminal with intent on doing evil give a second thought about his magazine capacity prior to committing a crime? No! Criminals commit crimes. It's what they do.

God's Word alone is truth and we each will stand before Him and give an account of the life we lived, either as unbelievers or believers in Jesus Christ. Last I checked, 100 out of 100 people will die.

The Word of God is innate truth because God and His Word are one and the same.

The more we go against His Word, the more we'll see Him removing His gracious hand of blessing from our once-great country. Now don't get me wrong; this is still a great country. We are truly blessed living here. But isn't the demise and disparity we're experiencing in increasing measure not enough to return humbly to God in repentance and faith? Instead of getting better and better by the day, the country is getting worse and worse.

Must we excavate deeper into sin to experience the truth of God's wrath? We're like a willful child, running out into traffic, touching the hot stove, and playing with electrical outlets after being warned, "Don't!" Such willful acts can seriously wound and be deadly! Yet, we "the people"—presumably adults with sound minds—are behaving exactly like a child who has been warned of everything that will harm and destroy them. We just don't get it.

On other issues of local politics, some residents here in the Vail Valley have written letters to the editor of *Vail Daily* regarding their desire to see a plastic bag ban. Are you kidding me? You have nothing else to spend your time and efforts on? There are global threats of the mass murdering of unborn human beings, men and women changing their gender identities as though changing their socks, and other more pressing matters than plastic bag use. What will a plastic bag ban accomplish amid such immense crises? What will banning plastic bags do exactly? We need plastic bags for garbage and dog waste! This is another example of people losing their minds.

Back when I lived in Milwaukee, a Sunday morning message at my church included thoughts about bad things happening to good people. God allows adversity in our lives to show His presence and work so we will glorify Him. He promises us: "In all things God works for the good of those who love him, who have been called according to His purpose" (Romans 8:28). Regardless of what's going on in our lives, God knows exactly what's going on at all times in and around us—right down to the exact number of the hairs on our heads (Luke 12:7). I am thankful to still have lots of hairs on my head at age forty-nine!

For so many years, I was admittedly selfish and perhaps egotistical and arrogant. I thought life was all about me rather than about my Creator. How wrong I was. We all fall short of the glory of God (Romans 3:23), but "if we confess our sins, he is faithful and just and will forgive us our sins and purify us from all unrighteousness. If we claim we have not sinned, we make him out to be a liar and his word is not in us" (1 John 1:9). God says He will reward the righteous (those whose hearts are united with His) and punish the wicked (Romans 2:6). With that being the case, why do believers even worry? (And that's coming from a worry wart!) Instead, we can accept His gift of grace and peace, knowing He has a great plan that is at work in our lives, in our nation, and in our world. We simply must trust Him and "pray without ceasing" (1 Thessalonians 5:17 KJV), and "not become weary in doing good" (Galatians 6:9–10). We know who will win in the end! To God be the glory!

Arab Spring

On January 25, 2012, peoples and nations "celebrated" the one-year anniversary of the so-called Arab Spring.[88] Many want us to believe that this movement was pro-freedom and pro-democracy. Not accurate. Arab Spring was a power-grab attempt by Muslim extremists in the Middle East to gain military and political power to (most likely) attack Israel in the effort to see Sharia Law spread and enforced throughout the Middle East. Not everything is as it appears, especially with our media.

Terrorism

My understanding is that the Arab Spring started in January 2011 with a young man setting himself on fire in Tunisia due to his unemployment and unhappiness with the Tunisian government. His act of self-violence in protest led to further civil unrest, protests, and demonstrations that quickly spread to other parts of Africa and the Middle East. Other countries in unrest were Libya, Egypt, Yemen, and Syria.

Though Libyan dictator and terrorist Moammar Gadhafi was an evil man who had a grip on Muslim extremists in his country, we were able to keep him at bay for years, and he eventually gave in to Western demands for peace. Much like Saddam Hussein of Iraq and President Hosni Mubarak of Egypt, Gahdafi served a purpose for the West. And it is this man back in 1986 that played a role in my taking an interest in current events when the US bombed Libya.

Hussein countered Iranian power in the Middle East and Mubarak used his military power to keep peace with Israel while keeping Muslim extremists under control.

Yemen may very well be the new Afghanistan as it appears to be a breeding ground for alQaeda.

> *Side Note:* My philosophy for a US military presence in the Middle East is to keep five-to-ten-thousand US troops stationed in Afghanistan to keep an eye on Iran and to support and protect Israel. I'd also like to see our troops come home and secure our southern border where drug violence and beheadings are daily occurrences. Secure the border!

The situation in Syria continues to be ugly and getting worse by the day. I would not at all be sad to see Syrian President Bashar Assad removed from power. However, much like in Tunisia, Egypt, and elsewhere, there are consequences to regime changes. Who exactly is behind the Arab Spring and the removal of those in power? Unfortunately, it appears to be Muslim extremists and The Muslim Brotherhood. Careful what you wish for.

While we should support regime change and democracy across the globe, we must also be aware of exactly who is coming into power. There are many bad actors vying for power. This world has no shortage of bad actors (and I am not talking about Keanu Reeves!).

The events in Syria are still concerning, to say the least. On one side are Syria, Iran, Russia, and the terrorist group Hezbollah, and on the other side are the rebels Al-Qaeda and Muslim Brotherhood. It's a lose-lose situation for the USA. I think the best course of action is to simply let them resolve their own issues in the Middle East. If Israel is struck and dragged into war, then we should act. Until then, we should not take a side in that civil war but be present and watchful. Had President Obama called for cruise missile strikes in Syria, we would have been on the brink of World War III. Liberal administrations have proven to foolishly support rebels. If the Syrian regime were to attack Israel and Israel wiped out Damascus, we would be in WWIII.

Expect terrorist attacks. Not only in Israel but here in the United Sates. Nothing good can come from our involvement in Syria.

Any day now, I expect that Israel (hopefully with the backing of the United States), will attack Iran's nuclear weapons facilities.

I would support such an attack on nuclear facilities, but not on the Iranian people and innocent civilians. Wipe out the facilities with bunker-busting bombs. Israel can and should do this, sooner than later. The longer they wait, the more likely Iran will resume building a nuclear weapon, not only to threaten Israel but the entire Middle East and the United States.

There are good or bad consequences for every action and inaction, including ignoring and showing apathy toward civil unrest. I hope and pray that the US will not suffer further domestic terrorist acts due to our government failing to recognize who is truly behind the Arab Spring.

What the Bible says about consequences:

- "Those who are wise will shine like the brightness of the heavens, and those who lead many to righteousness, like the stars for ever and ever" (Daniel 12:3).

- "Anyone who is angry with a brother or sister will be subject to judgment" (Matthew 5:22).

- "No one can see the kingdom of God unless they are born again" (John 3:3).

- "God cannot be mocked. A man reaps what he sows" (Galatians 6:7).

- "Just as sin entered the world through one man, and death through sin, and in this way death came to all people, because all sinned" (Romans 5:12).

- "The wages of sin is death, but the gift of God is eternal life in Christ Jesus our Lord" (Romans 6:23).

- "Whoever rebels against the authority is rebelling against what God has instituted, and those who do so will bring judgment on themselves" (Romans 13:2).

- "There is a way that appears to be right, but in the end it leads to death" (Proverbs 14:12).

- "Fools give full vent to their rage, but the wise bring calm in the end" (Proverbs 29:11).

- "We must all appear before the judgment seat of Christ, so that each of us may receive what is due us for the things done while in the body, whether good or bad" (2 Corinthians 5:10).

- "If we deliberately keep on sinning after we have received the knowledge of the truth, no sacrifice for sins is left" (Hebrews 10:26).

- "Do not be deceived: Neither the sexually immoral nor idolaters nor adulterers nor men who have sex with men nor thieves nor the greedy nor drunkards nor slanderers nor swindlers will inherit the kingdom of God" (1 Corinthians 6:9–10).

- "Whoever sows to please their flesh, from the flesh will reap destruction; whoever sows to please the Spirit, from the Spirit will reap eternal life" (Galatians 6:8).

- "Because of your stubbornness and your unrepentant heart, you are storing up wrath against yourself for the day of God's wrath, when his righteous judgment will be revealed" (Romans 2:5).

- "If we confess our sins, he is faithful and just and will forgive us our sins and purify us from all unrighteousness" (1 John 1:9).

- "Anyone who hates a brother or sister is in the darkness and walks around in the darkness. They do not know where they are going, because the darkness has blinded them" (1 John 2:11).

Are you choosing the path of Christ—love, forgiveness, and peace? Or are you choosing the path of the enemy of our souls—hatred, stubbornness, jihad, and violence? Regardless of the paths we choose, we will each one day give an account. The day to repent is now as people die daily.

North Korea recently (2023) launched a missile that supposedly gave them clout and power in the region by their capability to hit the US. North Korea's communist regime is evil. Their leaders spent millions of dollars from foreign aid to live lavish lifestyles while preparing their military for potential action against perceived foreign threats like South Korea and the United States. Clearly, they're paranoid. All the while, their people are cold and hungry, another sad situation pointing to the evil in our world. Those poor North Koreans that are suffering from starvation.

Keep in mind that though such leaders (Kim Jong Un) may have wealth and power, they will face eternity in hell for their evil against their fellow man—unless they humble themselves before God and ask for His forgiveness. God calls us to *serve* one another, not exploit. Do what is right.

We're seeing dangerous men and terrorist organizations take control of countries that are hostile toward the US. Yet, the Obama administration sent fighter jets to Egypt? That was a serious threat to our ally Israel. Are our US leaders so naive? The Arab Spring was not a good thing! Israel is surrounded by those who wish to eliminate the Israeli people and their land and impose Sharia Law.

We truly are living in scary and possibly the end times. Look at all the violence in our country and around the world. Look at the Middle East; Libya is spinning out of control post-Moammar Gadhafi, the killing of Benghazi, Egypt's US Ambassador, Benghazi now under the control of the Muslim Brotherhood who wants to impose Sharia Law, and Syria in the middle of a civil war where President Bashar al-Assad is killing his own people. Add to those the moral, ethical, and spiritual decline of individuals in every nation. All things considered, it's hard to not believe we're in the last days before Christ's return.

I saw the movie *13 Hours: The Secret Soldiers of Benghazi* with my niece. The movie was based on a true story, and it was a good movie that I'd give four out of five stars. However, I got really upset watching the inaction of American bureaucrats, neglecting to send in air support to our brave men in Benghazi while under attack at a Libyan compound. The Obama administration failed those Americans.

When we face evil, and innocent lives are at stake, we need to take decisive and overwhelming action.

We have the world's best military, so let's use it to defeat evil and protect what is good.

ISIS

The ISIS terrorist group wreaked havoc in Iraq (2014). They were ruthless. This is Genocide 101. We best wake up before ISIS exacts mayhem and death here in the US.

Many years later, we and our allies continue to war against terrorists. I understand that Islam claims to be "a religion of peace," but that is not what we've seen from them. We need to take Islamic threats seriously.

I prayed the US military would be authorized long-term to assist the Kurds in Northern Iraq, fighting ISIS, and that we'd get involved heavily militarily, perhaps along with Israel. Israel continues to be pummeled by terrorist organizations, in particular Hamas. Why not pummel another terrorist group—ISIS? These examples should be even more reasons for us as individuals, families, communities, and our nation—founded on God and His Word—to be on the Lord's side, fighting against evil.

Scary times are ongoing, as we know from the book of Revelation (there it is again). Does our knowledge of further decaying societies (by sin) give us pardon as Christians to simply throw up our hands and say, "We already know it's going to get worse, so why bother to try to do anything about what we can't prevent?" No! Why? Because the souls of countless human beings are at risk of not knowing the saving power of Jesus Christ that radically changes thoughts and hearts and further builds the army of God for the battles of today, tomorrow, and ongoing. Much of this is spiritual warfare.

As I see the progress of ISIS and other terrorists in the Middle East, I can't help but wonder when the US will again be attacked on our soil. I think it's a matter of when, not if. Time will tell.

The goal of Sunni extremists is world domination. Muslims are willing to kill other Muslims; so, of course they'll not hesitate to kill Americans. I pray that terrorists will not get their hands on a nuclear weapon. That's a scary thought.

As we look at everything going on in this world, we must remember that God is in control and sovereign.

Thanks to liberalism, tolerance, and political correctness, Islam is being accepted worldwide despite being a false religion with a false god. ISIS is on the offensive in the Middle East, persecuting, beheading, and otherwise killing those in their way. But, ISIS will not be on the loose forever; they will pay for their crimes, whether in this world or throughout eternity.

We'll each face a judgment-heavy price without repentance to God and faith in Jesus Christ.

I pray for the defeat, destruction, and annihilation of ISIS. They are pure evil—persecuting Christians, killing innocent people, and using women as sex slaves. Our nation has not yet truly taken the threat of ISIS seriously. Terrorists are minions of Satan who will soon be coming to our US shores unless we take a hard political and military stand.

Thank God for our Second Amendment rights as US citizens, and for the efforts of police officers nationwide. We must back the blue. The politician cowards in Washington D.C. and in our states and communities are more worried about re-election campaigns and political party affiliations than they are about the safety and survival of American citizens. But then, with this country going against and mocking God's Word, is it really any surprise that we continue heading down a path of irrelevance by our leaders and into further destruction? We reap what we sow.

Only God knows when the Lord Jesus Christ is returning, but looking at the world today makes me think Christ's return must be very soon. Transgenderism (a mental illness) really makes me think this.

What the Bible says about evil:

- "Woe to those who call evil good and good evil, who put darkness for light and light for darkness, who put bitter for sweet and sweet for bitter" (Isaiah 5:20).

- "Do not be overcome by evil, but overcome evil with good" (Romans 12:21).

- "Put on the full armor of God, so that you can take your stand against the devil's schemes" (Ephesians 6:11).

- "Our struggle is not against flesh and blood, but against the rulers, against the authorities, against the powers of this dark world and against the spiritual forces of evil in the heavenly realms" (Ephesians 6:12).

- "To fear the Lord is to hate evil; I hate pride and arrogance, evil behavior and perverse speech" (Proverbs 8:13).

- "Reject every kind of evil" (1 Thessalonians 5:22).

- "Hate what is evil; cling to what is good" (Romans 12:9).

- "The face of the Lord is against those who do evil, to blot out their name from the earth" (Psalm 34:16).

CHAPTER 11

Illegal Immigration and Drug Violence

I once conversed with a woman in Edwards, Colorado who shared that she was from Mexico. She didn't agree with the immigration laws being proposed and passed in various states (Arizona, Oklahoma, Alabama, . . .). I didn't bring up this issue, though I do feel strongly about US immigration. Of course, I wasn't about to ask if she was in the US legally. I assumed and hoped she was. She was very nice and, from our conversation, seemed to be a hard worker. The point is that our views on border security and immigration differed greatly. We are a sovereign nation. Not just anyone gets in.

Many people on the left claim that Arizona's laws on immigration are hateful or bigoted, yet the laws are a matter of common sense. I learned the following information regarding Arizona Senate Bill 1070, signed into law in 2010 and served as a model for other states, such as Alabama and South Carolina. SB 1070 contains several provisions that attempt to help the federal government enforce immigration requirements. The most controversial, at least from the standpoint of the Obama and Biden administrations, is a provision that requires police officers to check the immigration status of individuals when detaining officers have reasonable suspicion that the individual is in our country illegally. I raise this question: Shouldn't law enforcement officers take this step anyway as part of their duties, because it's common sense? Individuals in the United States *illegally* are, by nature of the term "illegal," breaking the law! Why don't states like Arizona and Texas (don't even get me started on California!) send the National Guard to protect the border with Mexico? I am afraid the answer is this: chaos is what the Biden administration wants. All of the chaos taking place is intentional.

Much like I expect local government to keep me and other law-abiding citizens safe in our communities through police services, I expect those at the federal level to do the same through immigration laws that protect US citizens—not the other way around. Those in authority in our federal government have a responsibility to keep US citizens safe. What's happening at the border is not okay.

Secure our borders!

While I support *legal* immigration, I have a big problem with illegally moving to the United States. That said, if a foreigner is here legally and they're working, paying taxes, and behaving as a law-abiding citizen, I have no issue with them living in this country. However, those who are here illegally and unemployed (or taking jobs from those who are here legally), not paying taxes, and breaking the law—which is the case when immigrants enter illegally—I have an issue with those individuals living in our country and relying on taxpayers' hard-earned money to fund their education and health care. Illegal immigrants are a drain on our economy. I'm reminded how the Apostle Paul addressed this issue to the early church, a premier example of how we ought to live:

> You yourselves know how you ought to follow our example. We were not idle when we were with you, nor did we eat anyone's food without paying for it. On the contrary, we worked night and day, laboring and toiling so that we would not be a burden to any of you. We did this, not because we do not have the right to such help, but in order to offer ourselves as a model for you to imitate. For even when we were with you, we gave you this rule: "The one who is unwilling to work shall not eat" (2 Thessalonians 3:7–10).

A coworker who grew up in Mexico couldn't stand the thought of returning to visit her family. She had lost family members to drug cartel kidnappings and murder. According to her, the government of Mexico is greedy and incompetent, the police are corrupt, and the drug cartels are ruthless killers, acting with impunity. We should not open our borders to them; we don't want to invite evil into our country. There's a long list of Mexican drug cartels. Just to name a few: Sinaloa, Jalisco, Gulf, and Los Zetas. Penetrating our southern border are heavily-armed, brutal drug cartels. Stop the cartels from entering and bringing with them fentanyl, other drugs, arms, and pursuing sex trafficking. We'll always have greed and corruption (mankind's sinful nature) to some extent, but let's place a strong emphasis on enforcing law and order. Bring back Donald J. Trump. He'll get it done.

Our ally Israel is surrounded by enemies—the Muslim Brotherhood, Hamas, Hezbollah. The Middle East is extremely unstable with Libya, Egypt, and Syria in disarray.

> *Side Note:* Why would our government send weaponry to Egypt? Just recently, in 2022, the Biden administration approved a $2.5 billion arms sale to Egypt![89] That makes no sense at all. The Biden and Obama administrations have proven incompetent and corrupt. It's frightening. Raising taxes won't solve a thing unless drastic *spending* cuts are made. We need to get our fiscal house in order.

Mexico's drug violence is a big concern for our country's safety. If I learned that my next-door neighbor is a violent, drug-addicted felon, I would alert law enforcement and expect them to keep our community safe. Second chances are great—we each have the choice to change our ways—but we know from records that many, if not most, felons are repeat offenders and most communities are inhabited with innocent civilians, including children, all of whom need to be protected.

Operation Fast and Furious was "designed to help the Bureau of Alcohol, Tobacco, Firearms, and Explosives (ATF) dismantle drug cartels operating inside the United States and disrupt drug-trafficking routes. Instead, it put into the hands of criminals south of the border some 2,000 weapons, which have been used to kill hundreds of Mexicans and at least one American, US Border Patrol agent Brian Terry."[90] In 2012, our House of Representatives held Attorney General Eric Holder in contempt of Congress for not releasing documents pertaining to the Fast and Furious scandal. He seemed to be rather corrupt, like many politicians, Democrats *and* Republicans. My thought was that Mr. Holder should resign immediately. The Fast and Furious gunwalking debacle was an embarrassment to our government that resulted in the death of a US border patrol agent. His death alone is worrisome, but it's also upsetting to learn that Mr. Holder would not release documents related to the case. I believe we'll eventually know the truth, who knew what, and when they knew it. Hold people accountable.

Among my hopes for President Trump, including building our military and defeating ISIS, was constructing "The Wall" on the Mexico border and, ideally, having Mexico pay for it. Building The Wall and securing the border would have directly impacted our economy by providing thousands of jobs to complete the project. Jobs are good! Trump needed continual prayer coverage in the wake of the Obama Administration's eight years of weak foreign policy and focusing more concern on liberal social issues than a foreign policy of "peace through strength" (President Ronald Reagan).[91]

I saved a page from our local newspaper's local and state news sections. Although the headlines represented only cities and towns across Colorado, in my view, the page summarizes the status and direction of the United States as a whole. I was astounded by all the anger, crime, and other sin listed for one state. We're seeing an increase in crime and a decrease in civility, not just in Colorado but sweeping our nation. I do not feel safe going to big cities.

Immigration and Our English Language

At my doctor's office and my bank's ATM were options to choose English or Spanish. I don't care for any option other than English. This is the USA and our language has always been and still is English. As a native English-speaking country, we should encourage and expect legal immigrants to learn our language and pass an English proficiency test as part of the legal immigration process of citizenship. There are plenty of resources available to learn a new language, including local libraries, apps, and countless English classes online and in local communities. For example, here in Colorado, I saw an ad for free English classes held at the local library. Take advantage of these free resources.

At a previous place of employment, there were some women who spoke very little English. They would tell me I needed to practice my Spanish. I wanted to roll my eyes and say, "No, if you want to live here in the US, *you* need to learn our English language." I did enjoy practicing my minimal Spanish-speaking skills with the women, but they needed to learn my language, not vice versa. I had taken two years of Spanish in college to meet the foreign language requirement at Marquette University and my employer offered Rosetta Stone language software. However, unless I plan an extended trip or move to a non-English-speaking country, I'm not the one in need of learning and practicing a second language.

My work supervisor was from Romania, and I give her a lot of credit for becoming a legal citizen of our country. She learned English proficiently, worked hard, and paid taxes. I admire and respect such diligence to do the right thing. She was in agreement with many of my conservative views I'd posted in my blog. We both agreed that if a person travels to the US, they're welcome, but for legal citizenship there are expectations, including completing the legal citizenship process, obeying US laws, working legal jobs, paying taxes, and learning the English language. Do you think I could go to Mexico or Romania and essentially demand that they accommodate my English-speaking ways? No! The right thing to do—which is what all issues boil down to—is to respect a country's history and culture, which includes learning their language.

What the Bible says about respecting culture:

- "Give to everyone what you owe them: If you owe taxes, pay taxes; if revenue, then revenue; if respect, then respect; if honor, then honor" (Romans 13:7).

- "In everything, do to others what you would have them do to you" (Matthew 7:12).

- "Everyone be subject to the governing authorities, for there is no authority except that which God has established. The authorities that exist have been established by God. Consequently, whoever rebels against the authority is rebelling against what God has instituted, and those who do so will bring judgment on themselves" (Romans 13:1–2).

CHAPTER 12

Homosexuality and the Gay Agenda

I responded to a social media post regarding Pridefest in Milwaukee, Wisconsin and my response started a controversy about homosexuality. To clarify, my issue is not with individuals as homosexuals but with the gay agenda that incessantly promotes and encourages sinful behavior. God makes very clear in His Word that homosexuality is a sin, and that He is *not* okay with any sin. A man in a sexual relationship with another man and a woman in a sexual relationship with another woman is sin.

Sin is not okay with God.

A high school friend posted a photo of a woman and wrote, "God is cool with homosexuality, much like He's cool with heterosexuality." That is not biblically true or accurate. I was compelled to respond in defense of the truth about God. We cannot let lies go by. We must call them out.

As I expected, I received some rather mean responses and I was further frustrated by the decline of our nation's morality and disregard for truth when only one person out of fifteen to twenty posted agreement with what I'd written. We now have generations of people who were not raised in knowledge of biblical truth, so they believe in political correctness. One commenter called me "ignorant" and a gay man asked, "Does it really matter who I sleep with?" Well, since God declared that homosexuality is a sin then yes, it does matter who you sleep with. For a man to sleep with another man brings about sin, disease, and ultimately death. "For the wages of sin is death" (Romans 6:23).

When you take a stand for truth, expect backlash. "Be on your guard; stand firm in the faith; be courageous; be strong" (1 Corinthians 16:13). I was attacked for my views. Get used to it.

The friend from high school also responded defensively to the biblical truth I posted. She asked if I had an "open mind." I responded that if an open mind requires me to be politically correct rather than biblically correct, then no, I do not have an open mind. All I ask is that people do not attach untruths about God. When they do, I will take a stand, especially in these last days.

She then asked, "Can't everyone believe in their own god?" Freewill answers that question; we get to choose who or what we'll believe and worship, but the truth is, there is only one true God and only one route to Him. To believe and live otherwise will not end well when eternity greets you and you stand before your Creator.

As for being called intolerant, I gave the term some serious thought, including that she may be the intolerant one—toward God, the Bible, and Christianity. Many who call for tolerance simply want us to tolerate their views while ignoring and mocking God's laws and those who serve Him. I'm not the judge; I'm simply a messenger by virtue of having given my heart and life to Christ. God is the Judge, just as He is the God of love and wrath (1 John 4:7–21; Romans 1:18), topics the woman was not happy to hear about. People oppose God because He calls out their sin. People don't like that.

Those of us who believe in biblical truth will be persecuted, in the least called ignorant and other names. We'll be mocked and criticized for our beliefs (1 Peter 3:16). I encourage believers to live above criticism. Doing so is living for Christ and being an overcomer. (Read Revelation 2.) It isn't easy. I get it.

A growing percentage of our nation has stepped away from the principles and commands of God's Word and a great percentage of recent generations are not knowledgeable about the specifics of God's Word. God's guiding principles and commands, once viewed by our nation as sacred, have morphed into what are now called "issues." One such deviation is homosexuality. Since Jesus Christ is the same yesterday today and forever (Hebrews 13:8), He has not changed His mind on any of His commands and principles, including homosexuality. Homosexuality is wrong.

How can we, mankind, then approve of gay "marriage?" We cannot. Please read the story about Sodom and Gomorrah (Genesis 19).

From the very beginning of time (creation), God's commission is for mankind, as male and female, to reproduce (Genesis 1:28). We know it's impossible for a same-sex couple to procreate. Yet, those who promote the gay agenda are advocating sin with disregard for their Creator, His commands, and His warnings. God gives us warnings because He loves us and is thereby "not wanting anyone to perish, but everyone to come to repentance" (2 Peter 3:9).

So, despite the claims by nonbelievers and activist liberals, faithful Christians are *not* "intolerant bigots" but simply "obedient believers," adhering to our Creator's unchanging principles, commands, and warnings. They took what is good and pure and perverted it.

Again, to be clear on my stance, I don't feel hatred toward homosexuals or any other people; I'm concerned for their souls. I'm not a "hater," or "bigot;" I'm simply tired of the gay agenda perpetually in our faces. The gay agenda is sweeping people to accept a lifestyle of sin and insisting that we all encourage sin. Wanting people to go to heaven is not hatred; it's actually love!

The Creator of mankind is the One who has determined what is sin—whether homosexuality, adultery, murder, stealing, lying, and any other actions and thoughts stated by our Creator as sins against Him. We are His creation, so we do not get to decide what is and is not sin.

The difference between the gay agenda and other sin is that adulterers, thieves, murderers, liars . . . are not calling for acceptance and encouragement of their sins. As human beings, we all sin, but let's not encourage and support sin, nor twist God's commands to fit our desires. Sin is sin, as He clearly listed for us because He loves us so much. A secondary good resource on this topic is the website Americans for Truth about Homosexuality. Peter LaBarbera does a great job warning people about that sinful lifestyle. Please check out his website.

Inclusivity in Church

True inclusivity means inviting and welcoming *all* people to learn the truths of God's Word—without sugarcoating. More and more churches have become slack in teaching biblical truths because they want attendees to feel warm and fuzzy, which encourages their ongoing lifestyles of sin, whether homosexuality, adultery, idolatry, gluttony, abortion.... The truth about sin has somehow become controversial. Because of this, some pastors would rather entertain, tickle ears, and bring in money. I don't attend church to hear how I am "a good person." I'm not. I am a wretched sinner!

Between ESPN, CNN, and Fox News, can we possibly get more mainstream media coverage on the gay agenda? The issue has filtered into every aspect of our society—even our education system. There are now classes offered on LGBTQ studies. While looking into master's programs at various colleges and universities, I came across the following undergraduate certificate programs offered at the University of Colorado:

> Lesbian, Gay, Bisexual, Transgender, and Queer (LGBTQ) Studies at the University of Colorado Boulder is an interdisciplinary program encompassing more than 20 courses in a dozen departments, involving the academic investigation of sexuality in established fields such as literature, history, theatre, law, medicine, economics, sociology, anthropology, political science, and the arts.[92]

The direction this world is headed has blown me away and caused me to take an even firmer stand as a conservative. Here is my LGBTQ study and thesis: You are a sinner. Repent before it is too late.

I recall the Boy Scouts of America standing by their position to not allow openly homosexual individuals into the organization. When I vocally defended their decision on social media, I sure took a liberal "intolerance" beating. Liberals want to make the ruling about so-called exclusion, discrimination, and equal rights, but I believe such a ruling is not theirs to make.

The greater issue is child safety, morality, and *private*, conservative organizations standing by their beliefs in God and the Bible. People are not born gay. It's a lifestyle they choose.

In support of the BSA's decision, I responded to a friend's social media post about the topic and, as expected, the liberals came after me with comments like, "I suppose you also don't want a black president."

If the candidate is liberal, then *no*.

"You're against women voting."

What? That one made no sense at all in the context of the post topic. See what liberals do? They paint as hateful, bigoted, sexist, racist those who stand for truth.

Liberals: for the record, I would absolutely support a conservative black president, and yes, women should and do vote.

I find that liberals are often unknowledgeable and naive to common sense and certainly to the truth of God's Word that trumps anything that mankind could think. Their brand of humility often prompts them to remind others that they are "right" (no pun intended) instead of God their Creator, and that Christians and conservatives are old-school and out-of-touch. This turning from God to self is tragic for them as individuals and is the ongoing cause of our nation's rapidly declining biblical morals, values, and freedoms on which our country was founded.

We really need a revival in this country, to get people to read the Bible, the Constitution, and the Declaration of Independence. Bibles for America will send you a free New Testament Recovery Version of God's Word. And Hillsdale College will send you a free copy of The Constitution (pocket size) and Declaration of Independence. These free resources are what every American needs! I encourage you to go online now and order them. (See "Recommended Resources.")

In another BSA conversation on social media, I responded to a friend who disagreed with BSA's ruling, calling it "discriminatory." I did some research and concluded that the BSA had the right to turn away (or, as some would say, "discriminate") openly homosexual individuals from participating in BSA's *privately* governed organization. Just as those who disagree with the policy have the right to disagree with, simply ignore, and not financially support the BSA. Likewise, it's my choice to not patronize liberal businesses. No one is forcing anyone to support or agree with BSA's policy, nor does anyone have a right to dictate the governing decisions of a private organization. They did the right thing.

I stand by my opposition of the gay agenda, my opposition to allowing homosexuals into the Boy Scouts of America, and my support of BSA's decision in 2012. However, since that time, the BSA has changed its policy to allow gay scoutmasters and transgender children. This is wrong. They caved to the woke mob.

A lot of my concerns are for the youth of this nation. They will become the future leaders.

My view is that parents allowing their children to "identify" as the other sex (or as no sex or anything else nonhuman) is child abuse and neglect. There's only one way to know the God-created sex of a child: by their external genital organs at birth. It is easy to know the sex of a child. Stop with the insanity already. These poor kids.

The question of gender identity is simple: If you were born with male parts, you are male. If you were born with female parts, you are female. How hard is that to understand? Perversion erodes understanding, smears and erases lines of definition, and creates confusion. This erosion is a tactic of Satan. The gay agenda and so-called tolerance has also eroded safety. For example, we're now faced with predators and perverts being welcomed to use the women's restroom! Consider the raging hormones of junior high and high school boys, and those boys across the US being welcomed and encouraged by adults (the so-called protectors and teachers) to use the girls' restrooms! Such new "policies" is an open invitation to rapists. Truly protecting "women's rights" is to not abort babies (millions of female babies murdered) and to not allow males into girls' restrooms. Common sense.

With countless schools accepting and teaching homosexuality, we are seeing more and more instances of little girls, young women, and aged women molested and raped by males who claim to "identify" as female. Public education has gone from educating to indoctrinating!

Because of mankind's free-will choice to turn against God and His Word (one and the same), the human heart is wicked and evil. This fact is why God instituted moral perimeters—in print—as rules for our physical, mental, emotional, and spiritual protection, safety, health, and well-being.

Our society is imploding. Liberal society is encouraging human destruction and eternal death—eternal separation from God. Consider the reality of being eternally separated from all of God's characteristics. What would that eternal reality actually look like? Here are just a few examples:

- Without God's eternal glory, there is unending total darkness.

- Without God's eternal provision and protection, there is unending decay.

- Without God's eternal forgiveness, there is unending regret.

- Without God's eternal presence, there is unending loneliness.

- Without God's eternal love, there is unending hatred.

- Without God's eternal hope, there is unending despair.

In other words, without God, there is eternal torment (weeping and gnashing of teeth). A televised GLAAD commercial ran in 2022 about "Max"—a girl who "identified" as a boy. GLAAD stands for Gay & Lesbian Alliance Against Defamation.[93] With that pursuit of willfulness against God's sovereignty as our Creator, Max's life and her family's life will be a mess. Her parents failed her miserably by allowing her to see herself differently than God the Creator formed her in her mother's womb, physically identifiable at her birth.

> For you created my inmost being;
> you knit me together in my mother's womb.
> I praise you because I am fearfully and wonderfully made;
> your works are wonderful,
> I know that full well.
> My frame was not hidden from you
> when I was made in the secret place,
> when I was woven together in the depths of the earth.
> Your eyes saw my unformed body;
> all the days ordained for me were written in your book
> before one of them came to be.
> How precious to me are your thoughts, God!
> How vast is the sum of them!
> Were I to count them,
> they would outnumber the grains of sand—
> when I awake, I am still with you.
>
> If only you, God, would slay the wicked!
> Away from me, you who are bloodthirsty!
> They speak of you with evil intent;
> your adversaries misuse your name.
>
> (Psalm 139:13–20)

Again, my issue is not with homosexuals but against all sin, including the sin of homosexuality and the promotion of sin, including *the gay agenda*. Homosexuality is now encouraged and promoted.

Regarding the BSA's 2012 policy controversy, another friend had said, "If it keeps just *one* boy from being molested by a homosexual, the policy was well worth upholding." Well said. Could not agree more.

My view is that scout youth (and all youth) safety is of utmost concern. The BSA's former policy was not a case of discrimination but rather one of safety and morality. Morality by nature ensures safety.

Why should the gay agenda be allowed to influence our impressionable youth and destroy safety? BSA was an organization of members who valued their religious faith and, upholding God's position (morality) on homosexuality, clearly stated in the Bible: homosexual activity is sin (Romans 1:18–32). Many homosexuals were probably neglected by their fathers. In an attempt to get that fatherly love, they turn wrongly to the love of another man. Perhaps they were abused. They need the gospel as they may have also been molested. They most likely have deep emotional pain.

If you were to search the Internet about the significant benefits of youths' involvement in scouting, you'd find such examples as staying away from drugs, morality, ethics, values (like helping at home and helping others), building self-confidence, and a strong sense of self-worth.

I read about a _six_-year-old "transgender" in Colorado being allowed to use the girl's bathroom in Colorado. Can anyone seriously tell me this is normal, moral, acceptable behavior? *What is wrong with parents and society that children are no longer being protected, even in their homes?* The turning away from God. It all starts in the home.

Parenting (one mother and one father) is the most important role in life, regardless of socioeconomic status. Having money simply gives a parent more options and opportunities for their children, which is great but has nothing to do with fundamental parenting: abundant time with your child(ren) in fun, teaching, practicing, and modeling moral, ethical, biblical behaviors, while providing for practical, emotional, mental, and spiritual needs, which includes protecting your child(ren) to your upmost ability. Parenting is, in my view, the highest calling in life. Kids are being used and abused—even by parents, teachers, and other leaders—and this is not okay. To echo a common phrase: there will be hell to pay.

There are serious eternal consequences for sin. Let's stop pretending that this lifestyle is normal and okay. It is neither. Homosexuality is leading many people down a path of hopelessness, despair, disease, and destruction, and will ultimately end in death and eternal separation from God.

I pray for the gay community, understanding that they chose the homosexual lifestyle out of tremendous emotional pain or out of desire to be part of the growing movement that helps them to feel accepted by others. In truth, their need is for true, godly love—the only love that is pure and satisfying—and the hope, healing, wholeness, and true freedom that only comes by following Jesus Christ as Savior and Lord over their lives.

Do not tell me you "love" the homosexual community when in truth that lifestyle means the individuals will spend eternity in hell unless they humble themselves and turn to Christ as their one and only Savior. Supporting the turning away from God is not okay. Whether or not you proclaim to be gay, you will one day stand before God and give an account of your life—what you supported and encouraged and what you didn't. Please stop encouraging this lifestyle. I'm sure many people regret having experimented in that lifestyle. Stop encouraging and supporting it! The homosexual lifestyle is hurting people!

It's sad to see former Christians turn from God's Word to homosexuality and "come out of the closet," as it's called. Parading sin. A true Christian knows their gender of birth, accepts and honors their birth gender as God's divine plan for them, and will commit themselves to abstain from the sin of homosexuality.

> No temptation has overtaken you except what is common to mankind. And God is faithful; he will not let you be tempted beyond what you can bear. But when you are tempted, he will also provide a way out so that you can endure it. (1 Corinthians 10:13)

I'm well aware of my own sinful nature, admitting to being a wretched sinner, especially lust for women, but as a believer in Jesus Christ, commissioned by God (as all believers are) to share the truths of God's Word, I do not and will not promote or encourage lust of any kind, including the lust of men for men and women for women. We each sin, and each need to repent humbly before our Maker. To choose a lifestyle of sin—whether homosexuality, lust, greed, abortion, or other acts of sin—is to mock God, mock His sovereignty over all of creation, and to mock His Word. Mocking God reaps everlasting separation from Him unless there is humble repentance and renewing the mind to be obedient to God's Word. In my personal life, I daily pray that my sexual thoughts and desires be removed from my mind and heart. I no longer want to live in sexual sin or view pornography. If you struggle with viewing pornography (which I did up until 2008), there are resources to help you. Ever Accountable and Covenant

Eyes software will hold you accountable. Check them out. (See "Recommended Resources.") Slay that sin. It is vile.

The gay agenda openly and blatantly mocks God in many ways, skewing what He has created and the purposes for what He created. The gay community has hijacked the rainbow as their symbol when, in truth, the rainbow is a symbol clearly set by God as an indication of His promise to not again destroy the earth by water (Genesis 9:16). Instead, His Word tells us that He will destroy everything on Earth by fire:

> The day of the Lord will come like a thief. The heavens will disappear with a roar; the elements will be destroyed by fire, and the earth and everything done in it will be laid bare. (2 Peter 3:10)

While mankind's self-destruction by sin is very concerning to me, I must remember that God is in control and will ultimately judge both the righteous and the wicked.

This is what the Lord says:

"Cursed is the one who trusts in man,
who draws strength from mere flesh
and whose heart turns away from the Lord.
That person will be like a bush in the wastelands;
they will not see prosperity when it comes.
They will dwell in the parched places of the desert,
in a salt land where no one lives.

"But blessed is the one who trusts in the Lord,
whose confidence is in him.

> They will be like a tree planted by the water
> that sends out its roots by the stream.
> It does not fear when heat comes;
> its leaves are always green.
> It has no worries in a year of drought
> and never fails to bear fruit."
>
> The heart is deceitful above all things
> and beyond cure.
>
> Who can understand it?
>
> "I the Lord search the heart
> and examine the mind,
> to reward each person according to their conduct,
> according to what their deeds deserve."
>
> (Jeremiah 17:5–10)

The dire consequences of the gay agenda are uglier and more terrifying with each passing day. Eternal life with God is at stake! I totally get struggling with sexual sin, but it can be overcome! I was sexually immoral with women and I viewed pornography, but by the grace of God that sin has been crucified.

To watch our federal government and our adult and youth citizens supporting homosexuality is beyond logic and my understanding. Whatever is illogical cannot be understood, for the root of illogical thinking is evil.

Our government's primary role is to protect Americans, and our role as adults is to protect one another, especially children, the widowed, and the elderly. Both roles (government and protecting others) are failing. Our leaders should be more concerned about protecting Americans from terrorism, destroying ISIS, and balancing our budget, and less concerned about welcoming males to use women's bathrooms and shower facilities. How did we become so woke?

The gay agenda is also selfish in that its followers care only about their political agenda, not about the well-being or health of homosexuals. The gay community wants to continue boycotting companies that don't agree with their agenda. That is fine. Go ahead.

Do whatever you desire in private—with the understanding that God sees your sins no matter where you are and will hold you accountable—but why promote and encourage sinful behavior in public?

At the time of this writing, 2023, Pope Francis clarified his stance on homosexuality, stating that while homosexuality is not a crime, any sexual act outside of marriage is a sin;[94] whereas in 2013 he said he won't judge priests for their sexual orientation.[95] This issue is another I have with the Roman Catholic Church. I grew up Catholic but left the church in 2007 over the fallout from the sex abuse scandal. I refuse to look to a mere mortal man, like the Pope, for truth. The Catholic church needs to better focus on the gospel, not on social justice issues. The gospel, the whole gospel, and nothing but the gospel.

I say cut out the middleman (the pope), and love and forgive homosexuals (and all people), but do not support or encourage sin, please. That's my two cents worth. I'd like to donate those two cents to the US government to reduce our federal debt; you're welcome.

While in Merrill, Wisconsin visiting Gram, I read the bulletin of St. Alphonsus Catholic Church (Greendale, WI) that included a support network listing for the gay community. Welcoming the gay community to church is important, but let's invite community members to know that homosexuality is an abominable sin to God and that He loves them, wants their humble repentance, and wants them to live their lives according to His Word. Invite the sinner to church, but do not welcome the sin.

Which is more important: filling the coffers of the Catholic Church or leading people to Jesus Christ?

I urge churches to teach the Word of God, love unconditionally while clearly pointing out sin, encourage parishioners to read and study the Bible, and pray for their turning from sin to Jesus Christ and a life devoted to Him in godly living. Such a life is not one of pompous perfection, not the "holier than thou" Christians, for all Christians (Christ followers) are sinners; but a life of humility and gratitude to God while striving to live a life that's pleasing to Him.

Humility and gratitude are vital in the Christian life.

The gay agenda (it is an agenda) daily and aggressively attacks society and persuades our youth into sinful living. There are many examples in every area of media, teaching, role modeling, and socialization. Let's pray for those influencers and followers. Let's lead them to the truth of God's Word. We don't want *anyone* to end up eternally separated from God. We are each responsible, and each have opportunities to present the gospel. And this comes from the world's worst sinner (me!).

My shared thoughts may appear to be obsessive, but in truth, my comments are primarily in defense of the gospel of Jesus Christ. I wouldn't feel the need to address the gay agenda issue so much if that lifestyle wasn't continually shoved and forced in the faces of Americans. Whether it be the Russian anti-gay laws to protect children or coming-out announcements by public figures, like football player Michael Sam, we're continually being manipulated by bombardment to approve this lifestyle, and the consequences of speaking out against sin is verbal persecution.

Enough with the influencing and encouraging of sin!

As the topic continues front and center at every turn, you can bet that this nation's conservatives and Christians are facing a greater persecution than verbal. For example, Michael Sam, while playing football at the University of Missouri, was eligible for the NFL draft until all the attention shifted to his personal lifestyle instead of his abilities on the football field. Some, like Michelle Obama, called his coming-out announcement "heroic." She posted on Twitter: "You're an inspiration to all of us, @MikeSamFootball. We couldn't be prouder of your courage both on and off the field. - mo."[96] What does athletic ability have to do with sexual preference? Absolutely nothing. And I must ask: what is so heroic about a man having relations with another man? It's not heroic; it's sinful.

Like each of us, Mr. Sam is a sinner in need of God's gift of salvation. None of us are heroes for sinning! Who in their right mind would call a murderer, adulterer, gossiper, or glutton a hero? If one's personal life is going to be brought into their professional life, every NFL prospect should come out and simply wrap up their lives with this single statement: "I'm a sinner." Would we then call them courageous? Such a person is not a hero any more than I am; we're both equally sinners. I am no better than Michael Sam.

My prayer is that public figures and all unbelievers come to know the truth found in Jesus Christ and follow God's Word, before it's too late, and take a stand for godly living. One such example is comedian and actor Kelsey Grammer who professed to giving his heart and life to Christ, reported in 2023 by Pureflix through which he's now involved in Christian films. He said:

> I don't know if I ever thought the family was cursed, but I cursed God for a while. I hated being alive, indulged in a great depression and a kind of aggressive approach to the streets at night. I was looking for trouble. . . . But I have come to terms with it and have found great peace in my faith and in Jesus. It's not cavalier—Jesus made a difference in my life.[97]

Another example is three-time MVP, two-time World Series champion Albert Pujols who "gives credit to God for all his victories. He is quoted saying, 'It doesn't matter if I hit a home run. It doesn't matter if we win a game. It doesn't matter if I go four for four; what matters at the end of the day, as long as I glorify His name, that's what it's all about.'"[98]

It's sad when sports fans consider athletes as heroes.

> *Side Note:* I love Charles Barkley, but he's not God and must never become a god to me!

> "Love the Lord your God with all your heart and with all your soul and with all your mind." (Matthew 22:37)

We sports enthusiasts pack stadiums to watch men display their God-given talents and abilities, and I get it—attending sporting events is exciting and enjoyable. Nothing better than nachos and a beer at a Milwaukee Brewers game! But are we keeping in mind that athletes are mere mortals? An athlete or any other human cannot save anyone from eternal separation from God. So, let's keep things in perspective: a sport is just a game and lifestyle that bears eternal consequences, good or bad.

While fans are willing to give up hours of their Sundays to support, cheer, and often get intoxicated, are they also willing to spend just an hour in church each week to hear about Jesus Christ? Sadly, the answer is most often no. Although I'm still a sports fanatic, I often consider as I grow older and wiser what's most important. Part of the renewing of my mind (Romans 12:2) includes a little prayer before watching each game. "Lord, may these men know you; and please keep them safe. I pray for their salvation and safety." I don't share that to appear lofty but to example how simple it is for us to keep our minds on Christ by including God in every area of our lives because there's is no eternal value to anything earthly. This is all passing, fleeting, temporary.

How our lives would drastically change for the better if we talked to God before everything we did through the day.

That's not only a relationship with God the Father but a strong deterrent against sin.

In 2014, President Obama sent three gay Olympic delegates to Russia for the Sochi Olympics. Did that administration not have bigger issues to address than supporting the gay agenda? Seriously! Our economy was in shambles and our military was being gutted.

The two Obama administrations could not have ended soon enough for our country. The truth is that gay activists will not quit until they've exhausted all means to get their way. An example is the demanded voter recounts and taking their demands to the courts in hopes that liberal judges would rule in favor of their perverted ways.

I used to worry much about what others did and about our legal system, but I've come to rest in the knowledge that God is the final judge and He's still in control, always has been and always will be. I really don't have much control in this life. And that's okay.

Make all the laws you want in support of sin, but in the end, we'll each stand before our Creator who will judge us for how we lived, thought, believed, and behaved. This fact is both reassuring and terrifying. The unrepentant will be sentenced to eternity—no end—apart from God and all His goodness and light. I often wonder if I'm getting in; but one cannot lose their salvation. We can backslide, but we cannot lose our salvation. Once saved, always saved.

My niece attended a high school that holds a "Diversity Week," which pushes the gay agenda onto the students. One of her teachers also pushed her political ideology on her students. If the teacher was pushing pro-global-warming views on my niece, what other views was she pushing onto these young, impressionable minds in addition to the school's "Diversity Week." These blatant wrongs prompted me to notify Brannon Howse, founder, broadcaster, and producer of Worldview Weekend. Subsequently, my niece and I were invited to discuss the matter on his national radio broadcast (February 2012). I appreciate any opportunity to share truth. I have severe social anxiety, so I do recall a shot of whiskey prior to the national interview. Turning to the bottle will never solve one's problems.

God hates sin, but not the sinner. Don't think for one second that God doesn't love the gay community. The late Fred Phelps (2014), founder of Westboro Church had publicly expressed, "God hates fags."[99] Wrong. That's biblically incorrect; God's Word tell us "For God so loved the world [every person] that he gave his one and only Son, that whoever believes in him shall not perish but have eternal life (John 3:16). God loves every person throughout the history and future of mankind. He loves us so much that His second greatest gift to us each is free will to either make choices that honor Him or dishonor Him in our daily living, and both have consequences. Mr. Phelps had made other mean-spirited remarks but claimed to be a Christian. True Christians will not have hatred in their hearts; they will have the love of God. Pray for the lost!

Our response to God's love and grace should be humble repentance, turning away from our sins, and lovingly calling out sin. While my thoughts expressed in this book may not at times come across as loving, I assure you that every thought comes from a heart of pleading to remove your blinders to sin and give your heart and life fully to Jesus Christ. You are not guaranteed a tomorrow or even another minute (every breath is a gift), which is why the apostle Paul quoted Christ when pleading with the lost:

> "In the time of my favor I heard you, and in the day of salvation I helped you."

> I tell you, now is the time of God's favor, now is the day of salvation. (2 Corinthians 6:2)

In December 2011, I attended the Brannon Howse Worldview Weekend Training Institute in Rockford, Illinois. The binder included a statement to this effect:

> The most telling aspect of the legalization debate, though, is that gays are not interested so much in marriage as they are in their agenda. Numerous studies document that the average homosexual has hundreds of sexual relationships. Given this reality, it stands to reason that homosexuals are not interested in getting married and having one life partner but in using the marriage issue to further a liberal, anti-family, anti-Christian political agenda.

State-by-state, the gay agenda machine is hard at work. And hundreds of sexual relationships? That is beyond sickening. I'll say it again: disease and death.

I occasionally read *USA TODAY*, which is nothing but liberal filth. On their front page, their Life section, and even their Sports section can be found articles supporting the gay agenda. An example that stands out in my mind is all that was published regarding Michael Sam (here he is again) as the first openly gay player to be drafted by the NFL—which had absolutely nothing to do with athleticism. Yet, the news was focused on hatred, bigotry, and conservatives regarding homosexuality—the gay agenda instead of football. The judgements should have been solely focused on Mr. Sam's physical ability and skills to contribute to an NFL team. I don't think his tenure in the NFL lasted long.

Despite claims by nonbelievers and activist liberals, Christian are *not* "intolerant bigots" but simply "obedient believers" adhering to our Creator's unchanging Word. He is the same yesterday, today, and forever.

I'm sick of the gay agenda, which has infiltrated headlines, schools, community activities, policy, and most critically, our mindsets, which influence our choices and actions. As for broadcast news, can we no longer cover truly relevant news without it being twisted in some way to leverage the gay agenda? Every day, as I look at MSN.com headlines, I see articles about gays, lesbians, and transgender individuals. I recall news of a Navy SEAL coming out as transgender. This is not "news" but rather heralding individuals' sex lives and distracting from relevant news. God made us either male or female (Genesis 5:2; Matthew 19:4) made evident by our distinguishing body parts and chromosomes. My plead is to stop fighting against fact. Our Creator has not changed His mind, nor will He, nor does He make mistakes.

Stop publicizing sex lives.

As I search news headlines for relevant news, I instead find more evidence that mankind is in a downward spiral with the weight of sin, taking unbelievers further and further from God's grace and patience. I pray that all people will come to see their sin and repent to God before it's too late. That's a big point of this book: to warn people because one day it will be too late!

While at work on a New Year's Eve (my birthday), I was introduced to a female coworker's same-sex "partner." The funny thing was after her girlfriend used profanity, the coworker said about me, "Watch your mouth. He's a pastor!" *Hilarious.* For the record, I am not a pastor, just a sinner saved by God's grace. I am a disciple, not a pastor. I must daily remind myself, *Just love them and pray for them.* We're all *sinners.* Every day, I blow it as a Christian because I'm a sinner. The difference is that I've chosen Christ as my Savior who promised forgiveness and an everlasting covenant with those who believe in Him. As the apostle Paul asked, "What does Scripture say? 'Abraham believed God, and it was credited to him as righteousness'" (Romans 4:3)

> "Blessed are those whose transgressions are forgiven, whose sins are covered. Blessed is the one whose sin the Lord will never count against them." (Romans 4:7–8)

It's our thoughts (hearts) that God judges. I'm thankful that "If we confess our sins, he is faithful and just and will forgive us our sins and purify us from all unrighteousness" (1 John 1:9). Being the wretched sinner I am, I have a long list of prayers on my Holy Bible App Prayer List.

I once tried to watch the TV show *Modern Family* but just didn't find it at all funny. One of my sisters finds the show hilarious, but I won't be sad if I never see it again. Two of the show's male characters are homosexual "partners." The show has a lot of homosexual overtones, which is not what we should be encouraging and promoting to our youth. Though some say that I'm a homosexual hater, I'm not; I'm a human being who loves God and wants all people to receive His gift of grace.

See how backwards this is: those claiming to love homosexuals are the very ones who are okay with gay people spending eternity separated from God. I want them to spend eternity in heaven. Therefore, I actually love them!

What worries me about the homosexual lifestyle—like any sinful lifestyle, be it alcoholism, theft, porn, . . .—is the eternal consequences for not humbly repenting to God and turning from sin: eternal separation from Him who is love and light incarnate, the Creator, and divine Judge. Such separation means eternal darkness, void of all the characteristics of love and light. Think of such a void in terms of "forever and ever and ever." This lifetime is but a blink in comparison to forever. Is your brief lifestyle and mindset against God worth eternal separation from Him? Our time here is short!

I also tried to watch an episode of *Saturday Night Live* and found it was also a waste of my time, no longer humorous to me. It isn't the show it was in the 1980s. It used to be funny!

I came across a cable show, *Gay USA*. Sickening. An older gentleman and older lady were providing positive commentary about the gay lifestyle and the "progress" made in the gay rights arena. I felt sad for the commentators, on a path that leads to destruction. I pray that the lost will hear and accept the gospel of Jesus Christ before it's too late.

The worship pastor of my church at one time said, "We could be raptured at any moment and taken home to spend eternity with the Lord. Let's go!" I am 100 percent with him but want all people to spend eternity with the Lord. I have friends who brush off their eternal souls. This greatly concerns me. Jesus said:

> "Not everyone who says to me, 'Lord, Lord,' will enter the kingdom of heaven, but only the one who does the will of my Father who is in heaven. Many will say to me on that day, 'Lord, Lord, did we not prophesy in your name and in

your name drive out demons and in your name perform many miracles?' Then I will tell them plainly, 'I never knew you. Away from me, you evildoers!'" (Matthew 7:21–23)

Oh, the godless time we're in. The filth on TV is not only an example that points us in the opposite direction of God's grace and truth but a waste of time. Bring back quality shows like *MASH*, *Family Ties*, *Growing Pains*, *Alf*, *Golden Girls*, *Frasier*, *The King of Queens*, and *Seinfeld*. A solid modern-day (2011–2021) show is *Last Man Standing* with Tim Allen. As a form of clean entertainment, I'm a big fan of the show. It's hilarious!

Laughter is good medicine.

A friend in Milwaukee made me aware of a 2012–2013 TV show *The New Normal*, showcasing the "family" as children with homosexual parents. That demonstration is so wrong. Children *need* to be raised by a mother and father in a shared home. The older I grow and the more research I do, I realize just how important parenting is and how crucial is the need for parents to live as God intended: husband (male) and wife (female)—the single greatest influence in the formative years of a child's life. Although I'm a single man, I am thankful for having morally traditional parents. In fact, without a doubt, the most important role a man and woman can have in life is parenting as husband and wife, paired as a team. Parenting matters.

From our respective childhood experiences, we know that parental influence—positive or negative—impacts a child for *life*, impacts our society, and the generations to come, which is why it's tragic to see single-parent homes and same-sex-parent homes rapidly increasing. This isn't emotionally healthy for a child. A child's foremost need in addition to food, water, clothing, shelter, and education, is a mother's love and affection alongside a father's protection and investment of time (sporting events, homework, and other family time). Think how much stronger and all-around better this nation would be with fewer divorces and more households with a mother and father.

I enjoy watching old-school cartoons like *Bugs Bunny*, *Looney Tunes*, and *Elmer Fudd* with his ever-present shotgun. It is funny! Every time there's a gun used or an explosion of some sort in the old cartoon, I think of leftists. Clearly, many liberals have worked to change such cartoons because children's broadcasts are now centered on political correctness. Cartoons are no longer funny. Watching old cartoons, I laugh more than I do when watching contemporary shows like *Modern Family* or an episode of *Saturday Night Live*. I've not laughed once watching politically correct cartoons and comedies. I'd just turned forty when I caught sight of an old cartoon, good comedy for laughter. I absolutely love how politically *in*correct they are. Oh, the good old days!

Our society, politicians, culture, TV shows, and other media and influences fail to honor and glorify God. How can we expect our children (future leaders) to be morally grounded? Without the current adult generations turning from sin, pride, and greed and regaining logical, moral thinking in alignment with our Creator, there is no such bright future. God is all-knowing (Romans 11:33) and has the final word of reckoning and rewarding. His sovereignty and plan cannot be abolished. Thereby, believers in Jesus Christ have hope and assurance regardless of what's happening in our nation and world.

Because of Christ, we need not be overly discouraged by political election results. He is the world's saving solution for all. We know the truth is God's Word (John 17:17). So, instead of living in anger and fear, we are to live in righteousness (right living) and courageously share the truth. So many people need to humbly repent of their sins.

> "Enter through the narrow gate. For wide is the gate and broad is the road that leads to destruction, and many enter through it. But small is the gate and narrow the road that leads to life, and only a few find it." (Matthew 7:13–23)

Leroy Butler of the Green Bay Packers (1990–2001) was once scheduled to speak at a church in Wisconsin. But the pastor wisely canceled the event after Leroy congratulated someone for living a sinful lifestyle. Nonbelievers want to claim that the church is intolerant; they cannot understand why Leroy's guest speaking at the church was canceled. Kudos to the pastor for standing up for biblical truth. The church *should* be intolerant—intolerant of sin.

The true church knows and teaches biblical truth. The true church stands for truth.

On the flip side, do you think a pro-gay "marriage" gathering would ask me or any other faithful Christ follower to speak? No. Hypocrites. If you're on the left, liberals will call you tolerant, and if you oppose the left, they'll label you as hateful and intolerant (bigoted) while preaching "inclusivity" of all people and beliefs. "Such a person is double-minded and unstable in all they do" (James 1:8).

When news of Leroy Butler's cancellation went public, one of my coworkers raged about religion, saying that religion is why this country is so messed up. My response was, "It's not normal or healthy for two men to have sexual relations." His counter was that he could not care less if two men have sex and marry. That mindset of sin acceptance and advocacy in direct contradiction to God is a perfect example of why our country is self-destructing, which includes the lack of good parenting and an increase in schools teaching and encouraging atheism, climate change, sustainability, homosexuality, political correctness, and the so-called "good" of big government.

Another example of our country's downward spiraling is once-gold-medalist decathlete Bruce Jenner "deciding" he was no longer a man and now living publicly as a woman. How do people decide to switch sexes? I just don't get it. There must be deep emotional pain.

Transgenderism is a tragically sad and destructive tool of the devil.

God made Mr. Jenner a man, and Mr. Jenner won all his athletic records as a man. I fear for him and the host of other people in desperate need of the truth and healing that can only be found in Jesus Christ. I feel sorry for all who have chosen paths of destruction, regardless of the sin. Sin is the "wide gate" and a sinful lifestyle is a "broad road," which is why we see more and more people taking that road. Transgenderism and "gender confusion" is on the rise in the greatest country in the world, the USA.

When former NBA player Jason Collins came out as gay in 2013, some people called him with *congratulations* as if he'd won a championship, including President Obama and Leroy Butler (former safety for the Green Bay Packers, my all-time-favorite sports team). Leroy sent a message on Twitter: "Congrats to Jason Collins."[100] Come on, Leroy; why? We're congratulating sin?

Seven years after Michael Sam "came out" as gay, football defensive end Carl Paul Nassib was praised by NPR (National Public Radio) as the "first active NFL player to come out as gay," and they applauded him as "making history."[101] *I just don't get the celebration of sin. This is not okay. I would be embarrassed to "celebrate" my sin. It is nothing I am proud of.*

Come on! Are porn stars congratulated for becoming sexually immoral? What about alcoholics, adulterers, gamblers, etc.? Do we post congratulatory messages to them for their sin? Perhaps Tom Brokaw should change his book's title from *The Greatest Generation* to *The Wussiest Generation* or write a book on that topic. One of my former coworkers was from Slovakia. He laughed when I asked him, "Would gay marriage ever pass in Slovakia?" His smirk was a mile wide, emphasizing that such an act would not happen in his country. There was a time when we wouldn't have believed our country would sanction gay marriage. The men in Slovakia are men, a good thing, and would chuckle at the gay agenda.

In Slovakia, like most countries apart from the US, men are men and behave as true men. They're attracted to women, and they fight to protect their country and families. That's what men do! I'm not encouraging womanizing, nor fighting without just cause, but the truth is that God designed men to be attracted to females, and vice versa, and should fight to protect rather than put on make-up and high heels, wondering how it feels to be a woman. Enough of this silliness!

Man up, men!

Read the website Authentic Manhood. (See "Recommended Resources.")

There's a local event in Colorado called Man of the Cliff—men behaving like men as they participate in various games of strength and agility, like axe throwing, instead of acting like wussies. Good for them! Our country needs more manly men and fewer silly male gooses running around acting like little girls. Would we find such a gross number of geese among ISIS, Taliban, and al-Qaeda? Their men are dedicating their lives, day and night, to refining their strength, agility, and other such characteristics toward taking over our nation and the world. We live in a scary age of self-destruction, less strengthened to defend our nation and the morals that made this country the most powerful in the world.

What's the solution? The conservative solution, of course.

Parents encouraging their boys to be boys, playing sports for example, and girls to be girls, playing Barbie. Our future generations of adult men are being told from a young age to stop being productively aggressive and that it's okay to hedge in on female sports and be stay-at-home dads—many out of fear of bullying Liberals who constantly jab society with terms like "inclusivity" and "home husbands," and concepts like "getting in touch with your feminine side." Men don't need a feminine side!

Encourage boys to be boys while teaching them the Word of God to ensure our up-and-coming generations are true and godly men who are taking back what the enemy of our souls is perpetually trying to steal: their God-given male traits. We have angry, lost, and confused boys and men because fathers have abandoned their God-given roles. Fathers matter.

Read the stats of fatherless boys at the website Fathers in the Field. (See "Recommended Resources.")

Once you read God's Word—begin with Romans 1—this fallen world (due to sin) and what's to come will make sense to you. I very much look forward to eternity with Jesus Christ, where there will be no more death, mourning, crying, or pain.

Look at all the sin in workplaces, for example. Whether it be gossiping, lusting, stealing, or slandering, sin is all around us—wherever we are, even in churches because that's the hospital for sinners! We don't attend church because we're good people! Having been in the workforce for decades, I've had a number of different jobs in varying environments. Looking back, I see more clearly all the sins that occurred in those workplaces. There is no place on Earth without sin. We need to beware and remember that we are to work for Jesus Christ, the Lord, not for man. "Whatever you do, work at it with all your heart, as working for the Lord, not for human masters" (Colossians 3:23).

The Hollywood stage had not changed since I last watched the Oscar Awards. It continues to be a showcase for liberals—those who say that gay rights is today's civil rights battle (it's not) and that gays are discriminated against, as blacks were in the 1960s. Give me a break; one cannot choose the color of their skin but one can and does choose sin, such as homosexuality. We are all born sinners but no one is born gay. The sin of homosexuality is a choice as racism is a choice. Sadly, those who are stuck in the lie that homosexuality is "who I am" are often those who had a poor relationship with the same-sex parent, an abusive childhood, or a no-parent relationship.

Those who choose homosexuality are hurting, and the good news is that Jesus is all about *healing* the brokenhearted.

Christ is the Great Physician who can heal our past wounds and present mental health issues. Choosing and remaining in a gay lifestyle is not God's design. He came that we might be "free" from the bondage of sin (Romans 6). Sin destroys.

The gay agenda is selfish in that its followers care only about themselves, sinful pleasures, and their political agenda, not about the well-being or health of homosexuals. Instead of supporting the gay agenda, we need to support and encourage good mental, emotional, physical, and spiritual health. A good book I recommend is *The Christ Cure: 10 Biblical Ways to Heal from Trauma, Tragedy, and PTSD* by Tim Murphy.

God created us to glorify Him and commissioned believers in Jesus Christ to share His salvation gospel with all of mankind. We are to love all people with the love of Christ, including our enemies. We are to pray for everyone, regardless of their beliefs, and, with love, we are to make known to others what God has specified in the Bible as sin, including homosexuality. Through Jesus Christ, we can each gain hope and freedom from sin.

Supporters of homosexual lifestyles either do not know God's Word yet, or do not believe the truth, and are thereby leading themselves and others down the wide road of lies, destruction, and eternal separation from God. Thereby, they are not truly *loving* people but adding to the misery of the hurting and blocking them from the freeing and healing salvation in Jesus Christ. So, in truth, the gay agenda is *not* authentically tolerant or loving; it is rooted in evil that produces selfishness and hatred. My intent is to help expose the gay agenda for what it is.

I urge you to visit the website Freedom in Christ. (See "Recommended Resources.")

Where are you standing in relationship with Jesus Christ the Savior and God your Creator?

What the Bible says about homosexuality and other sin:

- "God gave them over to shameful lusts. Even their women exchanged natural sexual relations for unnatural ones. In the same way the men also abandoned natural relations with women and were inflamed with lust for one another. Men committed shameful acts with other men, and received in themselves the due penalty for their error" (Romans 1:24, 26–27).

- "Do not be deceived: Neither the sexually immoral nor idolaters nor adulterers nor men who have sex with men nor thieves nor the greedy nor drunkards nor slanderers nor swindlers will inherit the kingdom of God" (1 Corinthians 6:9–10).

- "We know that the law is good if one uses it properly. We also know that the law is made not for the righteous but for lawbreakers and rebels, the ungodly and sinful, the unholy and irreligious, . . . for the sexually immoral, for those practicing homosexuality, . . . for whatever else is contrary to the sound doctrine that conforms to the gospel concerning the glory of the blessed God, which he entrusted to me" (1 Timothy 1:8–11).

- "The acts of the flesh are obvious: sexual immorality, impurity, and debauchery; idolatry and witchcraft; hatred, discord, jealousy, fits of rage, selfish ambition, dissensions, factions and envy; drunkenness, orgies, and the like. I warn you, as I did before, that those who live like this will not inherit the kingdom of God" (Galatians 5:19–21).

- "The wages of sin is death, but the gift of God is eternal life in Christ Jesus our Lord" (Romans 6:23).

CHAPTER 13

Same-Sex "Marriage"

State-by-state, the gay agenda machine is hard at work in the initiative to legalize same-sex "marriage." I'm concerned as I watch so many states giving in to gay "marriage" advocates. It isn't marriage! You need one man and one woman.

Current news is that "California will try to enshrine the right to same-sex marriage."[102] Other states are vying for same-sex marriage. Currently, thirty-seven of our fifty states, plus the District of Columbia, have legalized same-sex marriage. Thirty-seven! That leaves us with thirteen states holding true to moral values. But my guess is they eventually will cave in.

An interesting parallel regarding the number of remaining states—thirteen—is that our country gained ground toward freedom from Europe's governing by the pushback of thirteen colonies. It's not too late to reverse the course of our nation, just as Roe vs. Wade was reversed—to the shock of many. Let's also overturn Obergefell vs Hodges (2015).

Same-Sex "Marriage"

Iowa, a legal same-sex marriage state is pushing back strongly (2023) with state legislators proposing a ban. Here is the impacting statement from Iowa's "House Joint Resolution 8" introduced on February 28, 2023:

> In accordance with the laws of nature and nature's God, the state of Iowa recognizes the definition of marriage to be the solemnized union between one human biological male and one human biological female.[103]

Currently, many states allow civil unions and same-sex "marriage." At this writing, sixteen states no longer have a ban on gay "marriage." A July 2023 report on "Marriage and Civil Union" states:

> A civil union is a form of state-level relationship recognition for couples, regardless of gender, that entitles them to receive the same benefits and protections as married spouses. Unlike marriages, civil unions do not have any rights under federal law (such as federal income tax filing, survivor benefits of federal pensions, and social security). Same-sex marriage was legalized in 2015, but civil unions are still valid in Colorado.[104]

Effective in 2022, civil union laws were enacted in Hawaii and Delaware. These radical changes are taking place despite most[105] Americans being opposed to same-sex "marriage." Again, it isn't marriage!

The problem is that liberals like to use the courts to go against the American people's will. For example, Proposition 8: California's 2008 ballot proposition to ban same-sex "marriage" and still today has an anti-gay marriage law. However,

> Californians will vote on a proposal to amend the state Constitution on the 2024 ballot to reaffirm gay marriage rights—a cautious move that comes amid national anxiety after recent rulings by the conservative-leaning U.S. Supreme Court, including overturning Roe vs. Wade protecting the right to an abortion. . . . the Democratic-dominant state Legislature is seeking to remove language from California's Constitution that still defines marriage as between a man and woman.[106]

How many times must Californian residents vote no to gay "marriage," only to have the courts intervene and nullify those votes? President Biden signed a bill in 2022—the Respect for Marriage Act—to safeguard the legality of gay marriage. DOMA (Defense of Marriage Act) got kicked to the curb.

Watching the perpetual war between those who are against and for the moral decay of the United States is gravely upsetting and frustrating. State politicians are taxed with casting votes on their constituents' behalf, so it's critical that every conservative contact your representative to reinforce our unchanging conservative position on moral issues. It all starts at the local government level and every conservative voice makes a difference toward winning the war against liberalism. But we must speak up! Write a letter, make a phone call.

What a disappointing decision by the Supreme Court of the United States (SCOTUS) in 2015 to legalize gay "marriage." We are witnessing the mass devastation brought by this ruling. The chaos is out of control and most often the victims of suffering are children—our future leaders and law makers! They each need a mother and father of godliness to raise them in a healthy, stable, and safe environment. Have I said it all starts in the home? A good resource is Focus on the Family. (See "Recommended Resources.")

The roles of fathers and mothers are perpetually diminished and minimized by liberalism, hurting our children and causing serious trouble. A healthy society needs strong families. Dads are needed to do what God created and purposed them to do: lead, provide for, and protect the family and help to guide and teach the children. Moms are needed to do what God created and purposed them to do: nurture, raise, guide, and teach the children. The SCOTUS ruling in June 2015 was so devastating because children need a mom and dad as God instituted.

Kids are growing up confused, causing them to turn to drugs, the streets, crime, and homosexuality in search of healing they will not find in these. Little Johnny is more confused at school when Billy asks, "Who's picking you up from school today?"

"Well, one of my dads."

"What? You have *two* dads?" Billy is astounded and confused.

"Yes," Johnny replies with equal confusion.

"What about your mom?" Billy asks.

"Well, one of my dads says he's my mom."

Further confused, Billy says, "I don't get it. . . . You have two dads and one is your *mom*?"

Little Johnny hangs his head and responds, "Yeah."

"Dude, that's messed up!"

Conservative Solution

Homosexuality is devastating to a kid's self-esteem and overall grounding.

According to the US Census Bureau (2019), 15 percent of the 1.1 million same-sex couples in the US had a household with at least one child under age eighteen.[107] For a child to have two dads or two moms is unnatural. A child needs the God-designed characteristic of a male father and a female mother. Teach truth at a young age and that child will do well in life! Parents play a vital role in ensuring a healthy society in every respect. Our country is seeing a serious breakdown in the family structure designed by God for utmost health and safety. We are ruining His creation. We are ruining children.

We can thank feminism and the decline of male role models for a big chunk of the breakdown. Fathers matter. Society celebrates Mother's Day much more than Father's Day. We need to celebrate both equally. Both matter in the life of a child. Both roles are equally important. A child needs both parents.

In my opinion, feminism is a big contributing factor to the demise of society. Feminists demand abortion rights, gay rights, and essentially say a child doesn't need their father.

I read an article on feminism that mentioned the website Feminist Majority Foundation. Look it up. It is anti-God, anti-male, and anti-family. "Keep Abortion Clinics Open" is a link found on their website. Sickening. Very disturbing and outright scary for our nation and all aspects of our society. The traditional family, as I've said before, is the backbone of society.

The Supreme Court ruling is further hurting children. Just what we need, more confused kids, questioning their sexual orientation and gender identities. Being a kid is tough enough, living in dysfunctional homes with the added weight of homework, expectations to succeed, peer pressure toward drugs and sex, bullying, social media, and now the pressure, confusion, and fear brought on by adults who are attempting to normalize what can never be normal—homosexuality. This agenda is *not* the way toward a healthy society; it's the way of destruction.

Parents: step up with courage and boldness against immorality.

Liberal justices are doing the work of Satan by legalizing gay "marriage." He remains hard at work in this fallen world to "steal and kill and destroy" everyone who is not rooted in Jesus Christ as their Savior. But, God is sovereign over Satan, over all things and people, and longsuffering, "not wanting anyone to perish, but everyone to come to repentance" (2 Peter 3:9). For a time, He is allowing the human will and its consequences while He works "in all things . . . for the good of those who love him, who have been called according to his purpose" (Romans 8:28). He is always at work!

So, why worry about and fear mankind and man's laws when we have the certainty and faithfulness of God who will one day destroy the earth and make all things new? Let's instead honor and fear the Lord! He is the truth, the final judge, and the forgiver of those who repent to Him and turn from their wicked ways. He will win the war against Him and give eternal life to all who have put their faith in His Son, Jesus Christ. I pray that all who are in the gay lifestyle, and all who are supporting homosexuality, will repent and come to know the Lord before it's too late. I'll say it again: one day it will be too late.

The time is now. You could perish at any moment. Do not go to bed tonight unless you know you're saved!

Take a firm stand against the legalization of gay "marriage" and take a stand for truth. God is the authority on all things. When a man and woman follow God's specific design for marriage, the union works. Strong marriages matter.

In support of traditional marriage, a number of organizations, authors, and conversative media have quoted this powerful true statement: "Gays and Lesbians have a right to live as they choose, but they don't have the right to redefine marriage for all of us." Well said!

Knowledge is power. And choices have consequences.

Our foremost go-to for knowledge, truth, wisdom, and council should be the Word of God. Secondly, I encourage you to visit the following websites as both do a good job exposing the gay agenda: Nation for Marriage and Americans for Truth about Homosexuality. Also read *The Truth About Same-Sex Marriage: 6 Things You Need to Know About What's Really at Stake* by Erwin W. Lutzer and the websites of solid biblical teacher-pastors David Jeremiah and Charles Stanley. (See "Recommended Resources.")

God is as crystal-clear on marital relationships as He is on gender and gender relationships. Nowhere in the Bible can be found *husbands and husbands* nor *wives and wives*.

Again, whatever goes against the knowledge of the Word of God is, by His definition, sin (James 4:17).

Same-Sex "Marriage"

Discussing gay "marriage" at work once, a woman commented that she now supports gay marriage because "society has changed." Well, God hasn't!

My response was, "In other words, we're a society where morals no longer matter? Anything goes nowadays?" Essentially, that is what supporters of the gay agenda are saying.

While we're each sinners, let's not encourage others to sin, either by our words or in the way we live our lives. We should not be promoting or encouraging anything that God has stated as sinful. Let's use our words and lifestyles to lead people to the truth of God, found in His Word. The only truth we will find in the gay agenda is its devastating, deadly consequences.

I read an article that basically asked if a chocolate chip cookie requires chocolate chips. Well, duh, of course it does, otherwise it's not truly a chocolate chip cookie! Likewise, marriage must be between one man and one woman—according to mankind's Maker—otherwise, it's not a true marriage.

The Rose Bowl, Grammy Awards, and a host of other televised broadcasts, movies, and plays feature same-sex "marriage." A majority of actors and other Hollywood elitists are not shy in stating their support for homosexuality and gay "marriage," and mocking Christianity along the way. As an example, from the long list of mockers is actor Jamie Foxx who said to the audience of a televised awards show, "It's like church over here. It's like church in here. First of all, give an honor to God and our Lord and Savior Barack Obama"[108] This blatant idolatry is further evidence that we're near the return of Christ. We all know that Mr. Obama is a mere mortal man who cannot save anyone. Only Jesus Christ can save. What a danger to mock God.

Being the sports fanatic I am, I recall the 2013 Super Bowl between the San Francisco 49ers and the Baltimore Ravens. The Ravens' linebacker Brendon Ayanbadejo used the big game stage to promote gay "marriage," making it sound like the gay lifestyle is acceptable and normal. Public figures: please do something worthwhile and respectable, such as sharing the truth found in the Bible. It's no one's place or role to promote sinful behavior. While you think you're doing good by siding with sin while making people feel all warm and fuzzy, you're leading the world down the road of darkness. You have awesome opportunities to do what is morally right in the eyes of God. He is watching you and His judgement will be forever final.

I originally wanted the Ravens to win the Super Bowl, but having witnessed Brendon's influence toward sin, I considered cheering for the 49ers. As a Packers fan, that's not easy to do! After further review, I just wanted to see a good, hard-hitting game, without such influence to sin. Just play football!

Speaking of the NFL and public claims in support of gay "marriage" was a former Minnesota Vikings' punter who claimed he was cut due to his outspoken views. Mr. Kluwe, you, too, are leading people down the road of destruction. There's no such thing as the so-called "gay gene," and homosexuals can (and have) come to know the truth in Jesus Christ, and have repented and moved from their lifestyles of sin. People leaving that lifestyle is a beautiful thing! I pray more people will.

Stop supporting sinful lifestyles!

Supporting sin and the reality of the consequences—eternal separation from God—are what most concern me. Hell is a real place. I couldn't imagine spending eternity there.

Everything I share forms my worldview as a believer. The following list summarizes my belief that we're near the end times:

- Violence against law enforcement

- Mass shootings (The problem isn't guns; the problem is the condition of the human heart.)

- Unrest in the Middle East

- Hollywood elites who claim that a politician or other human being is their messiah

- Gay "marriage" and other social ills

God cannot be happy about the state of our world producing rapidly growing acts of evil. We each will one day face His judgment, regardless of our political or social positions. Now is the time to get right with God, before the hammer of His just wrath falls. Now is the time to repent:

> I tell you, now is the time of God's favor, now is the day of salvation. (2 Corinthians 6:2)

> The hour has already come for you to wake up from your slumber, because our salvation is nearer now than when we first believed. (Romans 13:11)

Why do we care so much when a public figure speaks out in favor or opposition of a particular law or policy? Because public figures have broad influence over people, young and aged. While there are a handful of public conservatives, the majority of influencers seem to be liberals (LeBron James; Hollywood).

Ignore the lies of humans and cling to the truth found in Christ Jesus.

While mankind presently has the free will to make whatever humanistic laws they want (e.g. abortion and gay "marriage"), in the end we'll see that God's laws are all that matter. I pray that when that day comes, many more unbelievers will have gained this truth and accepted Jesus as their Savior.

Those who think they're wise, God will one day reveal to them that they are utter fools (Romans 1:22). We probably know 1% of what He knows, and that may be generous!

As a sinful human being with free will, and witnessing all the chaos and uncertainty in the world, I understand that it's not easy to rest in the knowledge that God is in control. Regardless of how we feel at any given time, He is in control and He will bring us to stand before Him one day and we will give an account of how we lived our earthly lives. Our relationship with God and obedience to Him is what matters most in this lifetime—not Joe Biden's executive orders, not presidential elections, not influencer's views, not award shows, not human mandates like mask-wearing and vaccines.

The first gay "marriage" on a military base was in 2012. Following suite was our Navy in 2014, and its spread like the pandemic. Or should I say "the *plan*demic?"

In the same year (2012), eighteen pro athletes publicly showed their support for same-sex "marriage. By the next year, dozens of pro sports teams, major businesses, politicians, and other public figures were infected—showing their support for gay "marriage." In 2022, *Outsports* publicized a list of sixty-one NFL players, thirteen owners, and nine head coaches who are in public support of gay and "bi" athletes.[109]

The gay agenda is targeting all aspects of life. It's a machine, much like the Democratic Party is a machine.

The Colorado Avalanche won the 2022 Stanley Cup. Living in Colorado, it was fun for me to watch. However, watching them win made me think of two things: temporary happiness and idolatry. The Cup was passed around and raised over heads, making me think that the Cup was their idol, like an NFL ring, an Oscar, or a Pulitzer Prize. But, just like that, the hoopla is over, it's all history, and we move on to the next feat. It's all temporary.

The gay agenda has designated the month of June as "pride month" in which there are now many gay celebrations across our country—even in our schools. The gay agenda hijacked the rainbow as their symbol, ignoring the fact that God created the rainbow as His own symbol of promise: "I will remember my covenant between me and you and all living creatures of every kind. Never again will the waters become a flood to destroy all life" (Genesis 9:15). Ironic it is called pride month as man is destroyed by pride! Pride isn't a good thing, and we all struggle with it.

Marriage between one man and one woman is no longer the prominent view of our nation. Pew Research wrote, "Based on polling in 2019, a majority of Americans (61%) support same-sex marriage, while 31% oppose it." People just don't know the truth. Polls won't be taken in hell.

It does not matter what mankind thinks or how society wants to redefine marriage. What matters is only what God says in His Word: marriage is between a man and woman.

> The plans of the Lord stand firm forever, the purposes of his heart through all generations. (Psalm 33:11)

On social media years ago, an individual called me a "fag," a "Bible thumper," and even "Hitler" for expressing my biblical worldview. I called him out in response and sent him a message regarding his immaturity. I added that he had helped prove my point that he was the intolerant one.

We need to stand for truth and call people out in a loving and forgiving way. Ignorance does not mean someone is a bad person; they're simply uninformed of the truth.

A high school friend posted on social media that he thinks those who oppose gay "marriage" are "a——" The irony is that he calls for tolerance of gay "marriage" because he believes in respecting all people. Does that mean we should respect pedophiles, adulterers, murderers, arsonists, polygamists, . . .? The answer is no! Loving all people and praying for them does *not* mean respecting their perversity and sin. If I were to post on social media, "You're an a—— if you're against traditional marriage," liberals and other so-called tolerant people would call me every name in the book. Most liberals claim to be sensible and loving but, in truth, they often prove themselves to be hypocritical haters.

My response to the high school friend:

> Gave it some thought. Why am I the "a——" for believing in biblical truth and God's Word? In other words, you're

essentially calling Jesus Christ and His followers a——. Think about that. "Tolerance" is not a two-way street for liberals. It's their way and those who oppose them are deemed "intolerant."

How is that logical?

And "equality" between men and women doesn't mean we support and legalize immorality of any nature, including homosexuality and gay "marriage." Yes, many heterosexual couples damage the institution of marriage via divorce, cheating, adultery, etc., but that doesn't mean we're to give up marriage altogether and have a free-for-all. Let's say you're attracted to a sixteen-year-old high school cheerleader and you're an adult male. Your attraction to her doesn't make it right for you to have a romantic relationship with her. Nor should we legalize sexual relations between adults and young people. Where would such legalization end? If we're going to legalize same-sex "marriage," why not legalize marrying your brother-in-law *and* your neighbor's wife? How can one form of immorality be acceptable but not all forms? Legalize drinking and driving? Legalize sexual relationships with the underaged? Legalize murder? Legalize assault and battery? Legalize rape? Legalize theft?

Our free-will choices are black and white: we're either for God or against Him. The Democratic Party wants to take from God's hand what He gave us for optimal health and life that honors Him and put our human rights as free citizens into the hands of liberal lawmakers and justices. Continuing to go against God's Word simply puts us on the fast track to moral decay—which, sadly, in America, is ongoing.

Conservative Solution

When we deny God as sovereign Creator and deny His Word as truth, He will not continue to bless this nation. Rather, He is judging us for allowing this country to turn from and against Him; yet—for a time—He's graciously offering us the conservative solution:

> "If my people, who are called by my name, will humble themselves and pray and seek my face and turn from their wicked ways, then I will hear from heaven, and I will forgive their sin and will heal their land." (2 Chronicles 7:14)

CHAPTER 14

Abortion

Roe v. Wade has played a huge role in the heightening moral decay of the US. The overturn in June 2022 was a stunning victory for those of us who believe in the sanctity of human life, which begins at the moment of conception. This was big.

For decades prior to the 1973 legalization of abortion and since, women's so-called "rights" have relentlessly tried to dethrone God by picking and choosing who will live and who will die—by thousands daily. Regardless of mankind's laws, protests, and marches, God cannot be dethroned, and He *will* take vengeance on all who do not repent for their part in sanctioning and acting in the ongoing mass murdering of unborn children. What a victory that was the SCOTUS overturned Roe v. Wade! Yet, the war for women to decide which of their babies will live and die rages all the stronger. The Old Testament commandment that most of us know, "You shall not murder" (Exodus 20:10) still stands in the New Testament with this addition: "Anyone who murders will be subject to judgment" (Matthew 5:21). A friend of mine once said,

"The US Supreme Court legalized abortion, and therefore it cannot be a bad thing." Wrong. The truth is that "legal" doesn't equate to "moral" and "legal" doesn't equate to God's "commandment." God alone sets the standards for morality. Liberals continually try to change God's standards of morality—which cannot and does not change.

My friend is a moral relativist who believes that we can decide for ourselves as individuals what truth is and that "diversity," to him, means that it's okay that *his* truth may not be *my* truth. The truth is that there is One author of truth: God. *Life* is God's very essence and His purpose for mankind. The strong biblical case against abortion does not solely reside in God's commandment, "You shall not murder." The case resides in the very nature of God and what He says about death. He called death the enemy, and said, "The last enemy to be destroyed is death." And Jesus said,

> "The thief comes only to steal and kill and destroy. I came that they may have life and have it abundantly." (John 10:10)

None of us can trump God or His truth. Therefore, spawning from the belief of my friend that we each create our own truths is this question of example: If one person enjoys sexual relations with a minor, should we then recognize that behavior as acceptable and legalize it? Regarding abortion, how can we (the created) say that one life is more valuable than another life? We do not have that authority. God alone is the author of life and death.

We are not to play God.

> For you created my inmost being; you knit me together in my mother's womb. I praise you because I am fearfully and

wonderfully made; your works are wonderful; I know that full well. (Psalm 139:13–14)

God is still on the throne, overlooking His creation, granting us His grace, willing that no one perish but turn to Him for salvation before it's too late. The day of His wrath against evil is coming. He watches the United States, every person, and His Word makes clear His thoughts regarding sin and those who oppose Him. Based on what He's said to sinful nations as recorded in the Bible, I imagine His thoughts about the US are along this line: *You no longer teach or live by My Word—the truth; you mock Me and those who believe in Me; you redefine marriage; you've aborted 63 million unborn babies since 1973 and you're still mass murdering daily. My wrath is upon you; the day of my judgement is near.*

I once traveled to Denver to hear pastor and Bible scholar David Jeremiah speak. Please visit his website. The man is solid in his teaching. The event was great, with a powerful message about opposing abortion and standing for traditional marriage, family, and other godly life values. Pastor Jeremiah's message was relevant to the mess this world is in. Let's return to the Bible and obey God. As Pastor Jeremiah's message came to a close, it was very powerful to see nearly one hundred people go forward to accept Jesus Christ as their personal Lord and Savior. God is still in control and we're paying the price for ignoring His Word, mocking Him, and going against His divine design and plan for mankind that is for our protection. While the tendency toward sin is the result of our sinful nature, God always makes a way of escape from sin and has given us free will to choose His way over sin. Choose Him!

I know firsthand that sin destroys individuals and societies. Drunkenness and sexual immorality had me doing the work of the enemy prior to my salvation. I was miserable for decades and now I have the supernatural peace and hope of Christ in me. Sin isn't worth a miserable life and certainly not eternal separation from God. He heals the brokenhearted.

What the Bible says about murder and a child in the womb:

- "You shall not murder" (Exodus 20:13; Matthew 5:21; Matthew 19:19; Mark 10:19; Luke 18:20; Romans 13:9; James 2:11).

- "Out of the heart come evil thoughts—murder, adultery, sexual immorality, theft, false testimony, slander" (Matthew 15:19).

- "You [God] created my inmost being; you knit me together in my mother's womb. I praise you because I am fearfully and wonderfully made; . . . My frame was not hidden from you when I was made in the secret place, when I was woven together in the depths of the earth. Your eyes saw my unformed body; all the days ordained for me were written in your book before one of them came to be" (Psalm 139:14–16).

- "Surely I was sinful at birth, sinful from the time my mother conceived me. Yet you desired faithfulness even in the womb; you taught me wisdom in that secret place" (Psalm 51:5–6).

- "Before I was born the Lord called me; from my mother's womb he has spoken my name" (Isaiah 49:1).

- "The word of the Lord came to me, saying, 'Before I formed you in the womb I knew you, before you were born I set you apart'" (Jeremiah 1:4–5).

CHAPTER 15

Racism and All Lives Matter

The death of black teenager Trayvon Martin, shot and killed on February 26, 2012, in Sanford, Florida, birthed the radical social(ist) movement "Black Lives Matter." Only God knows exactly what happened that night when George Zimmerman shot and killed Trayvon Martin. I was not there. I like to think I have confidence in our justice system, although Mr. Zimmerman was essentially proclaimed guilty by the liberal American media before proven innocent. The loss of Trayvon's life was a tragedy. The truth of the circumstances will come out at some point—hopefully in this earthly life. It's sad losing a human life, but at times the loss of life is justified.

In 2015, the Justice Department closed the independent federal investigation due to "insufficient evidence to pursue federal criminal civil rights charges against George Zimmerman."[110]

If Mr. Zimmerman did in fact provoke the incident in any way—not acting in self-defense—justice should be served by a life sentence in prison. However, if he truly acted in self-defense, that act was justifiable and he should be a free man. Only God and Mr. Zimmerman know the truth. Trayvon is a corpse and he cannot share his side of the story. Just because the victim was black and the defendant was not, does not automatically mean racism is at play. All races commit crimes.

In connection with a crime here in Eagle County, Colorado, I received a text and email alerting me of a wanted man. It read something like this:

> Wanted subject. If you see a person matching description, call 911 – 25 young male, 5'05", dark glasses, red shirt and blue jeans. Last seen in Dotsero. Possibly armed/dangerous. DO NOT APPROACH.

I just have one minor question of detail for Eagle County: What is the man's race? Is he White, Black, Hispanic? That detail just might have helped us help law enforcement locate the wanted subject. I replied to the county email alert, asking that very question: "Was race left out due to 'political correctness' or simply a typographical error of omission?" I don't know, but I have a hunch that it's the former. It's all about feelings nowadays.

The Black Lives Matter movement insists that the lives of Black people are more important than the lives of other races. Be aware of such social movements; they are racist, socialist, and opportunistic. This is not a good organization.

When Major League Baseball held its 2016 All-Star Game in San Diego, controversy arose when a Canadian singer changed the lyrics of Canada's national anthem. He instead sang, "We're all brothers and sisters. All lives matter to the great."[111] Logically, how can the truth "all lives matter" be controversial? All lives do matter!

Our world has gone crazy with personal and political agendas and political correctness that's destroying our once-great Republic.

All lives matter!

All lives matter equally.

We do not get to pick and choose our skin color, so why would we think we can choose which lives have value, or more value, and which ones do not—no different from choosing which babies will live and which babies will be aborted. Racism is idiotic.

All lives matter because God, our Creator, made each and elected to do so in various colors.

It doesn't matter the color of an individual's skin—white, black, brown, yellow, purple, or green. God alone has control of our pigmentation, and He made clear that *all* lives matter. Enough with racism!

What the Bible says about all lives:

- "God so loved the world that he gave his one and only Son, that whoever believes in him shall not perish but have eternal life" (John 3:16).

- "God demonstrates his own love for us in this: While we were still sinners, Christ died for us" (Romans 5:8).

- "Peter began to speak: 'I now realize how true it is that God does not show favoritism but accepts from every nation the one who fears him and does what is right'" (Act 10:34).

CHAPTER 16

False Teachers

Here's an example of a false teaching alert. A local newspaper advertisement by a so-called church here in Colorado spoke of families, faith, culture, diversity of nations, harmony, stability, a peaceful life, and spiritual values—with no mention of God or Jesus. Red flag!

Here's another example. During a 2014 visit to my hometown, Milwaukee, I revisited a church I had attended regularly when I'd lived there. The morning of my visit, I had concerns when the church played a video by Rob Bell, a false teacher and former pastor. Ironically, he became an actor who starred in the movie *The Heretic*. As of 2023, you can officially put Andy Stanley in the category of false teachers. His dad, Charles, was so solid. Unfortunately, the son has gone away from the gospel.

The pastor of the church spoke falsely that morning about abortion.

The pastor I spoke of told a story of a twenty-two-year-old man and eighteen-year-old woman who were in a dilemma whether to continue the young woman's pregnancy or abort (kill) their unborn child. The father wanted her to keep their child and the mother wanted to abort the baby.

> **To be clear, abortion is not a political issue but rather a biblical one.**

Praise God the story ended well. The couple spared the baby's life and gifted the child to a loving family through adoption. However, because the pastor told the story with inferences rather than reading Scripture, his message wasn't altogether clear. Had he inferred that regardless of our sin choices, God forgives those who come to Him in repentance? Upon returning to Colorado, I listened to the message again, wanting to be accurate in my conclusion. What the pastor had said verbatim was, "This isn't a political stance on abortion. Whatever your opinion is on abortion, that's great, that's fine. This isn't some politicized thing. Shove that aside. Let's not worry about the stances or non-stances of abortion."

Whoa! False teaching! The pastor had an obligation and duty to stand up for the truth of God's Word—not his own opinions filtered through the lens of mankind. People have proved to want watered-down truth that makes them feel better about continuing in sin, and he'd done just that.

The apostle Paul addresses the issue of continuing to sin after seeking God's forgiveness:

Shall we go on sinning so that grace may increase? By no means! . . . we know that our old self was crucified with him so that the body ruled by sin might be done away with, that we should no longer be slaves to sin—because anyone who has died [to sin] has been set free from sin. . . . count yourselves dead to sin but alive to God in Christ Jesus. Therefore do not let sin reign in your mortal body so that you obey its evil desires. Do not offer any part of yourself to sin as an instrument of wickedness, but rather offer yourselves to God as those who have been brought from death [sin] to life [in Christ]; and offer every part of yourself to him as an instrument of righteousness [right living]. (Romans 6:1–14, author notations added)

All biblical teachers must be careful to be very clear in how they present God's Word to ensure there are no false inferences and statements that paint sin as acceptable. God has never sanctioned sin and will not ever sanction sin but will judge and condemn those who have chosen to continue in sin rather than in right living through Jesus Christ.

My response to the pastor's message would be to say to him: Don't give in to the lies of liberalism and this world! Be very clear with your abortion messages, reading aloud the truth as stated in the Bible. Speaking unclearly, or willfully taking God's Word out of context, can easily be avoided when we know God's Word.

I would also encourage that pastor, "Do not care what others think! Liberals demand 'human rights' while demanding 'abortion on demand.'"

Abortion (murder) isn't a human right.

The child in the womb is a life!

I emailed a church in the Rocky Mountains, calling them out for their false teachings. They claimed:

- all religions and faiths lead to God,
- guilt-free Christianity,
- humankind are good people, not necessarily sinners, and
- all are welcome into God's kingdom despite their sexual preferences and their self-defined sexual orientation.

In truth, according to our Creator:

- "[Jesus said,] 'I am the way and the truth and the life. No one comes to the Father except through me'" (John 14:6).
- "Let us draw near to God with a sincere heart and with the full assurance that faith brings, having our hearts sprinkled to cleanse us from a guilty conscience and having our bodies washed with pure water" (Hebrews 10:22).
- "All have sinned and fall short of the glory of God" (Romans 3:23).
- "Not everyone who says to me, 'Lord, Lord,' will enter the kingdom of heaven, but only the one who does the will of my Father who is in heaven" (Matthew 7:21).

Those verses of Scripture lead us to examine the difference between the *true gospel* of Jesus Christ and the *false gospel* shaped by human beings:

- **True gospel** states the hope that Christians (true believers in Jesus Christ as Savior) will spend eternity with Jesus Christ in Heaven, their sins covered, forgiven, and removed, by His blood.

- **True gospel** states that we do not get to Heaven through good deeds, but rather through our belief in Jesus Christ as Savior and His sacrifice on the cross as full payment for our sins. We only need to accept by simple faith His payment for our sins.

- **True gospel** states that eternal salvation comes to those who believe in Jesus Christ as the Son of God, resurrected from the dead, and that believers are resurrected from our old life of sin to new life of right living in Jesus Christ.

A false gospel states that (1) paradise can be found here on earth, (2) we can get to heaven simply through good deeds, (3) Jesus Christ is not the only way to God, and (4) Jesus was simply a "great teacher" rather than the Son of God, born of a virgin through the work of the Holy Spirit of God. These are false teachings. Beware! A good church will mention the blood of Jesus Christ. That is key.

Beware of false teachers!

A 2023 article by Will Graham shared the following "4 Ways to Spot False Teaching."

First, pride is a sign of false teaching.

Second, a false teacher is willfully ignorant.

Third, lust is a sign of a false teacher.

Finally, false teachers are covetous and are driven by greed.[112]

There's much to be said in explanation of each, so I encourage you to read the article (see the foot for the link).

My Colorado town of residence, and my hometown, Milwaukee, each have a free local newspaper. It's no wonder they're free; the contents are liberal. I wouldn't pay one cent for either paper. Because they're free, I read them to stay up to date on leftist views so I can counter with biblical truth in hope that unbelievers will repent to God, understanding that they probably won't.

The free Colorado newspaper featured writers who are, in my belief, false teachers. One was Dr. Jack Van Ens, who believed in social justice and supported President Obama. Another was Richard Carnes who contended that he was a Republican, yet often ripped the GOP and appeared to support a green energy policy.

I once read that it's worse to tell a half-truth than a full lie. I believe that half-truths were what Dr. Van Ens often produced. He really hammered away at class warfare and social justice. Biblical truth about money is one of several topics he needs to learn.

Third is Jeffrey "Biff" Bergeron who catered to the politically correct readership. He's a gay liberal who often commented about his "partner," and referred to God as a "she," though the Bible plainly describes God as "our Father" (Matthew 6:9), and the original Hebrew and Greek text for the term "God" is masculine. Oh, the rebellion!

I wrote to Biff:

> Just wondering, when did God have a sex change and become a woman? He is not a she. I pray you will learn biblical truth.
>
> God bless,
>
> Paul
>
> P.S. God is our Father (Matthew 6:9).

I also don't care for his public commentary on his sex life with his male "partner" (the politically correct term). Such public revelations cross the line of media ethics and morality. Keep your private life private! And the term is "boyfriend," not partner!

Many churches in my area lead people away from God with their false theology. Since Mr. Howse is among those who are unafraid to publicly call out false teachers, and believers must ban together as courageous truth teachers, I sent him this email:

> Hi, Brannon,
>
> False teachings of a Unity church were recently published in our local newspaper. My research indicates that the following is the shared belief of the Unity religion across our nation and the world:
>
> 1. "Our essential nature is divine and therefore inherently good."[113] *Wrong!* "There is no one righteous, not even one" (Romans 3:10).
>
> 2. "We see Jesus as a master teacher of universal truths and as our Way-Shower. In Unity, we use the term "Christ"

to mean the divinity in humankind. Jesus is the great example (rather than the great exception) of the Christ in expression." [114] *Wrong!* Jesus said, "I am the way and the truth and the life. No one comes to the Father except through me" (John 14:6).

3. "Heaven is not a place, but a state of consciousness; we create our own heaven and hell here and now."[115] *Wrong!* Actions on earth affect positions in heaven (Matthew 5:17–20), and our earthly bodies will be made complete in heaven (2 Corinthians 5:2).

4. "Christ is that part of God that is in every person. There is a spark of divinity within all people, just as there was in Jesus."[116] *Wrong!* "All have sinned" (Romans 3:23).

Be aware of media bias, especially regarding their anti-Christian views, and be aware of false teachers masquerading as Christians. There is no shortage of false teachers!

There are countless religions—a reported 4,000![117] So it's critical to measure everything you hear and read by the one and only reliable source: God's Word, the Bible, proven through historical accounts and sealed by the account of the virgin birth and the ultimate resurrection of Jesus Christ—the only One who has defeated death, the One, true, living, holy, infallible God, Creator of mankind and all of creation.

- "'You are my witnesses,' declares the LORD, 'and my servant whom I have chosen, so that you may know and believe me and understand that I am he'" (Isaiah 43:10).

- "In the beginning God . . ." (Genesis 1:1).

- "In the beginning was the Word, and the Word was with God, and the Word was God" (John 1:1).

- "The Word became flesh and made his dwelling among us. We have seen his glory, the glory of the one and only Son, who came from the Father, full of grace and truth" (John 1:14).

- "There is one God and one mediator between God and mankind, the man Christ Jesus" (1 Timothy 2:5).

- "I am the first and I am the last; apart from me there is no God" (Isaiah 44:6).

- "I, even I, am the Lord, and apart from me there is no savior" (Isaiah 43:11).

- "This is what the Lord says—he who created the heavens, he is God; he who fashioned and made the earth, he founded it; he did not create it to be empty, but formed it to be inhabited—he says: 'I am the Lord, and there is no other'" (Isaiah 45:18).

- "In him all things were created: things in heaven and on earth, visible and invisible, whether thrones or powers or rulers or authorities; all things have been created through him and for him" (Colossians 1:16).

- "There is but one God, the Father, from whom all things came and for whom we live; and there is but one Lord, Jesus Christ, through whom all things came and through whom we live." (1 Corinthians 8:6).

- "You believe that there is one God. Good! Even the demons believe that—and shudder" (James 2:19).

On a Sunday while visiting family members in Arizona, we attended a church service. I'm a very skeptical person, always looking out for churches that support false teachers. Right away, a few things caught my attention. Playing on a TV in the church was The Masters Tournament. Though I love sports and watch The Masters, I'm not sure how I feel about sports broadcasts (and Starbucks coffee) leading into corporate worship of God. If you entertain the masses, the masses will expect to be entertained!

At the 2013 Starbucks shareholder's meeting, "company officials told those who support Biblical marriage that they 'can sell [their] shares in Starbucks and buy shares in another company.'"[118]

I must include Rick Warren on my list of among many prominent false teachers. A book written by him waters down the Word of God. Yes, I tend to nitpick on every topic, individual, and groups that falsely teach the Bible. We are to seek God's Word—not mankind's opinion—in how we are to live our lives.

False teachers lurk among us in sheep's clothing as Satan does—to steal and kill and destroy. For many decades, I wrestled with severe anxiety. Looking back, I realize the root of my mental illness was spiritual warfare—Satan's work to steal and kill and destroy every person from the beginning of time. I realized that God was and continues to be for me, not against me. He waited patiently for me to come to know that I needed Jesus as Savior and to accept Christ as my Lord. I had often listened to and sided with Satan, living in the mindset of my own desires, known biblically as living for the flesh. I truly believe some of my anxiety was caused by my poor decisions of sin: acting out in anger, getting drunk, sexual immorality, unforgiveness, bitterness, jealousy, pride, etc.

No sin is greater or lesser than another sin.

God clearly defined sin for us: "If anyone, then, knows the good they ought to do and doesn't do it, it is sin for them." (James 4:17). I am 100 percent guilty of trying to rank sin. That's wrong of me; sin is sin.

I once watched a documentary on "Pastor" Jim Jones and his Peoples Temple who eventually left the US for Jonestown, Guyana. He was another of many false teachers who have fooled people. Where Jim Jones first went wrong—just like Lucifer—was thinking of himself as equal to or greater than God. There again is pride!

Pride, in some form, is the root of all sin.

Read Proverbs 11:2; 17:19; 18:12.

Many people blindly followed Jim Jones to Guyana and most died after consuming a poisonous drink, at Jones's persuasion, promising his followers an outcome that was false.

When we put our faith and trust in a human being, the guarantee is that we'll be thoroughly disappointed at some point. When we put all our faith and trust in a human being, the guarantee is eternal separation from God.

"Pastor" Joel Osteen, a false teacher since 1999, is contemporary Jim Jones who continues to lead multi-thousands of people weekly away from the truths of God, using his own version of "truth" centered on earthly prosperity rather than the gospel. Mr. Osteen is no different from Jim Jones and all other false teachers. Beware! Joel Osteen and Andy Stanley are leading people astray.

It's critical to look out for and know the difference between a true teacher or pastor of the Word of God and a false teacher or pastor!

Another false teacher of high prominence is the pope. Yes, I said it. People have deleted me from their social media for naming and speaking out against false teachers and churches. But, I'd rather have ten friends on social media and share the truth of Jesus Christ than five hundred friends who want their "itching ears" tickled. The truth over tickling.

> For the time will come when people will not put up with sound doctrine. Instead, to suit their own desires, they will gather around them a great number of teachers to say what their itching ears want to hear. (2 Timothy 4:3)

Jehovah's Witnesses

I once visited a Kingdom Hall for Jehovah's Witnesses (JW) in Colorado. Pulling into the parking lot, I second-guessed being there; I had a sick feeling in my stomach, but I knew what I was getting into. I'd already made the drive and figured I might as well head inside to see what the place had to offer. I knew I was entering a house of false worship.

Approaching the entrance, I introduced myself to a young man (probably in his mid-twenties) who was dressed in a nice suit. We engaged in small talk and he asked for my phone number "to keep in contact regarding future JW events." I gave him a previous phone number and felt somewhat bad, but the last thing I wanted was JWs calling me. Feeling convicted about the deceit, I repented. *Sorry, Lord.*

I felt underdressed for visiting a church, but suits are just not my style. I was wearing Nike flip-flops, casual shorts, and a Green Bay Packers t-shirt. I was soon approached by a man, then another, and then three more. I felt cornered but wanted to observe their false religion on their turf, like visiting a rival sports team. I listened to what the men had to say and then I asked for some literature. A few minutes later, I heard a woman's voice call out, "Hi Paul!" *Oh no, who knows me here?* I turned around and there stood the secretary from my dentist's office. Awkward!

The people were very friendly, but the sick feeling in my stomach lingered with the knowledge that the church was home to a false religion. In contrast, when I attend my Bible truth-teaching church, I feel the warmth of truth. My ill feeling at Kingdom Hall made me never want to visit again. And I haven't. I pray that Jehovah's Witnesses, and all other false teachers and believers, will come to know the truth before it's too late: Christ Jesus is not simply "a great teacher," as JWs believe. Christ Jesus is our Lord and Savior, God manifested in the flesh.

At work, I had noticed a coworker praying before his meal. Thinking he was a brother in Christ, I said, "It's good to see you praying!" In the course of the conversation that followed, he shared that he was a Jehovah's Witness. My heart sank for the man because, as I've said, JW is a false religion, much like Mormonism and Islam. I needed to give thought to how I could lead my coworker to the truth. Maybe an invitation to a service at my church or our night of worship where believers gathered to sing and play great music.

A different encounter at work was with a truck driver who'd pulled into the loading dock and we struck up a brief conversation about God. The man shared that he was an alcoholic and sober now for ten years. Praise the Lord! I thought of Matthew 9:26, "With God all things are possible."

> We are heirs—heirs of God and co-heirs with Christ, if indeed we share in his sufferings in order that we may also share in his glory. (Romans 8:17)

For many years, like many people, I tried to live with one foot in heaven and the other foot in this world. I learned that we can't live simultaneously in light and darkness. Righteousness and wickedness cannot "coexist!" (Maybe that should be the bumper sticker!) Hypocrisy gets us nowhere. For example, I can't be a true light of God's righteousness to the world while lusting after women.

> "Whoever is not with me is against me, and whoever does not gather with me scatters." (Matthew 12:30)

Are you in with Christ or are you in with the things of this world? You can't have both and the truth is that this life is short-lived and eternity is without end. I am guilty of wanting it both ways!

I heard Pastor Adrian Rogers ask that question, "Are you in or are you out?" He passed away in 2005, but his sermons can still be found online at the website Love Worth Finding. (See "Recommended Resources.") Get ready to be rattled by truth when you listen to his sermons. His website includes message series, resources for pastors and churches, and much more.

Speaking of hypocrisy, offered at my local community college was a Buddha class—"What the Buddha Taught." God forbid that a college would offer a class, "What Jesus Christ Taught." So many people are deceived by this world and its lies. Buddha didn't die for your sins. Nor did the Easter Bunny.

Mormonism

Every Sunday, as I drove or walked to church, I passed a Mormon church. I'm pained, knowing that the members are learning a false message within those walls. Again, I pray their members and leaders will come to know the truth of Jesus Christ before it's too late, and that they will turn against the lies established by a mere man, Joseph Smith, founder of Mormonism. There is only one truth—and it's *not* Mormonism, Catholicism, Islam, Buddhism, or Jehovah's Witnesses.

While attending college at Marquette University, I wrote a paper and gave a presentation on Mormonism. Even back then (1997), I thought, *This is a crazy cult.* I've since learned of many cults that pose as truth. May all members of the Mormon church and other false religions come to know the truth before it's too late.

While picking up dinner one night, I overheard a lady mention church to the restaurant owner. A few minutes passed and I asked her where she attended church. I cringed at her response, "The Mormon Church." I'm working on being more patient and loving in such circumstances where I have an opportunity to share the truth. People won't be receptive if I just jump in and say, "Mormonism is a lie!" The woman was also talking with another gentleman, sharing that she had a lot of gay friends (sinners like the rest of us) and that people really are good at heart. I don't agree, based not only on what I've seen of my own thoughts and actions and those of others, but on what God's Word says.

> Indeed, there is no one on earth who is righteous, no one who does what is right and never sins. (Ecclesiastes 7:20)

> For all have sinned and fall short of the glory of God, and all are justified freely by his grace through the redemption that came by Christ Jesus. (Romans 3:23–24)

We're all in need of repentance!

None of us will ever be without sin, but our sins can be covered by the shed blood of Jesus Christ, and we can strive to live in righteousness. I'm very aware that I'm still a sinner, in need of continued repentance, and that Jesus has saved me from the eternal death of sin. With that knowledge, I do my best (most times) to love people I come across while being courageous to speak the truth with kindness. I'm working on that! I am a work in progress.

In 2007, I left the Catholic Church. No church or religion should have sex abuse scandals! Many do, and there was barrage of sexual abuse accusations against priests that made me ask, *Why not allow priests to get married?* Think of all the pain that could have been prevented had priests been allowed to marry. The apostle Paul spoke to this solution in 1 Corinthians 7:9, "if they cannot control themselves, they should marry, for it is better to marry than to burn with passion."

If one takes a vow of celibacy and finds that such a vow is too difficult for them to adhere to, the (conservative) solution is for the individual to seek marriage.

There are two other major issues I have with Catholicism in addition to ongoing sex abuse. I spent years in catholic pews, going through the motions, but I don't recall ever learning the gospel. Secondly, the Pope is seen by Catholics as the final authority rather than God's Word. The pope is a human being like the rest of us. He is nothing special.

Pope Francis concerns me. I cringed when I heard someone on the radio refer to him as "his holiness." He is a mere mortal, thereby a sinner. He is a false prophet who stands on Marxist beliefs. The following excerpt is from a 2022 interview with Pope Francis by Fr. Matt Malone, S. J.

> [Malone] said to Pope Francis, "In the United States, there are those who interpret your criticisms of market capitalism as criticisms of the United States. There are even some who think you may be a socialist, or they call you a communist, or they call you a Marxist."
>
> The Argentine pope's answer is stunning: "If I see the Gospel in a sociological way only, yes, I am a communist, and so too is Jesus. Behind these Beatitudes and Matthew 25 there is a message that is Jesus' own. And that is to be Christian. The communists stole some of our Christian values."

> It is shocking for a pope to insinuate that the "Gospel [viewed] in a sociological way only" reveals that Jesus was a communist, and, therefore, he is too. . . .
>
> It is not surprising that Pope Francis states: "The communists stole some of our Christian values." It also explains his lavish praise for the late Cardinal Agostino Casaroli, the leading promoter of the Vatican policy of détente with communist regimes, who affirmed, "Catholics who live in Cuba are happy under the socialist regime." Ditto Pope Francis's satisfaction concerning the dialogue with China because, he says, the Chinese are "a people of great wisdom." Everyone knows he is not "dialoguing" with the Chinese people but with the Chinese Communist Party.[119]

Why do so many people oppose and hate the truth? Because truth holds us each accountable and convicts us of sin. As long as I'm in this human body, I'll continue to struggle with sin (especially lust), but I also know the freeing, forgiving, life-giving truth that is found in Jesus Christ! To know there is nothing I need to do to earn my way to heaven is powerful and freeing. No volunteer work or good deeds will get me there. A woman once raved about a friend that had recently passed. She said "He was such a good person. He did a lot of volunteer work." I wanted to roll my eyes. It is not about works.

The path to eternity with God in heaven is simply to honestly proclaim Jesus Christ as your personal Lord and Savior, giving Him your whole heart and life, knowing that He overcame sin on the cross by death for you and that His resurrection conquered death. Jesus paid the price for sin once and for all. Just before his physical death, He said, "It is finished" (John 19:30)—meaning the work of restitution of sin, for all of time, for all of mankind. We need only to believe and receive Christ as our Savior. What a relief to have such knowledge, new life, and sealed eternity with God by simple faith! Mother Earth, Buddha, and no other can give us those!

I urge you to find a Bible-teaching church and to socialize with Christians who have learned to differentiate between the one true gospel and the many false gospels. We must read the Bible to find *truth*; we must realize that God only—not human beings nor Mother Mary or other Catholic saints—is to be glorified.

The enemy of our souls is always at work to pull us away from truth. He is crafty and we must stand guard against him. One way is to be aware of what you're reading and who you're listening to in your quest for truth. The enemy will often lead you to false and weak teachers. There are countless pastors and so-called biblical scholars who are bending the truth to be liked by their listeners. They avoid the truth to avoid offending those who simply want their ears tickled to feel good about themselves as a "church-going" or so-called Christian. Such pastors and teachers bend for financial profit, to keep their parishioners and listeners coming back and giving money. Many pastors and teachers don't know truth because they've learned from other people instead of digging into the Word of God. Others know the Bible but don't believe it's the inspired and living Word of God.

> All Scripture is God-breathed and is useful for teaching, rebuking, correcting and training in righteousness, so that the servant of God may be thoroughly equipped for every good work. (2 Timothy 2:16–17)

> The word of God is alive and active. Sharper than any double-edged sword, it penetrates even to dividing soul and spirit, joints and marrow; it judges the thoughts and attitudes of the heart. Nothing in all creation is hidden from God's sight. Everything is uncovered and laid bare before the eyes of him to whom we must give account. (Hebrews 4:12–13)

It's wise to know your enemies. Study the Bible to be equipped to recognize false teachers and false doctrine and avoid falling into their traps of deception that may sound good but leads to eternal death (separation from God). Jesus said, "I am the way and the truth and the life. No one comes to the Father except through me" (John 14:6). Other religions (e.g., Mormonism, Jehovah's Witnesses, Islam, Buddhism) are false religions teaching the lie that there are other gods and other ways to heaven apart from Jesus Christ. Satan is using such falsities to accomplish his agenda here on earth that is leading millions of people to eternal separation from God.

I highly recommend *Fast Facts on False Teachings* by Ron Carlson and Ed Decker, a good read.

What the Bible says about false teachers:

- "There were also false prophets among the people, just as there will be false teachers among you. They will secretly introduce destructive heresies, even denying the sovereign Lord who bought them—bringing swift destruction on themselves. Many will follow their depraved conduct and will bring the way of truth into disrepute. In their greed these teachers will exploit you with fabricated stories. Their condemnation has long been hanging over them, and their destruction has not been sleeping" (2 Peter 2:1–3).

- "Watch out for false prophets. They come to you in sheep's clothing, but inwardly they are ferocious wolves. By their fruit you will recognize them" (Matthew 7:15–16).

- "Many will turn away from the faith and will betray and hate each other, and many false prophets will appear and deceive many people. Because of the increase of wickedness, the love of most will grow cold, but the one who stands firm to the end will be saved" (Matthew 24:10–13).

CHAPTER 17

Mental Illness

Another powerful tool used by Satan to steal, kill, and destroy mankind is mental illness.

> Batovsky, who was 39, died May 31 when he stepped in front of an Amtrak train—the day before his scheduled sentencing on 2011 child pornography charges. Batovsky, of Oak Creek, was charged last October with 11 counts of possession of child pornography and pleaded guilty in March to five of those counts. [120]

This article was about a man who'd attended my high school. A friend of mine thought the man was helpless to turn his life around. I disagreed and shared that Jesus Christ can do anything—He will save anyone who seeks Him. As with all of us, Mr. Batovsky had needed repentance and faith in Jesus and seeking biblical solutions to strongholds of sin in his life. Sin destroys and kills!

Earthly change came too late for the man, and only God knew his heart. Although Mr. Batovsky was in despair to the point of taking his life, my hope is that he had a salvation conversation with God in those final moments. You never know what happens in those last moments of one's life.

His coworkers harassing him was unacceptable behavior. To those coworkers: Put yourself in the man's shoes. Why did you not try to be his friend and help him with his life struggles?

Disregard for people's struggles is another example of how far from perfect we are. In the case of Mr. Batovsky, we find very immature adults who could have chosen to put childishness aside to help a fellow human being. Let this be a lesson to all. Millions of people are hurting and need help that we each can give through genuine care, concern, and love.

Mr. Batovsky's obituary reads:

> Age 39, Found Peace June 01, 2012. Loving son . . . . Proud brother . . . . Beloved uncle and godfather . . . . Further survived by his cherished friends . . . , his goddaughter . . . other relatives and many loving friends.[121]

I wonder if he found peace. I fear the opposite. When someone dies, there's an assumption by many that the individual is automatically in heaven, and many others believe there is no afterlife, or they believe in the lie of reincarnation—none of which is biblical. Jesus said, "Enter through the narrow gate. For wide is the gate and broad is the road that leads to destruction, and many enter through it. But small is the gate and narrow the road that leads to life, and only a few find it" (Matthew 7:13–14). I believe Jesus said that with pleading and grief, for He also said that He is "not willing that any should perish, but that all should come to repentance" (2 Peter 3:9) and the He came to earth "that they [all people] may have life, and have it to the full" (John 10:10). A Bible commentary states the following about suicide: "The Bible views suicide as equal to murder, which is what it is—self-murder. God is the only one who is to decide when and how a person should die."[122] And everything else is a matter of our free will. God is not about controlling us but protecting us, providing for us, healing us, and having deep relationships with us.

I sympathize with all those who battle mental illness, and for their family members. My own life story is riddled with mental illness, yet God is at work to heal! I invite you to read my transformation story—my first book, *A Perfect Walk*.

Prior to becoming a believer, I visited a friend's church in the small town of Carbondale, Colorado. Having been raised Catholic, the experience was different for me. People were freely going on stage to confess their sins and I wanted to do the same, but I held back because that visit was my first, and far more complicated was the fact that I greatly struggled with severe social anxiety.

Once I dug into God's Word, so many concerns made a whole lot more sense. That's what happens when a person steps deep into the living Word of God. Things started making sense and change ensued. Get into the Word.

Certainly, there are cases where individuals also need medication and counseling, but our foremost and fundamental need toward gaining a healthy mind and body is the living Word of God. We need to read it, believe it, study it, and apply it our lives. The Bible addresses everything—from anger, forgiveness, love, eternal life, food, taking care of our minds and bodies and relationships, to all other important issues of life. The answers to life's problems are all in the Word of God. All medical and mental treatments should therefore derive from The Source of all life, healing, wholeness, freedom, abundance, peace, joy, protection, security, hope. . . . Also, you cannot medicate a broken heart or sin.

After twenty years of medications and counseling, I had found the answer: Jesus Christ is the greatest physician, the One "who forgives all your sins and heals all your diseases" (Psalm 103:3). Amen!

What the Bible says about finding freedom from mental illness:

- "Do not be anxious about anything, but in every situation, by prayer and petition, with thanksgiving, present your requests to God. And the peace of God, which transcends all understanding, will guard your hearts and your minds in Christ Jesus" (Philippians 4:6–7).

- "Come to me, all you who are weary and burdened, and I will give you rest. Take my yoke upon you and learn from me, for I am gentle and humble in heart, and you will find rest for your souls. For my yoke is easy and my burden is light" (Matthew 11:28–29).

- "The God of all grace, who called you to his eternal glory in Christ, after you have suffered a little while, will himself restore you and make you strong, firm and steadfast" (1 Peter 5:10).

- "The righteous cry out, and the Lord hears them; he delivers them from all their troubles. The Lord is close to the brokenhearted and saves those who are crushed in spirit" (Psalm 34:17–18).

- "Those who hope in the Lord will renew their strength. They will soar on wings like eagles; they will run and not grow weary, they will walk and not be faint "(Isaiah 40:31).

- "Humble yourselves, therefore, under God's mighty hand, that he may lift you up in due time. Cast all your anxiety on him because he cares for you" (1 Peter 5:6–7).

CHAPTER 18

Firearms: Our Second Amendment Rights

> A well regulated Militia, being necessary
> to the security of a free State,
> the right of the people to keep and bear
> Arms, shall not be infringed.
>
> —Second Amendment, US Constitution

A liberal friend insisted that the US Constitution is a living, breathing document—in other words, it can be changed to reflect today's culture, society, and way of life. If this were true, this agenda would then apply to all legal documents. Therefore, what's the point of having any governing documents?

Imperative to citizens' freedom, our Supreme Court judges must make decisions based on the Constitution, not on personal beliefs, opinions, feelings, or emotions.

I'm very passionate about our Second Amendment—law-abiding citizens having the freedom to bear arms, enjoy a day at the shooting range, hunt, and most importantly, for self-defense. This world isn't getting any safer. Daily we see from news that violence is escalating. We're no longer in the 1950s; we're on the precipice of Armageddon and the return of Jesus Christ in judgement against vastly and deeply penetrating sin and evil as it was in the days of Sodom and Gomorrah. (Read Genesis 18:20–19:29.)

My liberal friend also thinks individuals should depend on the government for personal and national security. As far as national defense and patrolling the border, especially Mexico, I agree that the role of government is to protect its people. However, our Constitution makes it clear that citizens of the United States have the right to "keep and bear Arms," and that right "shall not be infringed." No room for misinterpretation. This individual freedom is a US constitutional *right*!

I once attended a very informative Hunter Education class in Colorado. Great class. We learned everything from hunter safety, hunting ethics, firearms safety and usage, to wilderness survival. The two days of eight-hour classes were time and money well spent. I encourage you to check with your local 4-H Club or county for a hunter education class. NRA (National Rifle Association) members can locate classes within their area. Being strongly pro-Second-Amendment, I'm a lifetime member of the NRA and GOA (Gun Owners of America).

Guns are cool. Criminals are not.

Liberals and anti-gun lobbyists (e.g., the Brady Campaign to Prevent Gun Violence) like to twist the Second Amendment to their benefit. Their goal is to restrict gun ownership to law enforcement officers and members of the military. How then will law-abiding citizens protect themselves in a home invasion, robbery, mugging, carjacking, and other such criminal acts of victimization? How does one protect themselves and family while enjoying an evening downtown? Check out this article, "2023 Top 100 Most Dangerous Cities in the U.S.," which also provides the probability of becoming a victim of a "violent crime."[123]

Are citizens supposed to just stay locked up at home instead of enjoying their cities? Even at home, the current rate of US home invasions is a startling 580,000.[124] Yet, a liberal response to gun ownership is *Why do you need a firearm? If someone robs you on the street or breaks into your home, just dial 911.*

As with most liberal views, that answer is naive, ignorant, and dangerous.

If you think the government is going to protect you and your family, think again.

For those who trust the government to protect them, are they aware that the Supreme Court ruled that law enforcement officers do not have a specific duty or requirement to protect people?[125]

Citizens trained in the proper and safe use, care, and storage of a handgun, rifle, or shotgun, their chances of survival and protecting their loved ones are significantly increased. When a criminal breaks into a home, carrying a knife, firearm, or any other life-threatening implement of assault, the situation is highly serious and potentially fatal, requiring immediate protection readiness. Consider that it typically takes the police several minutes to arrive at a scene after being dispatched. When a potentially violent criminal is in play, a few minutes is a long time to wait for police help! A lot can happen to defenseless individuals while waiting helplessly for police to arrive.

Minutes matter.

Protection by firearm doesn't necessarily mean shooting, but it's a very effective means of holding a criminal in place while you dial 911 and wait. The probability is greater that no one is physically harmed and the criminal gets cuffed and hauled to jail when police arrive. One less criminal off the street and countless citizens safer.

Immediate protection matters.

Better to have a solid and responsible means of protection than to be sorry (or dead).

Firearms safety is the most important rule, especially in a home with children. Parents must take responsibility to train and make sure guns are not loaded, no rounds are in the chamber, and the firearms are securely stored.

A plan is a critically important rule. There should be a solid plan for when you're on the streets, in your vehicle, and for the time when you suspect an intruder. The plan should be quick, easy, and as safe as possible for quick adult-only access to retrieve and load the firearm.

With most everything in life, accidents can happen, which is why appropriate safety measures—training in firearm safety—are critically important.

Firearms: Our Second Amendment Rights

Common sense is critical! Regarding firearms:

1. research,
2. purchase,
3. get professional training,
4. properly secure your gun,
5. and have a quick and easy (but safe) access plan!

I subscribe to the local county alert. One alert stands out in my mind, which reads something like this:

> The County Sheriff's Office and local PD are looking for two vehicles. One is a maroon and silver Subaru Outback, unknown plate, which was involved in a robbery in Eagle.
>
> The other is a white Subaru Outback station wagon with Colorado "Donate Life" plate number 497WAU (this was sent out by EC Alert last night), which was stolen from the owner while holding the owner at gunpoint.
>
> If you see either of these vehicles, please do not approach the vehicle or subject(s), but call 911 to report.

Such situations remind me to thank God for our Second Amendment rights. The left wants to take away our rights to keep and bear arms. It's not a privilege; it's a right!

We must defend our rights.

Locally, within a two-month period, we had a carjacking, a murder, and the shooting of a highway patrol officer. Even more reason for law-abiding citizens to have concealed carry licenses.

Highly concerning is that the murder was committed by a thirteen-year-old boy! He killed his dad with two gunshots to the head. Tragic.

As for the carjacking, thankfully the innocent wasn't harmed and the suspect was eventually caught. But both outcomes are the exception in such circumstances. The patrol officer who was shot, thank God, happened to be with another officer. Had the second officer not been in the patrol vehicle, the injured officer would have likely been killed in the line of duty during that "routine" traffic stop. I pray both officers are believers in Jesus Christ. Every moment of on-duty law enforcement is a risk. Such life-or-death incidents would be a wake-up call for me.

I'm so thankful for our country's law enforcement officers. We must support the men and women in blue. Encourage them by extending a wave, thanking them for their service, and buying them a coffee or a meal.

Encouragement instills confidence which grows courage, which gets the job done!

Here in Colorado, we have both open carry and concealed carry. I find it strange that gun owners in our state do not need a permit to open carry but need a permit to conceal carry. I do a lot of hiking and snowshoeing in remote mountain areas and I feel safer knowing I can legally carry a handgun in the event of a mountain lion or bear encounter, or worse, an attack. The chances of such an encounter are minimal, but as with all of life, we don't know what the next moment holds. Calling 911 in the remote mountains does a hiker no good when facing dangerous wild animals. Likewise, and far more prevalent, are the wild criminals on our streets who bear lethal weapons. Gun ownership by responsible citizens enables us to be prepared to defend ourselves and those we love when threatened by beasts or beastly humans. No one can help guarantee your safety except you. It's our sole responsibility as citizens to use the knowledge, wisdom, and other tools available to us under our constitutional rights.

Living in fear is also a choice. What abates fear is gaining knowledge, applying wisdom, practicing faith, and taking common sense safeguards like gun ownership. This world is getting eviler by the day. Society and our government are not getting better and safer; they're daily getting worse. It's up to us as individuals to become trained in self-defense, firearms, first aid, and home security, to be prepared, and to stand up for our constitutional rights.

Before moving from Wisconsin to Colorado, I took a four-hour concealed carry course taught by Great Lakes Firearms Safety Training, LLC. I learned a lot in that class, especially from a legal standpoint. Seeing the ways our country is sliding downhill morally, economically, socially, and in every other regard, it's imperative, now more than ever, to learn self-defense and firearm basics. Search the NRA website for local classes and training.

We have the right to protect ourselves, our loved ones, other citizens, and our homes and vehicles with responsible-use firearms. Join the National Rifle Association (nra.org). Take classes to learn the basics (at least) of firearms use and safety. Practice at your local shooting range. There's a range in Colorado that I occasionally use for target practice, which is fun.

Conservative Solution

Safety is paramount.

Owning a firearm is a big responsibility and carrying a gun is an even bigger responsibility. Become familiar with the laws in your state on open carry and concealed carry. It's interesting how different states have different gun laws. When I travel, I look up various states' gun laws to ensure I remain law-abiding as a gun owner.

> *Sidebar:* To learn how to protect yourself from aggressive prosecution in justifiable defense of your home and life, visit www.armedcitizensnetwork.org. I also encourage you to read *The Global War on Your Guns: Inside the U.N. Plan to Destroy the Bill of Rights* by Wayne LaPierre. There are people who are bent on taking away your right to self-defense. The Second Amendment (and all our rights) is worth fighting for!

During an Eagles-Cowboys football halftime, of all places and times, now-former NBC sportscaster Bob Costas spoke out against firearms, against the Second Amendment, and against gun ownership, politicizing the murder/suicide of a Kansas City Chiefs' football player and his girlfriend.

It was not Mr. Costas' place to publicly address the tragedy. His ranting was pathetic, which lost a lot of my respect for him. While listening, my brother-in-law and I looked at each other, mirroring that "Seriously Bob?" expression. Sure enough, his spouting became a hot topic across media the next day.

Hearing the constant stream of rhetoric about "gun violence" is maddening. Liberals: violence is violence, no matter the weapon used—gun, knife, vehicle, hands, bomb, etc. The human heart is what's wicked. You could confiscate every firearm in the world and still we'd have acts of violence. The government cannot possibly protect you during an act of violence against you or your loved ones. No one can, except you.

Yes, Mr. Costas, it was a tragedy, but keep in mind that the player could have killed his girlfriend with the brute strength of his bare hands, or a knife, machete, a vehicle, or any number of other means. There are many ways to brutalize and murder a person. Those who are intent on committing heinous, evil acts cannot be stopped, regardless of gun laws. Mr. Costas, shouldn't we also have strict knife control, machete control, hammer control, baseball bat control, all-blunt objects control, and vehicle control?

Many people who are anti-gun are naive (lack of experience) or ignorant (lack of knowledge) about the issues surrounding gun control and gun rights. Even more reason to join and support the NRA, GOA, and RMGO. What's crazy is that liberals find it hard to believe when an evil act is committed. Such ignorance no longer surprises me. Anyone with reading and listening comprehension knows that we live in a world of increasing violence and evil—not because of weapons but because of human free-will choices and the greatest influencer and instigator of all evil: Satan.

With approximately eight billion people on this earth, violence will happen daily. We see how evil choices have played out in Aurora, Colorado, Newtown, Connecticut, Boston, Massachusetts, Highland Park, Illinois, and other locations. Every day is fraught with violence by evil *human choices.*

What's going on in the US presently regarding the Second Amendment is purely political. Every state in our union still adheres to our Second Amendment, except for four who are hollering the loudest about gun control: Ironically, one of those exceptions, California, is the most populated state but ranked at 47 among the states with the least gun deaths while little ole Mississippi is ranked at number 1 for gun deaths! The issue is not about gun ownership but about human choices.

Connecticut is also ranked among the states with the least gun deaths; yet, when one deranged Connecticuter killed twenty-six people, our nation suddenly went into loud vigilance against gun ownership and to crack down on our right to bear arms rather than vigilance against criminals who make the choices to harm.

The solution is to enforce existing gun laws and *go after gangs, cartels, and criminals*! In the liberal mindset, that solution somehow makes less sense.

Jumping on gun control is a knee-jerk reaction to criminal tragedy. If someone were to yell "Fire!" in a crowded movie theater, would we go after the First Amendment of our US Constitution? No.

The Second Amendment was drafted to keep us *from* tyranny! Our founding fathers were brilliant men.

I encourage people to get their concealed carry permits and support the NRA, GOA, and RMGO. Law-abiding US citizens have the right and duty to protect themselves and others from the evil individuals roaming society with the intent to hurt or kill. Guns are here to stay and gun laws will always have loopholes that criminals will expose. I believe there are likely more guns than people in the US and certainly fewer crazies than law-abiding citizens.

Mass shootings (example, Highland Park, 2022) are an example of how wicked and evil a person can choose to be. Such massacres in America are not about guns, as some would like to otherwise think. Massacres in America are about mental illness and hatred, like the hatred of Islam and ISIS. Why do we not hear about gun banning in other countries where massacres have occurred? Because US politicians are not actually concerned about guns but about the power of control that greedy politicians seek. If the powerful can slowly erode our Second Amendment rights, disarming the American people, they will gain more power to control citizens, as we experienced with Coronavirus-related mandates.

As I watched the news and read the details of the Aurora, Colorado mass shooting (2012), I realized that James Eagan Holmes (the mass murderer), was truly psychotic. Watching him as he sat in court, even his orange hair kind of freaked me out, much less his brutal actions in that theater. When I first heard news of the shooting, I immediately thought two things: Evil exists in this world and gun control will quickly be the talk of the nation.

A liberal tactic is insisting that the Second Amendment is outdated and no longer relevant. Not true. Now, more than ever, with the threat of ISIS and other terrorists, liberals should be fully supporting our Second Amendment. And for the record, I would protect an innocent liberal in a heartbeat if they were being victimized by a criminal! Helping others without regard to political views, religious beliefs, race, or gender is a pillar of human integrity.

Opposite of integrity is people control—liberals feeding the media by stirring up talks and efforts regarding gun control rather than criminal control and labeling our Second Amendment as "outdated." What part of protecting one's self and others has ever been or will be outdated?

I'll say it a million times: gun control is people control.

A local newspaper published a letter to the editor written by a man who claimed to own firearms. But his article, in my interpretation, read as though he was anti-gun. Keep in mind that most people in this valley are non-believing liberals, like so many on social media that I tend to get into arguments with about gay "marriage" and the Second Amendment. I don't make a lot of friends online or through my submissions published in the local newspaper. But standing for truth is important.

I responded to the man's op-ed with my own:

> I respectfully disagree with Mr. Tom Backhus' letter to the editor, published on 12/31/12. He began his letter by name-calling those who are pro-gun as "Wyatt Earp." So, not a very mature response.
>
> Maybe this gentleman should voluntarily turn in his shotgun and high-powered hunting rifle. Perhaps he should drive to LA with those weapons and get a gift card from the government for 1/8th the value of those firearms he claims to own. Keep your BB gun and .22. As you would say, "Good luck with that."
>
> I believe the answer to the CT school shooting is addressing societal issues and mental health issues. This tragedy is not a gun issue, as many would like to claim. We do not value life as we should (e.g., abortion) and this lack of value is reflected in today's society.

Mr. Backhus mentions the Aurora shooting which, by the way, happened in a "gun-free" zone. Publicized gun-free zones notify criminal thugs that employees and patrons are not armed. As we've seen time and time again, gun-free zones are not effective. They are easy targets for those wanting to commit crimes. How about making a "crime-free" zone?

My place of employment in 2016 had a "no weapons on the property" policy, including the parking lot, indicated by a sign. Why post any kind of sign regarding weapons? Anyone intent on harming others will bring a weapon onto the property without regard to what the sign says. A more accurate sign would be: "Criminals, the Disgruntled, and the Mentally Ill, we are unarmed!" The only way to enforce a no-weapons policy would be to have security or law-enforcement on-site who send every person through a metal detector or pat-down.

Let's enforce existing US gun laws and crack down on gang activity and gunrunning. Heck, our very own government sent weapons to Mexican drug cartels (Operation Fast and Furious, anyone?), and now we should turn in our guns to this same government? What a joke. The Second Amendment protects us against the very government that's supposed to protect us. Americans have every right to purchase and own firearms, if they pass a background check, they're not felons, and not mentally ill, etc. We have laws and rules in place. Let's enforce them.

Why are automatic weapons being targeted when semi-automatic weapons were used in these tragedies? I'm surprised Mr. Backhus, as a gun owner, doesn't know the difference. Or perhaps he did and just decided to jump on the gun-banning wagon. Just goes to show that those without knowledge of firearms are the ones who want to crack down on gun ownership and ban certain weapons. The Second Amendment not only protects us from criminals but also from a tyrannical government. The government should fear the people rather than the people fearing the government.

To those who are anti-gun and pro-gun "control," here's an idea: Simply don't own them. If you're a gun owner, turn them in and try to depend on the government for your safety. As Mr. Backhus would say, "Good luck with that." But it's an option. You don't have to own a firearm, and you can always call 911.

Bottom line: There's so much focus on gun "control" when we should be focused on the gospel of Jesus Christ and all the issues that ail society (abortion, homosexuality, lack of morals), and mental illness. Those suffering from mental illness need help. There are many resources out there.

Like I tend to do on social media about liberal issues that are rapidly eradicating our nation's founding values and principles, I got into a debate about gun control. A girl I went to high school with said she just couldn't understand why someone would need to purchase an AR-15 semi-automatic rifle nor why an individual would be allowed to purchase so much ammunition that led to the cowardly act in Aurora. She also posted an anti-gun rant by *Seinfeld* actor Jason Alexander that asked why people needed firearms. I countered with, "Why does Jason Alexander need that fancy car and big home in LA?" The point being that he has the right to spend his money as he wishes. Likewise, the gunman (who only had a speeding ticket on record) had the right to purchase firearms and ammunition. We cannot stop law-abiding citizens with no criminal record from purchasing firearms and ammunition, any more than we can stop citizens from buying anything—including items that can be used as weapons. How often have people been strangled or stabbed to death with household items? We wouldn't blink an eye about purchasing switch blades, butcher knives, rope, duct tape, and cellophane.

Some people who hear the term "semi-automatic," think it's a machine gun. It's not; a semi-automatic firearm does not automatically fire an additional round until the trigger is released and re-pressed by the person firing it. In other words, one cannot simply hold down the trigger and continuously spray bullets. There's intent in every trigger pull. A fully automatic weapon, on the other hand, differs greatly from a semi-automatic and the automatic is highly regulated. People unfamiliar with guns simply don't know the terminology, and that lack of knowledge feeds their emotions when they hear about gun tragedies. In turn, they immediately go after guns—which, by the way, are inanimate objects that aren't making the decisions any more than a butcher knife. Guns and knives don't get up on their own and hurt people. Human beings make those decisions because the human heart is wicked.

My social media friend then tried to make the analogy that there seems to be stricter laws with OTC medication and alcohol purchases than for firearms. She said she could not buy Sudafed in bundles or purchase alcohol after 9:00 p.m. in Milwaukee. My response was that there are loopholes in every law. As for medications, I can go into Walgreens, then Walmart, then Target, and the grocery store and load up on Sudafed. How would anyone know? They wouldn't. Likewise, I could go from liquor store to liquor store and load my trunk with beer and Jim Beam and have a basement full of Sudafed and liquor. In other words, a person with intent can and will find ways around laws and guns are no exception.

Someone chimed into the posted conversation and added that she was pretty sure the founding fathers did not intend for individuals to be able to purchase so much ammunition and the AR-15. I responded that the Constitution does not specify which gun types are permitted to be purchased. The Second Amendment states: "the right of the people to keep and bear Arms."[126] We're continually hearing people twist that amendment to fit their own views and agenda—everything from firearms specific to our military versus citizens only having access to pistols and rifles. One friend thinks we should only own muzzleloaders!

Everyone has an opinion, about everything, but opinions do not change our constitution nor the intent of any person who desires to harm others.

When there's a mass shooting, the left calls for stricter gun control. Instead of removing our constitutional rights, we need to continue working to identify people who are evil and those who commit crimes out of severe mental illnesses while continuing to enforce existing US gun laws. People cannot legislate or prevent evil.

Interesting fact I uncovered from doing some research: Mexico, Russia, and Brazil have stricter gun-control laws than the United States and their murder rates are much higher. Israel and Switzerland, on the other hand, have a higher percentage of gun ownership than the US but much lower murder rates. What do those facts tell us?

More guns = less crime; fewer guns = more crime.

Another fact reiterated: the criminally-minded will *always* find a way to access firearms and other means of weaponizing to harm others. Let's not prevent people from retaining the right to purchase what we feel is necessary to protect and provide for ourselves, our loved ones, and other freedom-loving Americans.

So-called "gun control" is, in fact, an assault on law-abiding citizens and their right to keep and bear arms.

There's also a critical issue with signage that publicly announces a premises is a "gun-free zone." What does such a sign say to psychotic individuals like James Eagan Holmes whose intent is to do harm? Such advertisement confirms for criminals and psychotics that nobody at that location is armed to protect themselves. That was the case at the Aurora massacre location.

Most mass shootings happen in gun-free zones.

Breaking news: criminals don't obey rules and laws.

I'm not-at-all making light of the Aurora tragedy, but such circumstances beg the question, had that gun-free policy not been in place, would some of those lives have been saved? A law-abiding citizen carrying their concealed weapon would have likely saved lives, and in accordance with our Second Amendment, "A well-regulated Militia, being necessary to the security of a free State."

Those with evil intentions will never be stopped from carrying out evil acts, so why remove the freedoms of law-abiding citizens who can help to protect other citizens?

With the increased attention on the gun control movement and publicly posting premises as "gun-free zones," we've seen an increase in mass shootings, which include elementary schools.

The two most recent (at this writing) are Covenant School in Nashville, Tennessee on March 27, 2023, where twenty-eight-year-old Audrey Hale shot and killed three students and three staff members.

Just forty-three days earlier, on February 13, 2023, a man unassociated with Michigan State University strolled onto campus and killed three people and wounded five others before killing himself.

Ten months prior was the May 24, 2022, shooting at Robb Elementary in Uvalde, Texas by eighteen-year-old Salvador Ramos, who shot and killed twenty-one people: nineteen students between the ages of 7 and 10, and two teachers. And he also shot and wounded his grandmother!

Losing a child must be the most devastating loss in life. Tragically sad, which takes me back to two points: (1) evil does exist and (2) evil will remain active regardless of gun laws.

Watching the Robb Elementary post-shooting new coverage video was very disturbing. More than twenty heavily-armed police officers were shown standing in the school hallway, for almost an hour, during which more shots by the active murderer were heard. Unacceptable! As much as I support law enforcement, they dropped the ball there. An active shooter must be immediately stopped rather than allowing more time for the murderer to kill. The police chief badly mismanaged this event and, though the gunman was eventually killed, lives could have been saved had the chief of police taken decisive action.

The day of the Sandy Hook shooting, December 14, 2012, I had lunch with my sister. While discussing that morning's tragedy,

I made two points: If I were evil and had evil intentions to kill, I could use any means, which makes gun control senseless. Just look at what happened in Waukesha, WI, during the Christmas parade attack on November 21, 2022. A man killed six people with his SUV. Anyone could drive up to a school and run kids over with their vehicle as the children are waiting for their rides home.

I used to pick up my nieces from school about once a week. Standing along the curbs were many kids, waiting for their rides. If a psychotically angry or evil driver stepped on the gas in their direction, a group of kids would be killed in a short moment, and the driver could get away quicker than if he or she was carrying a loaded gun into a school.

One could just as easily drive to Denver for a Nuggets NBA home game and do the same thing—step on the gas and run people over who are waiting in line for the event.

Guns are not the problem; evil and psychotic people are.

Because human beings have free will and Satan lurks around, seeking those he can use to destroy others, every individual on Earth is capable of horrific acts, which are happening more and more frequently. Because most people choose good, moral behavior, we do not go out and do heinous things. We fear punishment from our criminal justice system, and some of us (like me) also fear the wrath and judgment of God. There is no doubt in my mind that God's wrath has come upon all who have not repented of their sins. Likewise, I believe all the murdered children—including the thousands aborted every day—are in the loving arms of our Lord.

The evening of the Sandy Hook shooting, I spoke with a good friend by phone. He's a liberal, but we agreed on one very important point: Those with evil intentions will follow through with their desires when they've determined to do so. My friend also said he would be in favor of heavy cost for ammunition. I disagreed, countering that if ammunition was expensive, anyone hell-bent on destruction could easily grab a $5,000 line of credit, go to the local gun shop, purchase ammunition, and not care less about the debt because such a person is evil and would not likely bother with paying the debt. Most likely, as we've seen in some cases, the evil person would either take their own life after killing others, or die in a shootout with law enforcement, or perhaps go to prison for the rest of their life.

Likewise, a crazed individual could simply walk into a Walmart with full-body armor and demand all the ammunition at gunpoint. Why? Because criminals do not care about people; they do not value human life.

So, what are we to do since evil will always find a way around obstacles? Gun control, capping credit card limits, or putting hefty price tags or taxation on ammunition are all pointless—just like it's pointless to blame guns for tragedies. The blame lies with Satan and the willful choices of evil individuals and those with mental illness. The mental health of millions of Americans is ignored due to the stigma associated with mental illness—and yet there is a faction who want to disarm law-abiding citizens and place the blame on inanimate objects? Illogical! Insane!

A social media friend said guns are too easy to buy. Well, in the case of Sandy Hook, the deranged gunman didn't purchase the firearms he used. He stole them from his mother who legally owned them. Criminals always find a way to cause mayhem.

Three months after the Sandy Hook shooting was March Madness. Milwaukee's Marquette University (my alma mater) had reached the Elite 8 and lost to Syracuse. As always, I watched the event—in my opinion, the best sporting event. In an SB Nation article by college sportswriter Jared Smith quoted Syracuse head coach (at that time) Jim Boeheim: "If we in this country as Americans cannot get the people that represent us to do something about firearms, we are a sad, sad society. I'm a hunter. I've hunted. I'm not talking about rifles. That's fine. If one person in this world, the NRA president, anybody, can tell me why we need assault weapons with 30 shots in the thing. This is our fault. This is my fault and your fault, all of our faults if we don't go out and do something about this."[127]

How was that our fault? To Mr. Boeheim: killing people is an issue of sin, crime, and evil. Encourage people to search for truth rather than going after inanimate objects like firearms. We live in a fallen world where there will *always* be crime. Address immorality, not our constitutional right to bear arms. Tell people to find a good local church and to serve in that church, tithe to that church, and read the gospel. A friend told me that fewer guns would equal less crime. "Let's try to cut gun ownership by twenty percent," he said.

"That won't make a difference in crime." Regardless of the eighty percent of guns remaining, criminals will still commit crimes. "Whether there are five million or four million guns in the United States," I added, "people with evil intentions and mental illness will commit heinous and cowardly acts. We need to focus on the real issues: mental illness and evil choices."

Extreme gun control measures were passed in Colorado, a knee-jerk reaction to the Connecticut school shooting in late 2012. Such proposals lack common sense. What will limiting magazine capacity to fifteen rounds do? Nothing. Will criminals and gangbangers care about such new laws and respect those? No. Whether criminals have fifteen- or thirty-round magazines, they'll continue to choose evil and commit crimes, including gang members killing other gang members. In addition, higher round magazines, in my experience, jam easier and more often than magazines with fewer rounds. Like a local gun dealer told me, "If citizens cannot buy high-capacity magazines, neither should law enforcement be able to." Good point, sir. If those in power want a policed state, citizens and law enforcement should be on equal footing. I like to think that most police officers support the constitutional right of citizens to keep and bear arms.

During my research on previous Colorado gun laws, I found the following about concealed carry on the CO State Patrol website:

> Title 18: Colorado allows a person to carry a firearm in a vehicle if its use is for lawful protection of such person or another person or property. [C.R.S. 18-12-105(2)] Colorado law also allows a person to possess a handgun in a dwelling, place of business, or automobile. However, when you carry the weapon into your home, business, hotel room, etc. it must be in plain view. Local jurisdictions may not enact laws that restrict a person's ability to travel with a weapon. [C.R.S. 18-12-105.6] The Act permits the nationwide carrying of concealed handguns by qualified current and retired law enforcement officers and amends the Gun Control Act of 1968 (Pub. L. 90-618, 82 Stat. 1213)

to exempt qualified current and retired law enforcement officers from state and local laws prohibiting the carry of concealed firearms."[128]

So, when I enter my home, my firearm must be in plain view? To whom?

Our Second Amendment is powerful and can't be taken for granted. One primary purpose of the Second Amendment is to protect us from a tyrannical government. We live in interesting times, especially since 9/11, the Occupy Wall Street movement, Antifa, Covid-19, the 2020 election, the increase in civil unrest, student violence in school against each other and against teachers (whose hands have been tied against discipline), and acceptance—even encouragement—of the sin of homosexuality.

Returning for a moment to prepping for social chaos, it's no longer a far-fetched or bad idea, a discussion I recently had with family members. Having an escape plan and prep for an uncertain future here in America appears wise. The Bible warns that the future will grow darker, and we are witnessing that by the decline of morals, values, principles, ethics, and reverence for God and His Word that laid the foundation for right living, which is fundamental to peace and prosperity. Instead, our nation is accelerating in the opposite direction. We see a rise in mental health issues that have a lot of Americans addicted to prescription drugs, which decreases mental clarity and logic.

While there are people who legitimately need prescription drugs, a vast number of users do not. The most beneficial "drug" for all people is exercise. Find the physical activity you enjoy, be daily consistent in that, and you'll be amazed by the improvement in your mental, physical, and emotional health. I enjoy walking, the rowing machine, the spin bike, and weightlifting. Just walking is a great start, then add some other physical activities.

As I mentioned, I became a lifetime member of Gun Owners of America (GOA) and National Rifle Association (NRA). Liberals view conservative believers and supporters of the Second Amendment as "domestic terrorists." Do leftists not often say, "Let people live as they please," only to then speak out of the other sides of their mouths, essentially saying that those who own firearms should not live as they please? And if you believe in God and traditional marriage, should you not live as you please? Liberals consider themselves tolerant until conservatives share their views. It truly is a one-way street.

We live in a society where firearms are more and more viewed as bad, and Islam and sin as good. Twisted. The Obama and Biden administrations have pursued importing Muslims and deporting Christians and firearms. As a gun-owning Christian, I have a lot of concerns with the direction of our country. Good is now bad, up is now down, and right is now wrong.

Firearms ownership and safety comes down to two things: common sense and personal responsibility. I own firearms, but I keep them secure with one exception, a handgun in the event someone breaks into my home. Home invasion is a frightening reality! President Obama did wonders for the firearms industry when he opposed legal gun ownership. Those who desire to retain our Second Amendment rights are stepping up and partnering in support of the NRA's work to preserve our rights.

We cannot take the right to bear arms lightly. We must support the NRA's efforts to uphold this very important citizens' right. Let's not allow those in leftist power to erode US citizens' constitutional right of freedom to keep and bear arms.

What the Bible says about self-defense:

- "When a strong man, fully armed, guards his own house, his possessions are safe" (Luke 11:21).

- "If you don't have a sword, sell your cloak and buy one" (Luke 22:36).

- "Give justice to the weak and the fatherless; maintain the right of the afflicted and the destitute" (Psalm 82:3).

CHAPTER 19

Crime and Law Enforcement

Among the root causes of our nation's rising crime and declining law enforcement is gross lack of quality political leaders who bow down to "political correctness." A prime example is the epic failure of leadership by Baltimore's mayor and state officials following the April 2015 arrest and subsequent death of Freddie Gray, age twenty-five. Public protests by West Baltimore citizens against law enforcement officers sparked a wildfire of protests, riots, and looting across our nation. Hundreds of police officers were needlessly injured in the line of duty, which is unacceptable, angering, frustrating, and disappointing.

When the death of Mr. Gray led to rapidly growing protests, the Baltimore mayor essentially gave a free pass to thugs and looters by not immediately calling in the National Guard. In the end, 113 police officers were injured, 486 people were arrested, and a number of local businesses were destroyed.[129]

One officer injured is one too many. Officers had to use force to protect themselves and innocent residents. The National Guard should have been brought in ASAP and told to do whatever it would take to contain and arrest those responsible for the violence. Weak leadership in that prolonged chaos also led to the shutdowns of schools, businesses, and city-wide activities. Though the Baltimore Orioles played one out of three scheduled games (two postponed), no fans were permitted to attend. That game should have been open to the public. Watching ESPN's highlights of the game with empty stands was odd and disturbing.

The next year, there was rioting, looting, burning, and the tipping over of vehicles when the Denver Broncos won the 2016 Super Bowl against the Green Bay Packers. As a Packers fan living in Colorado, my grudge over that loss and senseless destructions by fans still stands. These incidents demonstrate our country's lack of respect for people, property, and the law.

When I consider our country's worst convicts (many housed in Florence, CO), I think of Alcatraz and why we stopped using such well-placed, well-secured prisons for our hardest criminals. The answer? "The Federal Government found that it was more cost-effective to build a new institution than to keep Alcatraz open."[130]

You cannot put a price tag on the safety of Americans.

Where are our tax dollars going that's more critical than locking up prisoners in harder-to-escape facilities? Liberals care more about the welfare of dangerous convicts than they do about the daily mass murdering of innocent babies in the womb, hideously making Alcatraz and other "hard prisons" look like playgrounds, which brings me to the topic of Guantanamo Bay (a.k.a. Gitmo),

Cuba. Liberals want that US military prison shut down, citing it as a "symbol of lawlessness and human rights abuses."[131] In other words, "lawlessness" in terms of how prisoners are treated. The fact remains that there are bad and evil people in this world who need to be securely locked up for the safety, protection, and well-being of our law-abiding citizens. Hopefully, the current House of Representatives (2023), led by Republicans, can act on getting things done to put this country back on the right track.

I watched an episode on The Bio Channel regarding a white supremacist prison gang. The episode affirmed the fact that there are some bad dudes who need to be well-secured from society! Case in point regarding weapons, the broadcast showed where one inmate was stabbed close to a hundred times by two others who'd made weapons from PVC pipe. Another example of why law-abiding citizens should have legal gun ownership, and why lockups like Alcatraz and Gitmo are important. I don't want such monsters turned loose on society to further prey on innocent civilians. Such criminals did not become evil in prison or because of imprisonment; they entered prison as full-fledged evil people and simply continued that evil in prison.

I specifically think of the need to protect children and the elderly, the most vulnerable citizens in society.

I watched a lot of CNN news coverage about Ferguson, Missouri's then police officer Darren Wilson after he shot Michael Brown in 2014. This case was a demonstration of trying to force an outcome. Like all citizens of our country, Mr. Wilson had every right to due process and a verdict rendered on evidence and law by a jury of his peers. If he was justified in shooting the reportedly unarmed, black teenager, the jury got it right by not convicting him. If he was not justified in using deadly force, he should have been held accountable for his actions. Based on the presented evidence and the law, I believe Mr. Wilson acted with justifiable cause.

People: stop committing crimes and start complying with police officers' orders! Get a job, join a gym, abide by the law, and obey police orders. Pretty simple!

Regarding Michael Brown being an unarmed, black teenager:

> Unarmed: At 6'4" and 250-plus pounds, Mr. Brown was physically big enough to inflict serious bodily harm to another person.
>
> Teenager: Mr. Brown was an eighteen-year-old man and thereby considered an adult by law. He was legally able to vote.
>
> Black: What does a person's skin color have to do with human acts and the law? Absolutely nothing. Regardless of a crime suspect's race, officers of the law have a tough job: primarily dealing with society's lawbreakers while never knowing if their approach toward a person is a danger to them and others.
>
> When deadly force is necessary, responding officers need to exercise that lawful authority. Then, the duty of the justice system is to examine the case and determine what is and what is not lawful and do the right thing in their decision making.
>
> Bottom line: This was a justified shooting.

**It's our duty as citizens and human beings to
do the right thing in the eyes of the law.**

Jurors also have a tough job in determining who's innocent and who's guilty, and the responsibility of our justice system is to present evidence of fact. Every facet of society is comprised of fallible human beings, some of whom are unlawful.

I believe the vast majority of our law-enforcement officers are ethical, professional individuals. I'm so thankful for these brave individuals. They are local heroes.

Those who protested throughout the country in favor of Mr. Brown's innocence should have been more concerned about the root that ultimately led to his death. The root of society is parenting and, secondly, all adults leading by example. Parents, teachers, pastors, politicians, and other community leaders should consistently address with children and young people what choices and actions lead to crime.

Our country has a staggering growth rate of single-parent homes, primarily heaving the parenting load and household management upon the mom. Where is the dad? There's a good chance he's unemployed, uninterested, addicted to some drug, in jail or prison, or in a state of untreated mental illness.

**A strong, lawful, and united society begins
with sound and godly parenting.**

Despite the TV commercials, shows, and other media that minimize the importance of dads,

- we need dads to step up and be the leading male role in the lives of their children;

- we need dads to provide for their families;

- we need dads to involve their children in playing sports and then actually show up for their children's sporting events and cheer their children while teaching them—in word and by example—to behave respectfully.

As a youth baseball and softball coach, I've seen countless parents act like absolute jerks toward the children, the coaches, and other parents. That's not the exampled behaviors that build a strong path for our youth. Adults demonstrating reckless (lack of self-control) behavior is not right and not healthy for kids or our society. Adults: show respect! Be respectful toward everyone, regardless of the circumstance. Be respectful for your children and other children, for your spouses, for coaches and teachers, for civil authority, and for yourself.

Society needs to get back to strong, traditional family values where dad provides, protects, and supports his family, serving as the man of the household while honoring and loving his wife.

Is there a guarantee that raising children in a two-parent Christian home of true morality and ethics will produce lawful young adults? No, because we're each granted free will and we're each sinners (my life is a prime example). However, the probability of producing lawful young adults is exponentially greater when children are raised in two-parent Christian homes of godly morality, ethics, values, and principles. The only guarantee we get in life is the very one we should stand on throughout life and the one we should teach our children about: Jesus Christ "the solid rock" and His Word, the Bible.

Conservative Solution

As a young adult (in the eyes of the law) or as an aged adult, I cannot blame anyone else for my decisions. I can't blame God, my parents, my teachers, nor my peers, or circumstances. My decisions that led me down the dark road to destruction are my own. I share many examples in my first book, *A Perfect Walk*, but here's an example to make my point:

> As an adult, I chose to go to a clubhouse to grab some grub and ended up talking college football with some men I met at the bar. My choices. I consumed two beers, two mixed drinks, and two shots—a dangerous cocktail to uphold self-discipline. I ended up making more poor decisions by sticking around and drinking instead of heading home sober to watch the Wisconsin Badgers play the Nebraska Cornhuskers. I was the fool and the sinner in my choices—not someone else.

We're each responsible for our decisions and actions.

No matter your race, religious beliefs, political views, or socio-economic standing, show respect to others—all others. Avoid being in situations that may result in poor choices. Avoidance is key!

The following headlines exemplify the sin at work in America—murder, battery, assault, theft, greed, and more.

> Man found dead in apparent stabbing on Christmas Day
>
> Pastor punched in the face as he checks on burglary at neighbor's house
>
> Suspect shot, killed by police in Pueblo

Two paintings valued at $1,000 stolen from Loveland public art display

Man charged with stealing donated cash

Two US border agents shot, one fatally, in Arizona

Confronted about child porn, man shoots two deputies in San Diego County

Carjacking suspect shoots self during police pursuit

West Virginia state trooper, suspect killed in shootout following traffic stop.

St. Croix County deputies return fire, kill man

Douglas County deputy shoots, kills man

Officer wounded in Sikh temple attack still can't speak

If criminals are willing to attack law enforcement officers, what are they willing to do to you and me and our loved ones? I fear they would stop at nothing to get their way—get what they want, and do whatever they deem necessary to get what they want.

Let's stop coddling criminals and hold them accountable.

With our economy in shambles and immorality and crime on an accelerated rise, we can expect more criminal behavior unless we take *effective* actions.

Injustice

A friend of mine in Milwaukee, I'll call him Bob, is a man's man: a husband, father, teacher, coach, hunter, athlete, and tobacco chewer.

He and my friend "Michael" once saved me from a pummeling on Water Street in Milwaukee in 1999 when I came to fisticuffs with a man who was making fun of a friend with disabilities, which is not cool at all. I couldn't let such injustice slide, and we know that no civil authority is going to take such action. In the boxing bout with the abusing man, his two buddies jumped in, threw me against a fence, and threw punches at my head. Thank God Michael was there to knock out the little guy while Bob pummeled the other man. While senseless violence is not okay—I'm not an advocate of going around and punching people—neither is letting injustices against other human beings slide.

While we must lead our lives with the love of Christ, there are times when such injustices must be shut down for the sake of righteousness (right living). Such circumstances, as with Matthew 21:12–13, are where we got the term "righteous anger." Jesus was enraged when he found vendors selling their goods in the temple of God—desecrating (abusing) the holy house. In righteous anger, He commenced to overturn the moneychangers' tables and drove the abusers out while quoting Scripture, "'My house will be called a house of prayer,' but you are making it 'a den of robbers.'"

That's the only recorded time when Jesus expressed his anger physically, and that too should be our reminder that standing for righteousness with our words, as Jesus often did, is the first course of action. I should have grabbed my friend, spoken truth to the abuser, and walked away. Lesson learned.

We can help to change the world one encounter at a time by taking a bold stand against injustice with the words of truth.

Capital Punishment

At Marquette University, I took a course on our US criminal justice system. I had to give a presentation that was either in support of or against capital punishment. I was pro-capital punishment until I took that class and had to research and debate my point of view.

The biggest problem I've found with capital punishment is that innocent people too often get wrongly convicted and put to death, a horrible injustice I can't imagine. That said, the government does have an obligation to keep the public safe—hence the need for secure prisons. It's sad that the gunman in the Aurora, Colorado movie theater wasn't eliminated by law enforcement when they arrived on scene, and the Boston Marathon bomber wasn't riddled with bullets.

What the Bible says about justice and law enforcement:

- "Let everyone be subject to the governing authorities, for there is no authority except that which God has established. The authorities that exist have been established by God. Consequently, whoever rebels against the authority is rebelling against what God has instituted, and those who do so will bring judgment on themselves. For rulers hold no terror for those who do right, but for those who do wrong. Do you want to be free from fear of the one in authority? Then do what is right and you will be commended. For the one in authority is God's servant for your good. But if you do wrong, be afraid, for rulers do not bear the sword for no reason. They are God's servants, agents of wrath to bring punishment on the wrongdoer. Therefore, it is necessary to submit to the authorities, not only because of possible punishment but also as a matter of conscience" (Romans 13:1–5).

CHAPTER 20

Public Education

Back when my niece was in high school, her class read the book *Brave New World* by Aldous Huxley. I had read the book back in college and recalled its globalist theme. My niece's high school in a small town in Colorado was pushing climate change, homosexuality, and globalism on young minds. So how much more, especially in today's world, are our children being indoctrinated with lies and acceptance of sin as "good" in our nation's larger city schools?

Our country desperately needs education reform, which starts with parents and local school boards. We need to get conservatives on school boards! I recommend the website Parents Defending Education. (See "Recommended Resources.")

I believe that a majority of schoolteachers not only teach the liberal agenda but push their personal liberal agendas onto students: environmentalism, homosexuality, tolerance of sin, social justice, and all other lies and sin that are growing in acceptability. Liberal teachers are brainwashing our future leaders!

In addition to conservative school boards, we need to hire more conservative teachers who will teach the Constitution and the Bill of Rights, reinforce solid morality, ethics, values, and principles, as well as the fundamentals—reading, writing, math, and basic life skills, like computer use. While it's the job of parents to teach other fundamentals, like cooking, cleaning, laundry, budgeting, work ethic, and banking, there are tragically countless students who need these skills to be taught in school for lack of parenting.

I'm reminded of a 2015 article in the local newspaper about two boys, around age thirteen, who were out on the streets of Seattle demanding their city and state take immediate action against climate change. The article came to mind more recently when not *one* conservative was elected for any of the seven local school board vacancies! That's not only a shame and inexcusable, but scary. Our local Republican Party failed to make the community aware of the conservatives in the race. I had to rely on local conservatives to inform me who to vote for. The fact that seven liberals were voted in meant even more liberalism flooding our local schools.

When my niece was a high school senior, I wrote the following op-ed, published in the *Vail Daily* regarding political correctness at a local high school.

> Good morning.
>
> I was recently made aware that Eagle Valley High School's (EVHS) annual Powderpuff Football game has been cancelled. Based on conversations I've had with some students at EVHS, the reasons given to students

by the school's athletic director is that this event is not an "inclusive culture," the event risks injury to student-athletes, and is not in compliance with Title IX.

Instead of the girl's annual event, it's my understanding that a volleyball tournament of some sort is being considered to ensure both males and females (and transgenders?) will have an equal setting to compete. I threw in the word "transgenders" because I was initially told the game cancellation was due to "gender issues." That information led me to think there was possibly a transgender student attending EVHS. If so, let that individual participate and play in the game.

I also learned that over 100 students signed a petition to hold the game and keep the tradition, but that effort fell on deaf ears and the game will not be played.

Let's break this reasoning down. First, "an inclusive culture." The boys at EVHS have the opportunity to play football, and many of them do. Girls do not have that same opportunity because football is a male sport (though I occasionally hear about a female placekicker at the high school level). The girls thus look forward to their opportunity to play football with their female classmates and friends in a fun yet competitive atmosphere. Having fun while competing is a good thing and should be encouraged. The boys play football on Friday nights throughout the fall. Let the girls play their one football game of the year. They really looked forward to this game and are rather upset about it being canceled. Welcoming all girls at the high school to participate, and all students to coach or watch the game sounds inclusive to me.

Secondly, "a risk of injury to student-athletes." I spoke to two relatives who attended high school at EVHS. Both stated they never witnessed an injury during this annual football game. Could an injury occur? Of course, just as there are risks of injury in boy's football, in every other sport played by male and female students, and in everyday life, whether we're driving to work, simply attending school, or playing sports, etc. I was also informed the school is planning a bonfire during homecoming week. Isn't this more dangerous than a game of flag football? I would think so. We should not coddle our youth in hopes of them avoiding injury. It's a risk we take and accept when playing sports. If injury is a concern of the athletic director, simply have the students sign a release of liability as done for all other school sports.

Lastly, "lack of compliance with Title IX." I've been informed that Battle Mountain High School (BMHS) is still holding their annual Powderpuff Football game, thereby the athletic director at EVHS cannot say this a district-wide decision. If it was, BMHS is not in compliance, so I'm not buying this reason (or the first two reasons given for canceling the game). It sure sounds like one individual made this decision without input from other staff, administrators, or students. I could be wrong, but this is the impression I have after talking to several individuals associated with EVHS. The game should be played. Even some staff at EVHS think the cancellation of this game is ludicrous.

I don't know 100 percent the reasoning behind the decision to cancel the game, but the first thing that comes to mind is political correctness. This football game has been an annual tradition for many years. I graduated from high school over twenty years ago and remember this tradition back then. The girls at EVHS enjoy playing in this annual game and several boys from the high school football team help with coaching the teams (freshmen through senior). I've attended the game several times with relatives who attended the school. Parents came out to show their support in years past and to socialize with other parents. It was a fun tradition for the students, the school, and the community.

The cancellation appears to boil down to political correctness and so-called "inclusiveness." By being politically correct and claiming to be inclusive, EVHS is NOT being inclusive of the girls that want to play in this annual flag football game. I'm sure some girls take the game too seriously and may be overly competitive at times, but what's wrong with school spirit and competition? I feel this decision is a reflection on our society as a whole. It's becoming weaker because we want to make everything "equal" in our mission to be "inclusive."

Let kids be kids! Let them enjoy their high school years. They go by far too quickly.

Paul

Conservatives at every level have a responsibility to promote conservatism and truth to our kids, not only for the sake of what is right and good and godly as they grow into adults, but for the fact that in adulthood they will become our local, state, and federal leaders, teachers, professors, pastors, school administrators, and school board members.

What the Bible says about education and truth:

- "Teach what accords with sound doctrine" (Titus 2:1).

- "Apply your heart to instruction and your ear to words of knowledge" (Proverbs 23:12).

- "Let the wise hear and increase in learning, and the one who understands obtain guidance" (Proverbs 1:5).

- "The protection of wisdom is like the protection of money, and the advantage of knowledge is that wisdom preserves the life of him who has it" (Ecclesiastes 7:12).

- "All Scripture is breathed out by God and profitable for teaching, for reproof, for correction, and for training in righteousness" (2 Timothy 3:16).

- "How much better to get wisdom than gold! To get understanding is to be chosen rather than silver" (Proverbs 16:16).

- "An intelligent heart acquires knowledge, and the ear of the wise seeks knowledge" (Proverbs 18:15).

- "Give instruction to a wise man, and he will be still wiser; teach a righteous man, and he will increase in learning" (Proverbs 9:9).

PART 4

CHRIST: THE SOLUTION

CHAPTER 21

Christianity

My pastor doesn't sugarcoat the Bible or try to make us feel warm and fuzzy with watered-down, self-selected, or out-of-context Scripture. He states the biblical facts, such as we are all sinners and Jesus Christ is our salvation that creates the bridge for us to have right relationship with God who is holy and just. (I highly recommend reading the New Testament's Book of Romans and Book of Philippians). When I go back and read the notes I took during sermons, *boom!* —I recognize them as truths from the Bible and I know I'm attending a solidly biblical church. My pastor doesn't change God's Word to make us think we're inherently good people. God, through His Word and through solid teachers of the Word, hits us between the eyes with biblical truth.

I never tire of Jesus's statement in John 14:6: "I am the way and the truth and the life. No one comes to the Father except through me." Powerful stuff.

Know that God's Word is truth.

My pastor also compared Christianity to other religions, and he was spot on. Leaders of other religions fail their followers by denying God's existence or teaching that He is one of many gods, denying God as Creator and the one and only true God, denying Jesus Christ as *God the Son*, some religions lowering Him to a fully human position as "one of many historical teachers" rather than God's holy Son without sin, denying the validity of salvation by faith in Jesus Christ through God the Father's unmatched grace and love, and denying that the Bible is the living, holy Word of God. Here are three prominent examples of beliefs from among the 4,000 recognized religions around the world:

Buddhists	**Hindus**	**Muslims**
deny the existence of a personal God	believe in two major gods, Vishnu and Siva, as well as millions of lesser gods	believe in one God whom they refer to as Allah, and do not believe in the trinity
believe salvation is by self-effort only	believe salvation is achieved by devotion, works, and self-control	believe that people earn their own salvation and pay for their own sins
believe that Jesus was an enlightened human and wise teacher	believe that Jesus was one of many gods and a wise teacher	do not worship Jesus or consider Him divine but rather simply a messenger of God

Christianity

Those beliefs are lies. Truth cannot be found in the Tripitaka (Buddhist), nor the Veda (Hindu), nor the Quran (Muslim), nor the Book of Mormon, nor Dianetics (Scientology), nor any other human-created text touted as "sacred." Truth is found only in God's Word, the Bible.

All Scripture is God-breathed and is useful for teaching, rebuking, correcting and training in righteousness, so that the servant of God may be thoroughly equipped for every good work. (2 Timothy 3:16–17)

- [Jesus] "If you hold to my teaching, you are really my disciples. Then you will know the truth, and the truth will set you free." (John 8:31–32)

- [Jesus] "I am the way and the truth and the life. No one comes to the Father except through me." (John 14:6)

- "Sanctify them by the truth; your word is truth." (John 17:17)

A very good friend in Wisconsin is an agnostic who disagrees with and questions a lot of my views and beliefs. However, there's always a mutual respect between us, no matter how much we disagree. It's rather funny that we're such good friends despite our political, sociological, ideological, and faith differences. He's into music, movies, and art while I'm into politics, religion, current events, and sports. Though we're opposites, we have a truly great friendship that I'll cherish forever.

He and I primarily discuss Islam and homosexuality. Even though I speak out against the religion of Islam and the gay agenda, there is no hatred there—I do not hate Muslims or homosexuals but desire through outreach and prayer that all people will come to know Christ as their Savior, His Word as truth, and will follow His Word. Jesus Christ and God's Word are one and the same: Spirit and truth.

> In the beginning was the Word, and the Word was with God, and the Word was God. He was with God in the beginning. Through him all things were made; without him nothing was made that has been made. In him was life, and that life was the light of all mankind. The light shines in the darkness, and the darkness has not overcome it. (John 1:1–5)

> The Word became flesh and made his dwelling among us. We have seen his glory, the glory of the one and only Son, who came from the Father, full of grace and truth. (1 John 1:14)

I shared my heart with my friend by sharing the truths of the Bible regarding leading unbelievers to Christ, which is what believers are called to do. Leading others to Christ is evangelism of the gospel: Christ's death was payment for our sins and through faith in Him we receive the free gift of salvation from everlasting separation from God.

Many Muslims (and people of other religions) and homosexuals (and people with other strongholds of sin) have become believers in Jesus Christ through evangelism of the gospel. The truth has freed them from Satan's lies and the strongholds of sin.

Committing one's heart and life to Jesus Christ in faith *changes* the individual's heart and mind to the desire to please God.

> To the Jews who had believed him, Jesus said, "If you hold to my teaching, you are really my disciples. Then you will know the truth, and the truth will set you free. . . . Now a slave has no permanent place in the family, but a son belongs to it forever. So if the Son sets you free, you will be free indeed." (John 8:31–32, 35–36)

God made all persons (Jews, Gentiles, Muslims, homosexuals, murderers, liars, etc. [Romans 2:11–16]) and desires that *all*—every human being on Earth—come to Him in repentance and faith and follow Him in truth (2 Peter 3:9).

God is in the miracle business.

Once saved, we still struggle with our sinful nature but have the promise of forgiveness and eternal life with God the Father, Son, and Holy Spirit. I continue to struggle with sin's temptations (like lust). I've pretty much lived the gamut of sin and with the knowledge that no sin is lesser or greater than another sin.

We're all, each of us, God's creation, but not all people choose to follow Him as the One true God, holy Father, divine Creator, and Savior of humankind. We're all sinners who fall short of God's glory; but thankfully, there is complete forgiveness by His grace for our sins, freely given to those who accept Jesus as their Savior.

Following Christ, who calls us to practice self-control, I gave up drunkenness in 2018. While visiting Wisconsin, a friend and I went to a Green Bay Packers game at Lambeau Field. It was disappointing to see how drunk some of the fans were during a football game, and that reminded me of my own drunken days.

A man sitting in front of us at the game was so drunk by the fourth quarter that his eyes were bloodshot and his speech was slurred. Because of my past drinking, I knew how he would likely feel the next day and I pray that he has found Jesus. I'm so thankful to God every day that He saves sinners like me. My prayer is that all who are drinking their lives away (as I was), and otherwise living a lifestyle of sin, will come to know sobriety and self-control.

Please become familiar with the fruit of the spirit.

Read Galatians 5:22–23.

As believers in Jesus Christ, we work toward bearing the fruit of God's spirit.

By my outspoken faith in God's Word and Jesus Christ as truth, I am not saying or implying that I'm better than anyone else or that all Muslims, homosexuals, or any other group are all bad or evil people. God alone judges the heart of each person. I'm simply sharing that my hope and prayer is that all people will come to know the truth—Jesus Christ. Those who put their faith in Him receive the Holy Spirit within them, thereby giving us the means to know what is truly good and evil. God says we will recognize believers "by their fruit" (Matthew 7:16). In other words, we will know where we and others stand in relationship with Jesus Christ by our lifestyles. Believers continue to make mistakes and fall off the wagon, so to speak, but our charge is to get back up and live in obedience to God's Word.

What do Christians believe?

> 1. God is the One and only supreme being, the Creator of all things who created humans in His image, and the One

Christianity

who loves all of mankind and wants a personal relationship with each of us as our divine Father.

2. Jesus Christ is God made flesh, part of the trinity—Father, Son, and Holy Spirit—the Son of God, born of a virgin. He died for the sins of mankind, and rose to life as the One and only defeater of death.

3. Whoever trusts in Jesus as their Savior receives His Holy Spirit and will desire to follow God and live according to His Word. Believers have the promise of no more condemnation, eternity with God the Father, Son, and Spirit, and a host of other promises. *Have you tried to wrap your thoughts around the timelessness of eternity? Can you imagine spending forever and ever without hope, light, and love?*

4. The Bible is the infallible, holy, living Word of God to mankind, revealing His nature, character, plans, and purposes, including how we are to live as His beloved children.

While there are several translated versions of the Bible, for ease of reading and understanding, I highly recommend for new believers the NIV or NLT versions. The first Bible I read from cover to cover was the *New Believer's Bible New Testament: First Steps for New Christians*, which features notes by Greg Laurie, a solid Bible scholar and pastor. Other solid Bible teachers include Pastor David Jeremiah and the late (2023) Pastor Charles Stanley. I highly recommend these teachers. Their messages are easily accessible 24/7. (See "Recommended Resources.")

The Cross

I attended a Good Friday service with my sister and the message was powerful. The pastor spoke of Jesus dying on the cross, how He died, and why—His love for us was so great that He was willing to die as payment for our sins. The pastor knew biblical truth and did a great job relating Scripture to our everyday lives.

I have too many sins to even begin counting, so I'm thankful for all that Jesus did for me on the cross! The precious blood of Jesus Christ was spilled for us to have new life in Him on this earth and everlasting life with Him!

I got chills in church on Friday evening, hearing about all that Christ endured to save us from the death penalty of sin.

- "After they had mocked him, they took off the robe and put his own clothes on him. Then they led him away to crucify him" (Matthew 27:31–35).

- "Christ did not send me to baptize, but to preach the gospel—not with wisdom and eloquence, lest the cross of Christ be emptied of its power" (1 Corinthians 1:17–18).

- "His purpose was to create in himself one new humanity out of the two, thus making peace, and in one body to reconcile both of them to God through the cross, by which he put to death their hostility. He came and preached peace to you who were far away and peace to those who were near" (Ephesians 2:15–17).

- "Having canceled the charge of our legal indebtedness, which stood against us and condemned us; he has taken it away, nailing it to the cross. And having disarmed the powers and authorities, he made a public spectacle of them, triumphing over them by the cross" (Colossians 2:14–15).

- "For the joy set before him he endured the cross, scorning its shame, and sat down at the right hand of the throne of God. Consider him who endured such opposition from sinners, so that you will not grow weary and lose heart" (Hebrews 12:2–3).

Truth and Love

Just as the Bible states that we are to treat others equally, it also states that we are to share the truth in love. Though my words through this book and other publications may not sound as though they're from a heart of love, I assure you that my fervency is rooted in the love of Jesus Christ and God the Father and in concern for where you will spend eternity.

Out of love and concern for all people, I support churches that invite and encourage all people to attend, regardless of their lifestyles, origins, or beliefs, for we all are equally sinners and in need of Jesus Christ as Lord of our fallible lives.

My stance is not about being perfect or claiming to be perfect; I recognize my sin and my constant need for Jesus, God's Word, and practicing faith and the fruit of the Spirit in repentance and in commitment to avoid repeating a cycle of sin as a lifestyle. Due to my sinful nature, most days I found myself saying, "Come on, Paul!" Sin is real and has consequences. I recommend the book *Killing Sin Habits: Conquering Sin with Radical Faith* by Stuart Scott.

Creation

A former coworker of mine is an evolutionist who believes we evolved from fish. He made a statement that mankind is in trouble as the population grows and resources dwindle. My thought was, *God said to go multiply.* Why would the Creator of all things tell us to go multiply if His plan was opposite of that—to evolve from a different species? The first book in the Bible, Genesis, makes clear that God created fish and all other animals, apart from man and woman, and that specifically created man in His image and instructed him to procreate. The issue comes down to whether we believe God and His Word. We don't evolve from other species; God gave us dominion over other species!

Like the word "evolution," the term "population overflow" is another liberal phrase that's adversely impacting our US education system. Public education has deviated from teaching the fundamentals of a sound education and has instead become an institution for political agenda. The population of liberal teachers are growing and pushing evolution, environmentalism, the gay agenda, and other leftish beliefs.

Fly the American flag and teach truth in schools!

Death

Euthanasia (assisted death) is now allowed in eleven states—each are liberal states, treating the decision of human death as though we are God, picking and choosing who lives and dies. This is not our job or our right, nor the government's. Euthanasia breaks my heart.

Christianity

I think of my grandmother who lived to be one-hundred, on God's timetable. She was ready to go home to meet the Lord. She'd had enough of this life, having lost two children and her husband to major illnesses. She was one tough cookie and I loved her so much. She passed into heaven on October 8, 2016. She was a believer in Jesus Christ and I knew He had transported her into heaven. She was no longer suffering on this earth. She had diligently read her Bible, prayed, and lived a long and oftentimes tough life. I found sticky notes in her apartment, such as, "Take this cup from me, Lord. I can't go on anymore." She was what the Bible describes as an "overcomer" and she faithfully waited on the Lord's timing.

She was adorable, a wonderful woman, and a fighter. She was also amazing! Who tubes a river in their eighties and plays golf in their nineties? She was truly special. She had gone through much adversity and entered heaven peacefully in her sleep.

That's the way to go!

This life is tough but it's not our call to take shortcuts, like assisted death (or suicide). Sadly, many who are growing old are suffering without hope and peace in Jesus Christ. We will each eventually die and none of us knows what tomorrow or even the next hour will bring, but those who put their faith in Christ are given sufficient grace to wait on the Lord and honor Him in the waiting. Euthanasia is not God's way; it's a dishonor of His authority and sovereignty.

The essentials we must practice until our divinely-appointed time of death is to

- trust in the Lord with all your heart and wait on Him;

- seek Him, obey Him, and enjoy each moment of this life;
- share the gospel of Jesus Christ in words and in action with love;
- take nothing for granted;
- see all the blessings and give thanks to God in all things;
- love and forgive; and
- work hard.

The solution is not euthanasia; the solution is Jesus Christ our Savior.

For many years I feared death, and I know I'm not alone in this regard. However, it's comforting to know that Jesus conquered death (2 Timothy 1:10).

What the Bible says about death:

- "Before long, the world will not see me anymore, but you will see me. Because I live, you also will live" (John 14:19).
- "The wages of sin is death, but the gift of God is eternal life in Christ Jesus our Lord" (Romans 6:23).
- "Christ has indeed been raised from the dead, the first fruits of those who have fallen asleep. For since death came through a man, the resurrection of the dead comes also through a man. For as in Adam all die, so in Christ all will be made alive" (1 Corinthians 15:20–22).

- "We are confident, I say, and would prefer to be away from the body and at home with the Lord" (2 Corinthians 5:8).

- "For to me, to live is Christ and to die is gain" (Philippians 1:21).

- "Brothers and sisters, we do not want you to be uninformed about those who sleep in death, so that you do not grieve like the rest of mankind, who have no hope. For we believe that Jesus died and rose again, and so we believe that God will bring with Jesus those who have fallen asleep in him" (1 Thessalonians 4:13–14).

- "Just as people are destined to die once, [no reincarnation] and after that to face judgment, so Christ was sacrificed once to take away the sins of many; and he will appear a second time, not to bear sin, but to bring salvation to those who are waiting for him, but Christ offers salvation for His followers" (Hebrews 9:27–28, author insert).

- "You do not even know what will happen tomorrow" (James 4:13–14).

- "He will wipe every tear from their eyes. There will be no more death or mourning or crying or pain, for the old order of things has passed away" (Revelation 21:4).

Powerful stuff!

Hell

When I visited my home state, Wisconsin, for ten days, I visited my parents, grandmother, and some good friends. It was a good time, and getting out of town for a bit felt great. I had flown from Denver to Milwaukee via Denver International Airport, a rather bizarre place. The terminal had a futuristic design that felt somewhat eerie to me with its artwork radiating death and destruction and a new world order. One mural in particular caught my attention by its inscription that resembled a passage from *Journey to the Centre of the Earth* by Jules Verne. It read:

> "Is the master out of his mind?" She asked me. I nodded. "And he's taking you with him?" I nodded again. "Where?" she asked. I pointed towards the center of the earth. "Into the cellar?" exclaimed the old servant.
>
> "No," I said. "Further down than that."

Bizarre stuff. Were they referring to hell?

Hell is a real place and a destination a person makes of their own free will.

The steam room at my local rec center makes me want to avoid eternity in hell, at all costs. The thought of everlasting darkness and despair ramps up my desire for eternal life in heaven and I'm all the more thankful for Jesus and His assurance of heaven for all those who put their trust in Him.

At the rec center, thinking how horrid it would be to spend eternity in the fire of hell where there will be weeping and gnashing of teeth, I almost had a panic attack. My help and hope came from my faith in Jesus.

Where we spend eternity comes down to our choice. My prayer and hope is that you will choose faith in Jesus Christ as your Lord and Savior, with humble repentance of your sin, and that you will choose to forgive all who have wronged you and live in obedience to God's Word.

Eternity

I once saw a TV commercial advertising the services of a psychic. They have no clue about the future. Don't waste your time or money. Call me instead; I'll predict your future for half the price, based on your answer to one question: Where do you want to spend eternity?

A little league baseball team I was coaching played for the championship and lost 11–10 in extra innings. I hate losing. When my frustration ended, the truth hit me: As much as I love sports and coaching, the game means nothing compared to eternity. This life and activities are all temporary and eternity is ongoing, never ending, forever. I asked myself if I'd rather the boys have a temporary trophy or a permanent relationship with Jesus Christ. The answer was obvious. A baseball trophy has no eternal value whatsoever. The Bible, however, prepares kids for life, death, and eternity, and gives them solid hope and a solid future in Jesus Christ.

I emailed the team's parents and shared information about my church's Night of Worship. I expected some pushback, but oh well. It's better that kids learn the truth at a young age instead of going through life believing Satan's lies. Though the championship trophy would have been sweet, what was much more desirable and rewarding was leading the thirteen- and fourteen-year-old boys to the truth they could find in Jesus Christ.

Around the same time, I saw a truck on the freeway with a bumper sticker that read: Jesus Christ is Lord, not a swear word.

Amen to that! Cursing God is a direct route to literal hell.

While visiting my parents, I went through all of my stuff that was stored in their basement. Seeing all that I collected over the years, I thought, *What a waste of time and money to have all this stuff. I want to become a minimalist!* I really do. I don't need or want clutter. Material things no longer appeal to me. Did I really need all those CDs, DVDs, books, and all the other stuff I'd saved?

I felt compelled to donate the useful items to charity and throw the rest into a firepit and watch it burn. All I truly need are the basics of life: shelter, clothing, food, water, and other such staples. But, here's where I'd fudge as a sports fanatic: I'd want a TV and sports channels. Also, I'd hang on to my personal computer for writing books, blogging, and doing all the research that helps to keep me informed of current events. Beyond those desired "basics," everything else gets in the way of a meaningful life. Spending time with God, family, and friends. The stuff I was staring at in my parents' basement had no eternal worth whatsoever. I got rid of it all.

I find great peace of mind focusing on the Lord and sports rather than on myself and our decaying country and world; yet I am called to be a witness and messenger of that decay as God wills.

Regardless of the demise of society and economics, God is faithful to His children. He said we should not worry about food or clothing, for He will provide for all our needs. Likewise, He said we cannot serve both God and money, for we cannot serve two gods. Other than the basics, we can enjoy material things to an extent, but they simply do not matter. They are here today and gone tomorrow. Cars rust, houses collapse, clothes wear out.

What matters most is your relationship with God, where you'll spend eternity, sharing the gospel, family, and how you love and forgive others.

As I drove back to Colorado, I did a lot of thinking, which I tend to overdo. I thought of the Delete All option on my phone and how God deletes all our sins when we humbly repent and ask for forgiveness, giving our hearts and lives to Him. That truth is amazing!

No matter how low or down we get in life, we can simply ask God to Delete All our worries.

There's an indescribable weight lifted and freedom of heart and mind when we turn to God for forgiveness and for all our needs, and center our hearts, minds, and lifestyles in a personal relationship with Him. We'll still be prone to old habits, pick up our burdens of past mistakes and sin, and beat ourselves up. That's when we must remember that God no longer holds our sins against us—because we have turned our full hearts and faithfulness to Him as our powerful, heavenly Father. So, neither should we pick up the past to carry on our shoulders.

Consider all past sins and circumstances for what they are: good learning experiences. God doesn't waste any part of our past but uses that to further mold us to be like Christ. All we need to do to be in right relationship with God our Creator and Father is repent, have faith in Him, and, righteously through Him and by His Word, practice what pleases and honors Him.

Whether your past (or present) is riddled with a pornography addiction, drug addiction, sex addiction, gambling addiction, homosexuality, murder, hatred, lying, self-harm, unforgiveness—whatever your sins—Jesus alone is the answer to Delete All and fill you with His power, grace, and love to accomplish through you what He purposed for you.

Rather than focusing on the meaningless material stuff, mistakes, and sins of my past, I chose to give everything to God—and I feel free. We can be "confident of this, that he who began a good work in you will carry it on to completion until the day of Christ Jesus" (Philippians 1:6).

I want to focus on God's abiding forgiveness for all the sin I've committed, and those I will commit as a fallible but forgiven human. Instead of having a pity party, living in the past, or collecting material stuff, I want to collect treasures in heaven for when I arrive there. (Read Matthew 6:19–20.) I want to continue reading the Bible to learn more about God and right living. I want to continue spending quality time with family and friends. I want to continue making a difference in the lives of young people as a Little League baseball and softball coach, which I love to do. I want to become a firearms expert and continue reading and writing about current events in the hope that someone's life will be changed for eternity.

Love

Jesus died on the cross because He loves us with the greatest and deepest love. So . . .

> If God is for us, who can be against us? He who did not spare his own Son, but gave him up for us all—how will he not also, along with him, graciously give us all things? Who will bring any charge against those whom God has chosen? It is God who justifies. Who then is the one who condemns? No one. Christ Jesus who died—more than that, who was raised to life—is at the right hand of God and is also interceding for us. (Romans 8:31–34)

As I once heard my pastor say, Jesus's death for our sins was the greatest expression of love *ever* in the history and future of the world and will always be the ultimate show of love.

What the Bible says about love:

- "God is love. Whoever lives in love lives in God, and God in them" (1 John 4:16).

- "Love is patient, love is kind. It does not envy, it does not boast, it is not proud. It does not dishonor others, it is not self-seeking, it is not easily angered, it keeps no record of wrongs. Love does not delight in evil but rejoices with the truth. It always protects, always trusts, always hopes, always perseveres. Love never fails. But where there are prophecies, they will cease; where there are tongues, they will be stilled; where there is knowledge, it will pass away" (1 Corinthians 13:4–8).

- "I pray that you, being rooted and established in love, may have power, together with all the Lord's holy people, to grasp how wide and long and high and deep is the love of Christ, and to know this love that surpasses knowledge—that you may be filled to the measure of all the fullness of God" (Ephesians 3:18).

- "God so loved the world that he gave his one and only Son, that whoever believes in him shall not perish but have eternal life" (John 3:16).

- "I am convinced that neither death nor life, neither angels nor demons, neither the present nor the future, nor any powers, neither height nor depth, nor anything else in all creation, will be able to separate us from the love of God that is in Christ Jesus our Lord" (Romans 8:38-39).

- "Love the Lord your God with all your heart and with all your soul and with all your mind and with all your strength" (Mark 12:30).

- "Above all, love each other deeply, because love covers a multitude of sins" (1 Peter 4:8).

- "Love one another. As I have loved you, so you must love one another" (John 13:34).

- "Love your enemies and pray for those who persecute you" (Matthew 5:43–44).

- "Love must be sincere. Hate what is evil; cling to what is good" (Romans 12:9).

As for loving our enemies, I get that it's easier said than done. I still struggle with this! But it's important and necessary to love our enemies because God, our Creator, does and asks us to love as He loves (Ephesians 5:2). Hard to do when one is mocked, belittled, or bullied. But important.

Anger and Role Modeling

When it comes to youth sporting events, I found firsthand the truth behind this popular statement: "Parents are worse than the kids!" If you simply search the internet for "little league fight," you'll see just how pathetic some parents are at practices and games. Sad stuff. Parents are the problem in youth sports and too often the problem at home. I've mentioned the importance of solid, godly, two-parent parenting.

My friend I'll call "Jonathan" told me that he coached his son's football team. I regret not playing high school football. Back then, I was a skinny kid with major anxiety issues. We need more dads to step up and coach! To the dads who are coaching, thank you! Let's make sports fun again! Enjoy that time with your children on the field or court.

Be a positive role model.

Sports are great—they teach valuable life lessons to our youth about sportsmanship, attitudes when winning and losing, teamwork, work ethic, the importance of following rules, accountability, taking ownership, staying physically, mentally, and emotionally fit (with positive parenting), and more. I've long been a sports fanatic and coach and know the benefits.

Confession: I skipped high school classes to go home and watch March Madness, my favorite sporting event.

Parents: get your kids off of electronics and involved in sports.

As I said, I really enjoy coaching Little League baseball and softball. I often think I'm having more fun than the kids. Although it's time-consuming, the point is that you're investing in the lives of our youth, our future leaders, which is well worth the time and effort. And there's no place in any sport for anger! It's a learning opportunity that should remain fun.

I volunteered to help coach a local all-star baseball team of twelve-year-old boys. What a sad experience from the very first game—the parents of the opposing team were bad role models, rude and, quite frankly, jerks. I had to bite my tongue several times (as I'm not one to keep my mouth shut). However, I kept in mind that if I confronted the rude parents in front of the team and onlookers, I would also be a bad role model. Instead, I emailed the local president of Little League after the game:

> I'm the first base coach for TRLL. I felt uncomfortable due to the parents' comments toward me and the first base umpire. On a close play early in the game, I signaled "safe" (a part of the game), and people got excited. When the runner was ruled safe, a parent chirped, "Hey blue, don't listen to the first base coach! Don't let him call the game!" Whether right or wrong, the umpire's decision needed to be respected.
>
> A short time later, Durango made a phenomenal defensive play—a double play. I heard from the bleachers, "Hey first base coach, that's how we play baseball!"
>
> I'm just a volunteer coach, not otherwise part of the game, and I'm a single man with no kids, volunteering my time because I love the game of baseball and enjoy working

with youth. However, this experience made me question if I want to return next year. I'd often heard about obnoxious parents and found out firsthand their immature behavior. Their continuous banter made me realize how parents can be worse than their kids.

Halfway through the game, during a stop in play, the field umpire spoke to one of our players at first base. A parent yelled, "What? Is that grandpa talking to his boy? What's that all about? Hey grandpa, call a fair game! What are you saying to him?" That was so rude to call the umpire "grandpa." He's a very nice and competent umpire who was simply warning the player about possible defensive interference and coaching him on properly getting out of the way when a runner makes the turn at one. That's all.

Lastly, and unfortunately, two of the Durango boys got beaned in the head (helmet). They were okay, which is all that matters. There was no intent by our pitcher (he's wild) and I'm glad the boys were okay. The last thing I want to see is an injury/concussion. After the second beaning, I went to first base to coach and a father yelled, "Hey first base coach, how do you let that happen?"

I stated, "There was no intent."

The father proceeded, "That's ridiculous. Why wasn't he taken out? And you know what I'm talking about!" The man was rather aggressive and confrontational. I decided to ignore him, but he continued to rudely chirp.

Had I been immature, like I was in my twenties, I'm quite certain I would have been a lot more vocal and confrontational toward the people in the stands. It could have gotten ugly, but thankfully I was the bigger person and did my best to remain calm.

The chirping parents are not good role models for these boys and I'm disappointed in their behavior. They need to stop living vicariously through their boys. Games and practices should be about baseball fundamentals, good sportsmanship, and fun—not about heckling the opponent, umpires, and opposing coaches.

I didn't know if the email would make a difference in the future, but I had to say something and I'm glad I did. The situation really irked me. I believe we (adults) can help prevent children from growing up to be angry, argumentative, and disrespectful members of society. These behaviors bleed over into every other aspect of their lives. Discussing the matter with the local president of Little League didn't hurt the situation. I spoke my mind and hopefully, something positive came from that experience.

The Bible says the following about anger (angry parents), arguments (oh, they wanted to argue!), children and parents (I felt bad for the kids whose parents were disrespectful), and respect (little was shown during the game).

- "'In your anger do not sin': Do not let the sun go down while you are still angry, and do not give the devil a foothold" (Ephesians 4:26–27).

- "Slow to become angry" (James 1:19).

- "The tongue also is a fire, a world of evil" (James 3:6).

- "Avoid foolish controversies . . . and arguments" (Titus 3:9).

- "Do not exasperate your children; instead, bring them up in the training and instruction of the Lord" (Ephesians 6:4).

- "Children, obey your parents in everything" (Colossians 3:20).

- "Honor your father and mother" (Ephesians 6:2).

- "Show proper respect to everyone" (1 Peter 2:17).

Our hope? The Solution? "God did not appoint us to suffer wrath but to receive salvation through our Lord Jesus Christ" (1 Thessalonians 5:9).

Forgiveness

At an airport job I had, I was amazed at the lack of two coworkers' maturity, both in their thirties. One would hold a grudge like you would not believe. For example, I made a mistake on the ramp and apologized profusely, but the coworker refused to acknowledge or accept my apology. Part of doing what's right, good, and pleasing to God is learning how to better communicate with others, be aware that mistakes will be made, and the need for forgiveness and practicing forgiveness. The unforgiving individual was then involved in an accident where another coworker got injured. Of course, I wondered if the unforgiving employee at fault apologized to the injured coworker. I hope so, and I hope the injured individual accepted the apology. This incident again reminded me of the fact that we're all human, we all make mistakes, and we all need to extend and receive forgiveness.

At a different place of employment, the environment was darkened by a vindictive employer. If your boss is a jerk, chances are you'll want to leave that job. Dealing day after day with greedy, unethical, or unprofessional bosses is not easy, but we need to remember that all work should be done as though we're working for God rather than humans (Ephesians 6:5–9). Yes, easier said than done, but nonetheless, it's crucial to stay in obedience to Christ by adjusting our mindsets to glorify Him by exampling Jesus in our mindsets and choices. Along the same line, our work for God is never wasted (1 Corinthians 15:58). He will reward our faithfulness to Him (Ephesians 6:8).

A boss can make or break a job! I had zero issues with my coworkers; the problem was in management, a serious dysfunction by the employer. I had to remind myself that bosses and coworkers are not the true enemy, Satan is! He and his demons are completely evil (John 8:44) and for the time being, Satan and his band have temporary rule over this world (Ephesians 2:1–2).

Christ has forgiven our sins, so why would we not forgive others, as He asked us to do? Read "The Parable of the Unmerciful Servant," Matthew 18:21–35. It's not always easy to forgive, but the truth is that our unforgiveness hurts ourselves, not the people we're refusing to forgive.

The Bible says the following about forgiveness:

- "If you forgive other people when they sin against you, your heavenly Father will also forgive you. But if you do not forgive others their sins, your Father will not forgive your sins" (Matthew 6:14–15).

- "Bear with each other and forgive one another if any of you has a grievance against someone. Forgive as the Lord forgave you" (Colossians 3:13).

- "Through Jesus the forgiveness of sins is proclaimed to you" (Acts 13:38).

- "Without the shedding of blood there is no forgiveness" (Hebrews 9:22).

- "If we claim to be without sin, we deceive ourselves and the truth is not in us. If we confess our sins, he is faithful and just and will forgive us our sins and purify us from all unrighteousness" (1 John 1:8-9).

Persecution and Serving Others

Christians around the world are being persecuted for their beliefs, just as the Bible says. Persecution is okay! God is greater than all and said, "Blessed are you when people insult you, persecute you and falsely say all kinds of evil against you because of me" (Matthew 5:11). He also said to us, "Love your enemies and pray for those who persecute you" (Matthew 5:44).

I had a great conversation during a walk with my sister. She was concerned with everything that's happening in Ukraine and the worldwide persecution of Christians. I agreed. I'm also concerned. But we both know that God is in control and the situations of this world will ultimately play out exactly as the Bible states as a warning and urging to unbelievers, and to prepare and direct believers.

> "Be always on the watch, and pray that you may be able to escape all that is about to happen, and that you may be able to stand before the Son of Man." (Luke 21:36)

A court in Wisconsin purportedly ruled that a public school could not hold graduation ceremonies at a local church. God forbid that the public associate with a place where one can find the truth! This world is upside down, trying to force Christianity out of the public square and replace God with temporary things (like material "stuff" and status),

- numbing things (like legalizing marijuana),
- distorting things (like news and gender),
- sinful things (like gay "marriage" and homosexuality), and
- hateful things (like Christian persecution), and so on.

The more we go against God's Word—the truth—the sooner we will face His judgment.

I highly recommend we practice repentance and forgiving others, now, before it is too late. Time is ticking.

There's so much animosity and hatred towards Christians. A 2021 *Christianity Today* article reported that there are fifty[132]—50!—countries where following Jesus is most dangerous. The top ten listed are North Korea, Afghanistan, Somalia, Libya, Pakistan, Eritrea, Yemen, Iran, Nigeria, and India. The article gave the following 2021 stats, so imagine how these numbers are increasing:

Christianity

Every day, 13 Christians worldwide are killed because of their faith.

Every day, 12 churches or Christian buildings are attacked.

And every day, 12 Christians are unjustly arrested or imprisoned, and another 5 are abducted.

Open Doors identified three main trends driving last year's increase:

- "COVID-19 acted as a catalyst for religious persecution through relief discrimination, forced conversion, and as justification for increasing surveillance and censorship."

- "Extremist attacks opportunistically spread further throughout Sub-Saharan Africa, from Nigeria and Cameroon to Burkina Faso, Mali, and beyond."

- "Chinese censorship systems continue to propagate and spread to emerging surveillance states." [133]

There's a palpable rise in Christian persecution in our own country—the nation founded on God's Word and faith in Him.

Many people hate the truth, so they hate the believers in Jesus Christ. We must remember that the world hated Jesus before it hated His followers. Be comforted in knowing that Jesus overcame the world, and will return to avenge sin, chain up Satan and His demons, destroy the wicked, and take control over the world. He's biding His time because He loves all people and desires that none will perish due to unbelief—the discarding of Christ, His love, and the price He paid for our sin.

This life is indescribably short, temporary. Turn to Christ, keep looking upward in prayer, and believing that the truth of God will indeed prevail in all His glory.

I recall a woman in Sudan who was sentenced to death because she refused to convert from Christianity to Islam (touted as the religion of "peace"). For her courage and commitment to Christ, she's eternally rewarded by the Lord. While I was sad about her circumstances, I rejoice in her faith and eternal life. God bless her. She is now in Heaven with Jesus.

Even in death, mankind is limited in what we can do as human beings, mere mortals. In the end, mankind doesn't win. God wins. The government could physically take away our guns, our Bibles, and our other freedoms, but no one can touch the souls of those who have put their faith and trust in Jesus Christ. We belong to God, untouchable beyond our physical bodies, and untouchable throughout eternity.

We each get to choose how we will respond to God and His Word. This life is short and eternity is forever. Seek Him today while He can still be found, and spend the rest of your designated earthly days planting the seed of truth!

What the Bible says about judgment:

- "Everyone will have to give account on the day of judgment for every empty word they have spoken" (Matthew 12:36).

- "Stop judging by mere appearances, but instead judge correctly" (John 7:24).

- "Why do you judge your brother or sister? Or why do you treat them with contempt? For we will all stand before God's judgment seat" (Romans 14:10).

- "We must all appear before the judgment seat of Christ, so that each of us may receive what is due us for the things done while in the body, whether good or bad" (2 Corinthians 5:10).

- "I saw the dead, great and small, standing before the throne, and books were opened. Another book was opened, which is the book of life. The dead were judged according to what they had done as recorded in the books" (Revelation 20:12).

What the Bible says about serving others:

- "Even the Son of Man did not come to be served, but to serve, and to give his life as a ransom for many" (Mark 10:45).

- "Give, and it will be given to you" (Luke 6:38).

- "He poured water into a basin and began to wash his disciples' feet" (John 13:3–5).

- "The Lord Jesus himself said: 'It is more blessed to give than to receive'" (Acts. 20:35).

- "God demonstrates his own love for us in this: While we were still sinners, Christ died for us" (Romans 5:8).

- "Keep your spiritual fervor, serving the Lord" (Romans 12:11).

- "Share with the Lord's people who are in need. Practice hospitality" (Romans 12:13).

- "Jesus came, took the bread and gave it to them, and did the same with the fish" (John 21:13).

- "In your relationships with one another, have the same mindset as Christ Jesus . . . taking the very nature of a servant" (Philippians 2:5–8).

- "Offer hospitality to one another without grumbling" (1 Peter 4:9).

- "Each of you should use whatever gift you have received to serve others, as faithful stewards of God's grace in its various forms" (1 Peter 4:10).

- "He will not forget your work and the love you have shown him as you have helped his people and continue to help them" (Hebrews 6:10).

- "Not looking to your own interests but each of you to the interests of the others" (Philippians 2:4).

- "Serve one another humbly in love" (Galatians 5:13).

Prayer

After the tragic shooting in Connecticut at Sandy Hook, I noticed a lot of people posting online, "Where is God in all of this?" Liberals, non-believers, and even Christians ask of any tragic situation, "Where is God when something bad happens?"

God allows all people, from their births to their deaths, to exercise the gift of free will He gave us, beginning with the first human beings, Adam and Eve. Unfortunately, as we see, humans use their gift of free will to commit acts of evil that further Satan's agenda to kill, steal, and destroy human beings and gather them into the pit of hell for all of eternity.

We each have free will and we each are capable of evil acts. Nonetheless, God is faithful, wooing people to Him for salvation, protection, provision, and eternal life with Him. He says He will never leave us, that He's always with us. Yet, we choose to ignore Him and His desires for us—all the goodness He wants to lavish on His children.

He is allowing evil choices for only a season, and then, in His perfect time (unknown to mankind), Jesus will return, rescue those who believe in Him, and destroy evil in a phenomenal display of His holiness, righteousness, and glory. And "at the name of Jesus every knee should bow, in heaven and on earth and under the earth" (Philippians 2:10).

The prophet Isaiah gave us God's directive and a sneak preview of what's to come:

> Comfort, comfort my people, says your God. . . . Every valley shall be raised up, every mountain and hill made low; the rough ground shall become level, the rugged places a plain. And the glory of the Lord will be revealed, and **all** people will see it together. For the mouth of the Lord has spoken. (Isaiah 40:1, 4–5, author emphasis)

I'm bothered when people say and post the well-intended thought, "My thoughts are with you," to those who are hurting or in need. What does that sentiment even mean in terms of making a difference in someone's life? Does it mean the well-wisher is thinking so hard about their friend's situation that they hope their thoughts will positively change the sufferer's adversity?

By merely saying, "My thoughts are with you," isn't that essentially admitting there is a higher power than themselves—though many new-agers believe their thoughts are powerful enough to change circumstances? Can a human being's "positive thinking" change their friend's situation to a positive conclusion? Shouldn't we instead acknowledge that God works in our lives and the lives of others through our prayers? Shouldn't we acknowledge and put into action what God says about prayer?

By the declining condition of the world, including the persecution of Christians, we can assume that saying, "You are in my prayers," is politically incorrect. What a tragic, lost world we're living in.

When we state, "You are in my prayers," are we following through with that promise, truly committed to praying for that individual?

> The prayer of a righteous person is powerful and effective. (James 5:17)

Are we remembering that prayer is one of our greatest weapons against our greatest enemy, Satan?

I often think, by the scary direction our country is headed, that we'll one day have no gun shows or public church services. Praying—which no one can take from us—is the most powerful spiritual action we can take as believers in Jesus Christ.

Again, the time is short. Now is the time to repent and stay in right relationship with the Lord.

Compassion for Pets and People

While walking my sister's dog, I came across two people walking their dogs and we briefly talked. Their dogs looked miserable and in pain. Curious, I asked their ages. One woman shared that her dog was seventeen! The poor dog had cysts as big as softballs (not kidding), and his legs were at an angle. I'm a dog lover and felt awful for him. It was past time to extend compassion by putting the dog to rest, out of his misery.

I had to make that compassionate decision in late 2011, to put down my pit bull, Bruno. It wasn't easy, but it was necessary because he was in ongoing pain that couldn't be resolved.

The other lady said her dog was fourteen. He, too, was moving slowly and appeared to be in pain.

Stop being selfish. At the time that's best for your pets in their suffering, do the right thing: show compassion by putting them down. Yes, it's very sad and depressing, but when Bruno entered into unstoppable pain, I knew I had to take that compassionate step for his sake. I'm thankful for the time we had together. Bruno was quite the character and would have soon been thirteen. He had a very aggressive form of cancer (lymphoma) that caused diarrhea and no appetite, and his pain became obvious—like the two dogs I met along my walk. Because I loved him, I made the hard but compassionate decision to end his suffering rather than feeding my selfishness to keep him alive a little longer.

Our pets are living creatures who feel pain and deserve to be treated with compassion.

God shows compassion for animals, so imagine the greater compassion He has for you and me:

> "Look at the birds of the air; they do not sow or reap or store away in barns, and yet your heavenly Father feeds them. Are you not much more valuable than they?" (Matthew 6:26)

> In his hand is the life of every creature and the breath of all mankind. (Job 12:10)

Accidentally, I maimed a bird with a power tool at work. I felt awful about it and then I thought about this remarkable truth: If I care so much about this bird, how much more does God love me?

> "Indeed, the very hairs of your head are all numbered. Don't be afraid; you are worth more than many sparrows." (Luke 12:7)

> Because of the Lord's great love we are not consumed, for his compassions never fail. They are new every morning; great is your faithfulness. (Lamentations 3:22–23)

His directive to us? "The righteous care for the needs of their animals" (Proverbs 12:10).

Both dogs I met along my walk had lived long, but their pain was evident. Human beings are selfish by nature. The owners were doing what was best for themselves rather than best for their suffering dogs. Please do what's best for your pets rather than what's best for your happiness by holding onto them in their suffering.

I heard that animals at the Humane Society don't get enough exercise, being caged for most of their stays. Being a dog lover and having owned an American Staffordshire Terrier for twelve years, I was more than qualified to take a dog or two for a walk. So, I headed down to my local Humane Society to volunteer as a dog walker. I was told by the receptionist that I had to complete a dog training class to be allowed to walk the dogs, but that I could take a dog to the pen area and let him run around. *What?! Are you kidding me?* That's our government for you—a bureaucracy even at the Humane Society. I know how to control a dog and pick up dog waste (plastic bag!), so give me a leash! The dogs needed a good walk, companionship, and compassion.

My pastor made a great point when he noted that many human beings care more about animals than they do about their fellow human beings, which reminded me of a local front page news story. Over a million dollars ($1.2) was being donated to a horse rescue organization. What if we used such grand amounts to place orphans and unwanted babies in good, loving homes? If we were to return to valuing human life more than anything else created by God, we would be far better off as a society.

Unfortunately, we have an adversary who prowls about, seeking those he can devour. Satan is alive, he does exist, and he is actively and relentlessly attacking mankind, 24/7. Just watch the news and read the newspaper!

The term "compassion" appears eighty-two times in the NIV Bible. Here are just a few:

- "But you, Lord, are a compassionate and gracious God, slow to anger, abounding in love and faithfulness" (Psalm 86:15).

- "As a father has compassion on his children, so the Lord has compassion on those who fear him" (Psalm 103:13).

- "As God's chosen people, holy and dearly loved, clothe yourselves with compassion, kindness, humility, gentleness and patience" (Colossians 3:12).

- "Be sympathetic, love one another, be compassionate and humble" (1 Peter 3:8).

Public "Awareness" month is another area of compassion that's important but out of balance. Being a big fan of the NFL, and especially my Green Bay Packers, I watch a lot of football, which happens to coincide with October's breast cancer awareness month. NFL players and officials show their support by wearing pink shoes, pink armbands, wristbands, etc.

The show of support is great, but I don't understand why only breast cancer is brought to the forefront. Certainly, breast cancer is an awful disease; two of my aunts had breast cancer. But my point is that there are other types of cancer equally as devastating. My uncle died at the very young age of two, due to complications with Leukemia. My good friend's mom and my grandfather both died from lung cancer. A former coworker had stage four prostate cancer. Awful stuff. Absolutely devastating. I just simply wonder why other cancers don't get the same publicity as breast cancer. Compassion should be a part of all areas of suffering, including mental illness and caring for orphans and widows.

> Religion that God our Father accepts as pure and faultless is this: to look after orphans and widows in their distress and to keep oneself from being polluted by the world. (James 1:27)

Traditional Family and Parenting

At church, I saw a man who presented himself as a man's man—a husband, father, leader, and protector. He was a big guy, probably 6'3" and 250 pounds. He was affectionate with his wife and two boys (about ages eight and twelve), rubbing their shoulders often and hugging them. I thought *That's the kind of man I respect.* I could see that he was a man who led his family as the loving and honoring patriarch. That demonstration of male qualities, by God's design, was so cool to see and exactly what this country needs from men, now more than ever: real men.

Thanks to feminism, encouragement of homosexuality, and political correctness, our society has a rapidly growing number of effeminate males—so-called "men" who prefer other men over women, "men" who are into fashion and design (metrosexuals), and "men" who would rather play patty-cake than watch sports or go hunting.

Man up, males!

Watching the husband and father in church, I may have had a little jealousy. He seemed to have it all, including the image of an all-around man's man. It was great to see. We need for our males to be *men*.

The mentality among many today is that teachers, others, and the government should play the role of parent while parents chase their big-dollar careers and dreams, and deadbeat parents go out and get drunk and sleep around. Their children are left with gaps and must decide how to nurture themselves, though they lack knowledge of the essentials needed to become whole, healthy adults. So, they absorb what they can from their parents' leftover energy, time, attention, and nurturing (if any), and survive with less or no structure, direction, values, morals, ethics, or a sense of their value as human beings.

Part-time parenting leaves children in practical, emotional, and mental seclusion that encourages inactivity—playing video games for hours rather than playing outside, not getting the sunshine and fresh air they need, not discovering and learning from nature and the experiences brought by climbing trees, exercising in outdoor play, kicking the can, running with the dog, bike riding, and neighborhood pickup games. A vast number of children are latch-key kids or sat with by other adults or teens and tragically left to easily wander into and digest all that is unhealthy, warping, and life-threatening. They become exposed to the traps of pornography, scams, and other lures for the vulnerable to fall into the hands of those who seek to do harm: molesters, sex traffickers, cults, false religions—even within their schools and churches and clubs with unwilling and part-time parents as convenient sitters.

The root of a collapsing society is the lack of dedicated, committed, hands-on, invested, godly, full-time parenting.

Without such parents tending to their children, a kid's mind quickly becomes stagnated and warped. Their overall health and safety is at risk across the board, emotionally, mentally, physically, and spiritually.

Christianity

Be a dedicated, full-time, godly parent.

I heard a commercial to this effect: "See, a woman *can* raise a man."

The question isn't whether a mother can raise a son into manhood (which she cannot fully) but rather the quality of raising children without a father. A boy needs his father to instill in his boy what a mother was not created to instill (and thereby cannot instill).

In my observation, a boy raised solely by his mother or grandmother (which is increasingly the case) turns a boy into an indecisive, shy, introvert. Children need their respective fathers to be fully involved in their lives! The lack of fathering is why society is in such a sad state today, including in the black community—which isn't racist but fact. I would love to see the black community thrive, which starts with dedicated dads.

Too many families are broken, leaving the mother to raise the children. And society complicates and confuses homelife all the more by redefining the family to include two "dads" or two "moms." Essentially, redefining fathers, and the absence of fathers, teaches children that dads are not needed. We see this teaching and mindset in a lot of movies and TV series. The man is frequently portrayed as either a bumbling idiot or some mean ogre. What happened to creating TV shows and movies that portray moral, invested, intelligent fathers, like the show *Father Knows Best* with Robert Young and *Leave it to Beaver* with Hugh Beaumont? Watching *Leave it to Beaver* makes me happy.

I give credit to single mothers; that's a tough road. *Fathers* need to be available, accessible, and invested in their children's upbringing.

Absent fathers and mothers fail society.

Fathers matter. Mothers matter. The traditional family matters.

I'm repeating myself because this truth is critical:

Traditional parents and families are the backbone of society.

Without two-parent, heterosexual parenting, society suffers and erodes morally. Again, just watch and read the daily news and trace the childhood backgrounds of criminals.

This country does not need a president or priest to save us from our demise, we need to turn to God in humble repentance and faith. We need strong, traditional families with a father and mother dedicated to their biblical, traditional roles.

Parenting matters. Traditional values matter.

Conclusion

During the 7th inning stretch of the 2012 World Series between Detroit and San Francisco, I was listening as "God Bless America" was being sung. But God will not continue to bless our nation as long as we're continuing to go against His Word. Dispute and argue this point all you want, but He will not forever stand by, nor idly, as we see gay "marriage" legalized and the increase in violence, greed, corruption, and other sin. Ironically, "God Bless America" was sung in San Francisco, a city known for its liberal views and increasingly ungodly lifestyles. A comparable city is Las Vegas, home to gambling, greed, and prostitution.

A year later, I watched the Boston Red Sox defeat the St. Louis Cardinals in the 2013 World Series in Boston and found it ironic that "God Bless America" was sung in the seventh inning. Can a city be any more liberal and anti-God than Boston and San Francisco? We can look at the state of Massachusetts, too, with their liberal views on gun control and gay "marriage."

Say all you want about God blessing America, but He's proving to be who He is: long-suffering. He's also just and hates sin, and there will come a time of judgement. God continuing to bless our country is unlikely unless our nation of individuals repents and returns to our formerly godly roots as a nation. God wants mankind to return our hearts and lives to Him so we can be all that He created us each to be, for His glory and purposes. The question should not be, "Where is God?", but rather, "Why would we not choose God?"

I pray our country will turn back to Jesus, repent of sin, and humbly return to right living. We can do this!

Furthermore...

- We must teach children the truth of Jesus Christ in schools.

- We must enforce the Defense of Marriage Act (DOMA).

- We must ban euthanasia.

- We must let the free market run its course regarding health insurance.

- We must remove government from our personal health care decisions.

- We must defend our Constitution.

- We must vote into office at every level—from school board and city councils to the presidential administration—those whose hearts and lives are clearly dedicated to Jesus Christ.

**Christian conservatives know the solution:
the gospel of Jesus Christ.**

Conclusion

Are you ready for Christ's return? Are you ready to meet your Maker if you were to die today? Only He knows those dates.

Before me every knee will bow; by me every tongue will swear. They will say of me, "In the Lord alone are deliverance and strength." All who have raged against him will come to him and be put to shame. (Isaiah 45:23–24)

God's "Epilogue: Invitation and Warning"

---

through the apostle John

[Jesus] "Look, I am coming soon! My reward is with me, and I will give to each person according to what they have done. I am the Alpha and the Omega, the First and the Last, the Beginning and the End.

"Blessed are those who wash their robes, that they may have the right to the tree of life and may go through the gates into the city. Outside are the dogs, those who practice magic arts, the sexually immoral, the murderers, the idolaters and everyone who loves and practices falsehood.

"I, Jesus, have sent my angel to give you this testimony for the churches. I am the Root and the Offspring of David, and the bright Morning Star."

[Apostle John] "The Spirit and the bride say, 'Come!' And let the one who hears say, 'Come!' Let the one who is thirsty come; and let the one who wishes take the free gift of the water of life.

"I warn everyone who hears the words of the prophecy of this scroll: If anyone adds anything to them, God will add to that person the plagues described in this scroll. And if anyone takes words away from this scroll of prophecy, God will take away from that person any share in the tree of life and in the Holy City, which are described in this scroll.

"He [Jesus] who testifies to these things says, 'Yes, I am coming soon.'

"Amen. Come, Lord Jesus.

"The grace of the Lord Jesus be with God's people. Amen."

(Revelation 22:12–21)

How to Talk to God and Receive Jesus as Your Savior

Simply start speaking from a sincere heart, either aloud or from within. He is with you. He is listening. He will answer.

Example Prayer of Salvation:

"Dear God, I know I am a sinner. I want to turn from my sins, and I ask for Your forgiveness. I believe that Jesus Christ is Your Son. I believe He died for my sins and that You raised Him to life. I want Him to come into my heart and to take control of my life. I want to trust Jesus as my Savior and follow Him as my Lord from this day forward. In Jesus' Name, amen."

—Billy Graham "Peace with God"

www.peacewithgod.net/steps

Recommended Resources

Must Reads

Free Bible – www.biblesforamerica.org

Free Pocket Constitution of the United States – https://lp.hillsdale.edu/free-pocket-constitution/

Books

Killing the Deep State: The Fight to Save President Trump by Jerome R. Corsi, PhD

The Blueprint: How the Democrats Won Colorado (and Why Republicans Everywhere Should Care) by Rob Witwer and Adam Schrager

Biblically Solid Teacher-Pastors (my starting 5)

Ronald L. Dart – www.borntowin.net

David Jeremiah – www.davidjeremiah.org

Greg Laurie – www.harvest.org

Adrian Rogers – www.lwf.org

Charles Stanley – www.intouch.org

Christian Radio News

WVCY, Milwaukee, Wisconsin – www.vcy.org

KLTT, Denver, Colorado – www.670kltt.com

Websites

Alliance Defending Freedom – www.adflegal.org

Authentic Manhood – www.authenticmanhood.com

Christian Information – www.vcy.org

Covenant Eyes – www.covenanteyes.com

Ever Accountable – www.everaccountable.com

Fathers in the Field – www.fathersinthefield.com

Focus on the Family – www.focusonthefamily.com

Freedom in Christ – www.freedominchrist.com

Parents Defending Education – www.defendinged.org

Ramsey (financial fitness) – www.ramseysolutions.com

Government and Conservative News

American Policy Center – www.americanpolicy.org

Americans for Limited Government – www.getliberty.org

Recommended Resources

Family Research Council – www.frc.org

Imprimis – A Publication of Hillsdale College – www.imprimis.hillsdale.edu

Media Research Center – www.mrc.org

Nation for Marriage – www.nationformarriage.org

The Heritage Foundation – www.heritage.org

The New American – www.thenewamerican.com

World Net Daily – www.wnd.com

Worldview Weekend – www.worldviewweekend.com

Get Involved

40 Days for Life (a pro-life organization) – www.40daysforlife.com

Act for America (a grassroots movement dedicated to preserving America's culture, sovereignty, and security) – www.actforamerica.org

Fraternal Order of Police (the voice of our nation's law enforcement officers) – www.fop.net

Gun Owners of America (a no-compromise gun lobby) – www.gunowners.org

The Republican Party (better than Marxism!) – www.rnc.org

Endnotes

1   "The Pledge of Allegiance - the U.S. Constitution Online," The Pledge of Allegiance - The U.S. Constitution Online - USConstitution.net, accessed May 19, 2023, https://usconstitution.net/pledge.html.

2   "Heritage Foundation Releases 2023 Index of U.S. Military Strength, Gives U.S. Military First-Ever 'weak' Overall Rating," The Heritage Foundation, accessed May 19, 2023, https://www.heritage.org/press/heritage-foundation-releases-2023-index-us-military-strength-gives-us-military-first-ever.

3   Ibid.

4   Ibid.

5   Ibid.

6   U.S. Department of The Treasury, "Debt to the Penny," U.S. Treasury Fiscal Data, accessed May 17, 2023, https://fiscaldata.treasury.gov/datasets/debt-to-the-penny/debt-to-the-penny.

7   Ibid.

8   "NET Interest Will Total $10.5 Trillion over the next Decade," Committee for a Responsible Federal Budget, accessed May 19, 2023, https://www.crfb.org/blogs/net-interest-will-total-105-trillion-over-next-decade.

9   "President Obama Welcomes Gay Marriage Ruling," BBC News, accessed May 22, 2023, https://www.bbc.com/news/av/world-us-canada-33287079.

10   MJ Lee, Betsy Klein, and Kevin Liptak, "Biden Signs into Law Same-Sex Marriage Bill, 10 Years after His Famous Sunday Show Answer on the Issue | CNN Politics," CNN, December 13, 2022, https://www.cnn.com/2022/12/13/politics/white-house-same-sex-marriage-signing-ceremony/index.html.

11   National Geographic, "Doomsday Preppers," *YouTube*, https://www.youtube.com/watch?v=cSfxmOS3Naw.

12   About our party | GOP - Republican National Committee | GOP, accessed May 22, 2023, https://www.gop.com/about-our-party/.

13   Alec Torres, "Cuomo: Pro-Lifers Not Welcome in New York Remark Was 'Distorted,'" National Review, October 10, 2017, https://www.nationalreview.com/corner/cuomo-pro-lifers-not-welcome-new-york-remark-was-distorted-alec-torres/.

14   Jeffrey M. Jones, "U.S. Political Party Preferences Shifted Greatly during 2021," Gallup.com, September 21, 2022, https://news.gallup.com/poll/388781/political-party-preferences-shifted-greatly-during-2021.aspx.

15   Jeff Diamant, "What the Data Says about Abortion in the U.S.," Pew Research Center, January 11, 2023, https://www.pewresearch.org/short-reads/2023/01/11/what-the-data-says-about-abortion-in-the-u-s-2/.

16   Democrats, accessed May 23, 2023, https://democrats.org/where-we-stand/party-platform.

17   Ibid.

18   Ibid.

19   Ibid.

20   "Guttmacher Institute Releases 2020 Abortion Provider Census with Important Data on US Abortion Landscape before the Fall of Roe," Guttmacher Institute, February 8, 2023, https://www.guttmacher.org/news-release/2022/guttmacher-institute-releases-2020-abortion-provider-census-important-data-us.

21   Jeff Diamant, "What the Data Says about Abortion in the U.S.," Pew Research Center, January 11, 2023, https://www.pewresearch.org/short-reads/2023/01/11/what-the-data-says-about-abortion-in-the-u-s-2/.

22   Abortion rates by state 2023, accessed May 23, 2023, https://worldpopulationreview.com/state-rankings/abortion-rates-by-state.

23   Democrats, accessed May 23, 2023, https://democrats.org/where-we-stand/party-platform.

24   Justin Worland, "John Kerry Says U.S. Should Help Address Climate Damages," Time, October 28, 2022, https://time.com/6225834/john-kerry-loss-and-damage-climate-interview/.

25   "Climate Change Deniers Should Be in Prison...," YouTube, September 21, 2015, https://www.youtube.com/watch?v=go33Llz8hFs.

Endnotes

26 "Kim Davis, Kentucky Clerk, Held in Contempt and Ordered to Jail," NBCNews.com, September 3, 2015, https://www.nbcnews.com/news/us-news/kentucky-clerk-kim-davis-held-contempt-court-n421126.

27 "Sexually Transmitted Infections (Stis)," World Health Organization, accessed May 23, 2023, https://www.who.int/news-room/fact-sheets/detail/sexually-transmitted-infections-(stis).

28 Tea party. Accessed May 24, 2023. https://teaparty.org/about-us/.

29 Dr Tim Dean, "What Is Moral Relativism? An Ethics Explainer by the Ethics Centre," THE ETHICS CENTRE, February 17, 2021, https://ethics.org.au/ethics-explainer-moral-relativism/.

30 "Platform," Libertarian Party, June 1, 2022, https://www.lp.org/platform/.

31 Ibid.

32 Ibid.

33 Tea party. Accessed May 24, 2023. https://teaparty.org/about-us/.

34 Jimmie D. Martin, "Tea Party Principles from Teaparty.Org....15 Non-Negotiable Core Beliefs," Tea Party principles from teaparty.org....15 Non-negotiable Core Beliefs, accessed May 24, 2023, https://webteaparty.blogspot.com/2014/12/tea-party-principles-from-teapartyorg15.html.

35 "About," *OccupyWallStreet*, http://occupywallst.org/about/.

36 "Acorn," InfluenceWatch, September 29, 2020, https://www.influencewatch.org/non-profit/acorn/.

37 Christian Schneider, "City of Madison Thanks the Occupy Movement," National Review, October 10, 2017, https://www.nationalreview.com/corner/city-madison-thanks-occupy-movement-christian-schneider/.

38 "As the Website of Saudi Tourism Authority States LGBTQ Are 'welcome in the Kingdom,' Jihadis Suggest ISIS-Style Execution, Opposition to Saudi Government Decry 'Moral Decline,'" MEMRI, May 8, 2023, https://www.memri.org/jttm/website-saudi-tourism-authority-states-lgbtq-are-welcome-kingdom-jihadis-suggest-isis-style.

39 "What Is the Employer Mandate?," healthinsurance.org, February 27, 2023, https://www.healthinsurance.org/glossary/employer-mandate/.

40 Common core states [updated May 2023], accessed May 26, 2023, https://worldpopulationreview.com/state-rankings/common-core-states.

41 Kristan Hawkins, "Remove Statues of Margaret Sanger, Planned Parenthood Founder Tied to Eugenics and Racism," USA Today, July 23, 2020,

https://www.usatoday.com/story/opinion/2020/07/23/racism-eugenics-margaret-sanger-deserves-no-honors-column/5480192002/.

42   Planned Parenthood, "The Maggie Awards Recognize Contributions Made by the Media and Arts That Enhance the Public's Understanding of Reproductive Rights and Health Care Issues.," Planned Parenthood, accessed May 26, 2023, https://www.plannedparenthood.org/about-us/newsroom/campaigns/ppfa-margaret-sanger-award-winners#.

43   Planned Parenthood, "Campaigns," Planned Parenthood, accessed May 26, 2023, https://www.plannedparenthood.org/about-us/newsroom/campaigns#.

44   Denise Burke, " Protecting it's abortion business," September 4, 2019, *USA TODAY*, https://www.usatoday.com/story/opinion/2019/09/04/planned-parenthood-whistleblower-lawsuit-abortion-choice-rights-column/2208047001/.

45   "Constitution of the United States, First Amendment," Constitution Annotated, https://constitution.congress.gov/constitution/amendment-1.

46   "Woke Definition & Meaning," Merriam-Webster, accessed June 1, 2023, https://www.merriam-webster.com/dictionary/woke.

47   "gay," *Online Etymology Dictionary*, https://www.etymonline.com/word/gay/.

48   "DSD :: Resources - Publications - Core Publications," United Nations, accessed May 28, 2023, https://www.un.org/esa/dsd/agenda21/.

49   "What is the difference between global warming and climate change," *USGA*, https://www.usgs.gov/faqs/what-difference-between-global-warming-and-climate-change-1?qt-news_science_products=0#qt-news_science_products/.

50   Devin Willems, "Furries in Wisconsin Schools? Districts Respond to Alleged 'Furry Protocols,'" WFRV Local 5 - Green Bay, Appleton, April 27, 2022, https://www.wearegreenbay.com/news/local-news/furries-in-wisconsin-schools-districts-respond-to-alleged-furry-protocols/.

51   "A-38. Persons Not in the Labor Force by Desire and Availability for Work, Age, and Sex," U.S. Bureau of Labor Statistics, accessed May 29, 2023, https://www.bls.gov/web/empsit/cpseea38.htm#cps_eande_m38.f.1/.

52   "Entitlement Programs," Federal Safety Net, February 21, 2023, https://federalsafetynet.com/entitlement-programs/.

53   FNS-prod.azureedge.us, accessed May 30, 2023, https://fns-prod.azureedge.us/sites/default/files/data-files/keydata-february-2023.pdf.

Endnotes

54   "February 2023 Medicaid & Chip Enrollment Data Highlights," Medicaid, accessed May 30, 2023, https://www.medicaid.gov/medicaid/program-information/medicaid-and-chip-enrollment-data/report-highlights/index.html.

55   March 2022 Medicaid and Chip Enrollment Snapshot, accessed May 30, 2023, https://www.medicaid.gov/medicaid/national-medicaid-chip-program-information/downloads/march-2022-medicaid-chip-enrollment-trend-snapshot.pdf.

56   "Log into Facebook," Facebook, accessed May 31, 2023, https://www.facebook.com/notes/3281898858572186/.

57   Brannon Howse, *Grave Influence: 21 Radicals and Their Worldviews That Rule America from the Grave* (Collierville, TN: Worldview Weekend Pub., 2009).

58   Craig Wilson, "'Feminine Mystique' at 50: Timelessly Revolutionary," USA Today, February 12, 2013, https://www.usatoday.com/story/life/books/2013/02/11/betty-friedan-feminine-mystique-50th-anniversary/1899371/.

59   Betty Friedan, *The Feminine Mystique*, 27, (New York: Dell Publishing, 1983).

60   Ibid, 67.

61   Author Archives, zb163054, "Extra Credit," "History 1000: American Society and the Individual, Fall 2013," December 14, 2013, Blogs@Baruch, https://blogs.baruch.cuny.edu/his1000fall2013/?author=14442/.

62   "Power to the People Plan," My WordPress, accessed October 27, 2023, https://jillstein.org/power-to-the-people-plan/.

63   Ibid.

64   Contributors to Alvin and the Chipmunks Wiki, "Going Green," Alvin and the Chipmunks Wiki, accessed October 27, 2023, https://alvin.fandom.com/wiki/Going_Green/.

65   "Earthstock," *Stony Brook University*, https://www.stonybrook.edu/commcms/campus-operations/recycling/events/earthstock/.

66   Child trafficking Statistics, *Ark of Hope for Children*, https://arkofhopeforchildren.org/child-trafficking/child-trafficking-statistics/.

67   "How Much Does the U.S. Contribute to the UN?," Council on Foreign Relations, accessed July 4, 2023, https://www.cfr.org/article/funding-united-nations-what-impact-do-us-contributions-have-un-agencies-and-programs#/.

68	Nile Gardiner, "Kofi Annan's Legacy of Failure," *American Heritage Foundation*, https://www.heritage.org/report/kofi-annans-legacy-failure/.

69	"Kofi Annan's Legacy of Failure," The Heritage Foundation, accessed October 27, 2023, https://www.heritage.org/report/kofi-annans-legacy-failure.

70	Element Books, Ltd., *Agenda 21: The Earth Summit Strategy to Save Our Planet*, EarthPress, 1993, https://www.google.com/books/edition/Agenda_21/8LsyAAAAMAAJ/.

71	"President's Council on Sustainable Development," *National Archives*, https://www.archives.gov/files/federal-register/executive-orders/pdf/12852.pdf

72	Pacific Freedom Foundation, "Crimes Against Humanity (You) Are Being Executed Right Here—Right Now—in Your State and Town," https://olis.leg.state.or.us/liz/2013R1/Downloads/CommitteeMeetingDocument/19055/.

73	Raven Claybough, "UN Small Arms Treaty Targets Second Amendment Rights," *The New American*, https://thenewamerican.com/un-small-arms-treaty-targets-second-amendment-rights/.

74	"Understanding The Teen Brain," *University of Rochester Medical Center*, https://www.urmc.rochester.edu/encyclopedia/content.aspx?ContentTypeID=1&ContentID=3051/.

75	Thurgood Marshall, "The Bicentennial Speech," *Thurgood Marshall*, http://thurgoodmarshall.com/the-bicentennial-speech/.

76	Michael C. Dorstewitz, "A Baker's Dozen of Trump's Top Accomplishments," Newsmax, June 14, 2021, http://www.newsmax.com/bestlists/donald-j-trump-accomplishments-america-first/2021/06/14/id/1025067. 1. Michael C. Dorstewitz, "A Baker's Dozen of Trump's Top Accomplishments," Newsmax, June 14, 2021, http://www.newsmax.com/bestlists/donald-j-trump-accomplishments-america-first/2021/06/14/id/1025067.

77	"Biden's Budget: A Future That's Built on Government Dependence," The U.S. House Committee on the Budget - House Budget Committee, March 15, 2023, https://budget.house.gov/press-release/7582/.

78	Andrew Clevenger, "Congress Made $80 Billion-plus in Changes to Defense Budget," Roll Call, October 4, 2023, https://rollcall.com/2023/10/04/congress-made-80-billion-plus-in-changes-to-defense-budget/.

79	Remy Tumin, "Same-Sex Couple Households in U.S. Surpass One Million," The New York Times, December 2, 2022, https://www.nytimes.com/2022/12/02/us/same-sex-households-census.html.

Endnotes

80   Kimberly Amadeo, reviewed by Somer G. Anderson on March 21, 2021, "National Debt Under Obama," *The Balance*, https://www.thebalance.com/national-debt-under-obama-3306293/.

81   Republican Governors Associationstated on April 29 et al., "Politifact - Republican Governors Association Says Mayor Tom Barrett's Policies Drove up Unemployment 27 Percent in Milwaukee," @politifact, accessed October 27, 2023, https://www.politifact.com/factchecks/2012/apr/11/republican-governors-association/republican-governors-association-says-mayor-tom-ba/.

82   "Tax Rates - 1984 to Present," Tax Rates - 1984 to Present, accessed October 27, 2023, https://city.milwaukee.gov/assessor/data/TaxRates1984toPresen725/.

83   "Eminent Domain," Encyclopædia Britannica, October 18, 2023, https://www.britannica.com/topic/eminent-domain/.

84   Ashira Ostrow, "Minority Interests, Majority Politics: A Comment on Richard Collins' "Telluride's Tale of Eminent Domain, Home Rule, and Retroactivity," Scholarly Commons at Hostra Law, 2009, https://scholarlycommons.law.hofstra.edu/cgi/viewcontent.cgi?referer=&httpsredir=1&article=1176&context=faculty_scholarship/.

85   "Where Do Abortion Rights Stand in the World in 2023?," Focus 2030, accessed August 4, 2023, https://focus2030.org/Where-do-abortion-rights-stand-in-the-world-in-2023/.

86   Usama Dakdok, "Islam," *The Straight Way of Grace Ministry*, https://www.thestraightway.org/learn-from-usama/frequently-asked-questions-and-answers/pages/islam/.

87   INC The Straight Way of Grace Ministry, "Women in Islam," The Straight Way of Grace Ministry, INC, accessed October 27, 2023, https://www.thestraightway.org/usamas-teaching/frequently-asked-questions-and-answers/pages/women-in-islam/.

88   The Takeaway, "Egyptians mark one-year anniversary of Arab Spring protests in their country," January 25, 2-12, *TheWord*, https://www.pri.org/stories/2012-01-25/egyptians-mark-one-year-anniversary-arab-spring-protests-their-country/.

89   Jennifer Hansler, "Biden Administration Authorizes $2.5 Billion in Arms Sales to Egypt despite Human Rights Concerns | CNN Politics," CNN, January 25, 2022, https://www.cnn.com/2022/01/25/politics/us-arms-sales-egypt/index.html.

90   Ian Tuttle, "El Chapo's Capture Puts 'Operation Fast and Furious' Back in the Headlines," January 22, 2016, *National Review*, https://www.nationalreview.com/2016/01/fast-furious-obama-first-scandal/.

91   "Peace through Strength," Ronald Reagan, accessed October 27, 2023, https://www.reaganlibrary.gov/permanent-exhibits/peace-through-strength/.

92   LGBTQ studies, accessed October 27, 2023, https://www.colorado.edu/lgbtq/.

93   "GLAAD TV Spot, 'Transgender Family: Max,'" iSpot.tv | Realtime TV Advertising Performance Measurement, accessed August 16, 2023, http://www.ispot.tv/ad/b1sD/glaad-transgender-family-max/.

94   Carol Glatz, "Pope Clarifies Remarks about Homosexuality and Sin," USCCB, January 30, 2023, https://www.usccb.org/news/2023/pope-clarifies-remarks-about-homosexuality-and-sin/.

95   "Pope Says He Won't Judge Gay Priests," POLITICO, accessed August 18, 2023, https://www.politico.com/story/2013/07/pope-francis-gay-priests-094854/.

96   USA TODAY Sports, "Michelle Obama: Michael Sam Is an 'Inspiration to All,'" The Indianapolis Star, February 10, 2014, https://www.indystar.com/story/sports/2014/02/10/michelle-obama-openly-gay-football-player-michael-sam-is-inspiration/5364653/.

97   Marissa Mayer, "How a Car Accident Reignited Kelsey Grammer's Faith & Saved Him from Addiction," Pureflix, August 10, 2023, https://www.pureflix.com/insider/kelsey-grammers-faith-addiction/.

98   Bryan Robinson, "Christian Athletes: Pointing Others to Jesus through Sports," 316Tees, January 17, 2022, https://www.316tees.com/blogs/316/christian-athletes#/.

99   Kate Dailey, "Fred Phelps: How Westboro Pastor Spread 'God Hates Fags,'" BBC News, March 21, 2014, https://www.bbc.com/news/magazine-26582812/.

100   Leroy Butler, @leap36, Twitter, April 29, 2013.

101   Sharon Pruitt-Young, "Carl Nassib's Experience Coming out Is Very Different from NFL Players before Him," NPR, June 23, 2021, https://www.npr.org/2021/06/22/1009180945/carl-nassibs-experience-coming-out-is-very-different-from-nfl-players-before-him/.

102   Sophie Austin, "California Will Try to Enshrine Right to Same-Sex Marriage," AP NEWS, February 15, 2023, https://apnews.com/article/california-state-government-scott-wiener-san-francisco-marriage-769914918583e62f3c186cbd52046f5a/.

103   Iowa Legislative Services Agency, Iowa legislature - billbook, accessed May 25, 2023, https://www.legis.iowa.gov/legislation/BillBook?ga=90&ba=hjr8/.

Endnotes

104   Marriage and Civil Union - Jefferson Center, accessed August 24, 2023, https://www.jcmh.org/wp-content/uploads/Civil-Unions-and-Marriages-1-1.pdf.

105   Same sex marriage states [updated May 2023], accessed August 24, 2023, https://worldpopulationreview.com/state-rankings/same-sex-marriage-states/.

106   "California Voters Will Be Asked to Reaffirm Gay Marriage Protections on 2024 Ballot," Los Angeles Times, July 14, 2023, https://www.latimes.com/california/story/2023-07-14/california-voters-will-be-asked-to-reaffirm-gay-marriage-protections-on-2024-ballot/.

107   Danielle Taylor, "Same-Sex Couples Are More Likely to Adopt or Foster Children," Census.gov, October 8, 2021, https://www.census.gov/library/stories/2020/09/fifteen-percent-of-same-sex-couples-have-children-in-their-household.html.

108   JC, "Jamie Foxx Calls Barack Obama 'Our Lord and Saviour,'" Praise 104.1, July 2, 2019, https://praisedc.com/1323603/jamie-foxx-calls-barack-obama-our-lord-and-saviour/.

109   Cyd Zeigler and Jim Buzinski, "These 61 Current NFL Players, 13 Owners and 9 Head Coaches Support Gay and Bi Athletes," Outsports, October 27, 2022, https://www.outsports.com/2022/10/27/23425352/nfl-gay-bi-players-straight-support-lgbt-rk-russell/.

110   "Federal Officials Close Investigation into Death of Trayvon Martin," Office of Public Affairs | Federal Officials Close Investigation Into Death of Trayvon Martin | United States Department of Justice, August 26, 2015, https://www.justice.gov/opa/pr/federal-officials-close-investigation-death-trayvon-martin/.

111   Camila Domonoske, "Singer Alters Canadian Anthem to Say 'all Lives Matter' at All-Star Game," NPR, July 13, 2016, https://www.npr.org/sections/thetwo-way/2016/07/13/485822835/singer-alters-canadian-anthem-to-say-all-lives-matter-at-all-star-ga/.

112   "Will Graham Devotion: 4 Ways to Spot False Teaching," Billy Graham Evangelistic Association, May 5, 2023, http://www.billygraham.org/story/will-graham-devotion-4-ways-to-spot-false/.

113   "About Us," Unity.org, accessed October 27, 2023, https://www.unity.org/static/about-us/.

114   Ibid.

115   Ibid.

116   Ibid.

117   "World Religion Day 2023: History and Significance," cnbctv18.com, January 15, 2023, https://www.cnbctv18.com/world/world-religion-day-2023-history-and-significance-15661981.htm.

118   Editor, "Starbucks CEO to Shareholder: If You Support Biblical Marriage, Sell Your Shares," Christian News Network, March 28, 2013, https://christiannews.net/2013/03/24/starbucks-ceo-to-shareholder-if-you-support-biblical-marriage-sell-your-shares/.

119   Luiz Sérgio Solimeo, "Pope Francis: 'If I See the Gospel in a Sociological Way Only, Yes, I Am a Communist, and So Too Is Jesus,'" The American TFP, December 19, 2022, https://www.tfp.org/pope-francis-if-i-see-the-gospel-in-a-sociological-way-only-yes-i-am-a-communist-and-so-too-is-jesus/.

120   Steve Schultze, "Panel backs contract for firm that hired sex offender, *Journal Sentinel*, http://archive.jsonline.com/news/milwaukee/panel-backs-contract-for-firm-that-hired-sex-offender-os5rk2s-159792565.html.

121   James A. Batovsky, *Milwaukee Journal Sentinel*, https://www.legacy.com/us/obituaries/jsonline/name/james-batovsky-obituary?id=3237874/.

122   "What does the Bible say about suicide," *Got Questions*, https://www.gotquestions.org/suicide-Bible-Christian.html.

123   "NeighborhoodScout's Most Dangerous Cities – 2023," NeighborhoodScout, September 5, 2023, https://www.neighborhoodscout.com/blog/top100dangerous/.

124   Rob Cirillo, "Home Burglary Facts and Stats for 2023," Securiteam, August 3, 2023, https://securiteam.us/2023/08/03/home-burglary-facts-and-stats-for-2023/.

125   Linda Greenhouse, "Justices Rule Police Do Not Have a Constitutional Duty to Protect Someone," *The New York Times*, https://www.nytimes.com/2005/06/28/politics/justices-rule-police-do-not-have-a-constitutional-duty-to-protect.html.

126   "Constitution of the United States, Second Amendment," *Constitution Annotated*, https://constitution.congress.gov/constitution/amendment-2/.

127   Jared Smith, "(Video) Syracuse Orange coach Jim Boeheim takes a stance in favor of gun control," December 18, 2012, https://newyork.sbnation.com/syracuse-orange-basketball/2012/12/18/3779280/syracuse-orange-coach-jim-boeheim-gun-control-comments-newton-ct-school-shooting/.

128   "Colorado Gun Laws," CSP, accessed October 6, 2023, https://csp.colorado.gov/i-want-to/colorado-gun-laws/.

Endnotes

129   Author: Katie Kyros, "Baltimore Back 'open for Business' despite Destruction," fox43.com, May 5, 2015, https://www.fox43.com/article/news/local/contests/baltimore-back-open-for-business-despite-destruction/521-643cf52b-9be6-4d07-8a66-0fdc56fd7248/.

130   "Prison Closure," *Bureau of Federal Prisons*, https://www.bop.gov/about/history/alcatraz.jsp

131   "Senators Urge Biden To Shut Down Guantánamo, Calling It A 'Symbol Of Lawlessness,'" *NPR*, https://www.npr.org/2021/04/16/988078547/senators-urge-biden-to-shut-down-guantanamo-calling-it-a-symbol-of-lawlessness/.

132   CT Editors, "The 50 Countries Where It's Most Dangerous to Follow Jesus in 2021," News & Reporting, January 13, 2021, https://www.christianitytoday.com/news/2021/january/christian-persecution-2021-countries-open-doors-watch-list.html.

133   Ibid.

Bibliography

"5 Things the Bible Says about Work." Billy Graham Evangelistic Association, September 1, 2022. https://billygraham.org/story/5-things-the-bible-says-about-work/.

"A-38. Persons Not in the Labor Force by Desire and Availability for Work, Age, and Sex." U.S. Bureau of Labor Statistics. Accessed May 29, 2023. https://www.bls.gov/web/empsit/cpseea38.htm#cps_eande_m38.f.1/.

Abortion rates by state 2023. Accessed May 23, 2023. https://worldpopulationreview.com/state-rankings/abortion-rates-by-state/.

About our party | GOP - Republican National Committee | GOP. Accessed May 22, 2023. https://www.gop.com/about-our-party/.

"About Us." Unity.org. Accessed October 27, 2023. https://www.unity.org/static/about-us/.

"Acorn." InfluenceWatch, September 29, 2020. https://www.influencewatch.org/non-profit/acorn/.

Agency, Iowa Legislative Services. Iowa legislature - billbook. Accessed May 25, 2023. https://www.legis.iowa.gov/legislation/BillBook?ga=90&ba=hjr8/.

"As the Website of Saudi Tourism Authority States LGBTQ Are 'welcome in the Kingdom,' Jihadis Suggest ISIS-Style Execution, Opposition to Saudi Government Decry 'Moral Decline.'" MEMRI, May 8, 2023. https://www.memri.org/jttm/website-saudi-tourism-authority-states-lgbtq-are-welcome-kingdom-jihadis-suggest-isis-style/.

Austin, Sophie. "California Will Try to Enshrine Right to Same-Sex Marriage." AP NEWS, February 15, 2023. https://apnews.com/article/california-state-government-scott-wiener-san-francisco-marriage-769914918583e62f3c186cbd52046f5a/.

"Biden's Budget: A Future That's Built on Government Dependence." The U.S. House Committee on the Budget - House Budget Committee, March 15, 2023. https://budget.house.gov/press-release/7582/.

"California Voters Will Be Asked to Reaffirm Gay Marriage Protections on 2024 Ballot." Los Angeles Times, July 14, 2023. https://www.latimes.com/california/story/2023-07-14/california-voters-will-be-asked-to-reaffirm-gay-marriage-protections-on-2024-ballot/.

Contributors to Alvin and the Chipmunks Wiki. "Going Green." Alvin and the Chipmunks Wiki. Accessed October 27, 2023. https://alvin.fandom.com/wiki/Going_Green/.

Caporal, Jack. "SNAP Statistics and Eligibility Changes for 2023." The Motley Fool, April 13, 2023. https://www.fool.com/the-ascent/research/snap-statistics-and-eligibility-changes/.

Cirillo, Rob. "Home Burglary Facts and Stats for 2023." Securiteam, August 3, 2023. https://securiteam.us/2023/08/03/home-burglary-facts-and-stats-for-2023/.

Clevenger, Andrew. "Congress Made $80 Billion-plus in Changes to Defense Budget." Roll Call, October 4, 2023. https://rollcall.com/2023/10/04/congress-made-80-billion-plus-in-changes-to-defense-budget/.

"Climate Change Deniers Should Be in Prison..." YouTube, September 21, 2015. https://www.youtube.com/watch?v=go33Llz8hFs/.

"Colorado Gun Laws." CSP. Accessed October 6, 2023. https://csp.colorado.gov/i-want-to/colorado-gun-laws/.

Common core states [updated May 2023]. Accessed May 26, 2023. https://worldpopulationreview.com/state-rankings/common-core-states/.

Dailey, Kate. "Fred Phelps: How Westboro Pastor Spread 'God Hates Fags.'" BBC News, March 21, 2014. https://www.bbc.com/news/magazine-26582812/.

Bibliography

Dean, Dr Tim. "What Is Moral Relativism? An Ethics Explainer by the Ethics Centre." THE ETHICS CENTRE, February 17, 2021. https://ethics.org.au/ethics-explainer-moral-relativism/.

"December 2022 Medicaid and CHIP Enrollment Trends Snapshot Center for Medicaid and CHIP Services." n.d. Accessed May 30, 2023. https://www.medicaid.gov/medicaid/national-medicaid-chip-program-information/downloads/December-2022-medicaid-chip-enrollment-trend-snapshot.pdf.

Democrats. Accessed May 23, 2023. https://democrats.org/where-we-stand/party-platform/.

Diamant, Jeff. "What the Data Says about Abortion in the U.S." Pew Research Center, January 11, 2023. https://www.pewresearch.org/short-reads/2023/01/11/what-the-data-says-about-abortion-in-the-u-s-2/.

Domonoske, Camila. "Singer Alters Canadian Anthem to Say 'all Lives Matter' at All-Star Game." NPR, July 13, 2016. https://www.npr.org/sections/thetwo-way/2016/07/13/485822835/singer-alters-canadian-anthem-to-say-all-lives-matter-at-all-star-ga/.

Dorstewitz, Michael C. "A Baker's Dozen of Trump's Top Accomplishments." Newsmax, June 14, 2021. http://www.newsmax.com/bestlists/donald-j-trump-accomplishments-america-first/2021/06/14/id/1025067/.

"DSD :: Resources - Publications - Core Publications." United Nations. Accessed May 28, 2023. https://www.un.org/esa/dsd/agenda21/.

Editor. "Starbucks CEO to Shareholder: If You Support Biblical Marriage, Sell Your Shares." Christian News Network, March 28, 2013. https://christiannews.net/2013/03/24/starbucks-ceo-to-shareholder-if-you-support-biblical-marriage-sell-your-shares/.

Editors, CT. "The 50 Countries Where It's Most Dangerous to Follow Jesus in 2021." News & Reporting, January 13, 2021. https://www.christianitytoday.com/news/2021/january/christian-persecution-2021-countries-open-doors-watch-list.html.

"Eminent Domain." Encyclopædia Britannica, October 18, 2023. https://www.britannica.com/topic/eminent-domain/.

"Entitlement Programs." Federal Safety Net, February 21, 2023. https://federalsafetynet.com/entitlement-programs/.

"February 2023 Medicaid & Chip Enrollment Data Highlights." Medicaid. Accessed May 30, 2023. https://www.medicaid.gov/medicaid/program-information/medicaid-and-chip-enrollment-data/report-highlights/index.html.

"Federal Officials Close Investigation into Death of Trayvon Martin." Office of Public Affairs | Federal Officials Close Investigation Into Death of Trayvon Martin | United States Department of Justice, August 26, 2015. https://www.justice.gov/opa/pr/federal-officials-close-investigation-death-trayvon-martin/.

FNS-prod.azureedge.us. Accessed May 30, 2023. https://fns-prod.azureedge.us/sites/default/files/data-files/keydata-february-2023.pdf.

Friedan, Betty. *The feminine mystique*. New York: Dell Publishing, 1983.

"GLAAD TV Spot, 'Transgender Family: Max.'" iSpot.tv | Realtime TV Advertising Performance Measurement. Accessed August 16, 2023. http://www.ispot.tv/ad/b1sD/glaad-transgender-family-max/.

Glatz, Carol. "Pope Clarifies Remarks about Homosexuality and Sin." USCCB, January 30, 2023. https://www.usccb.org/news/2023/pope-clarifies-remarks-about-homosexuality-and-sin/.

"Hamas at 35." The Washington Institute. Accessed October 6, 2023. https://www.washingtoninstitute.org/policy-analysis/hamas-35/.

Hansler, Jennifer. "Biden Administration Authorizes $2.5 Billion in Arms Sales to Egypt despite Human Rights Concerns | CNN Politics." CNN, January 25, 2022. https://www.cnn.com/2022/01/25/politics/us-arms-sales-egypt/index.html.

Hawkins, Kristan. "Remove Statues of Margaret Sanger, Planned Parenthood Founder Tied to Eugenics and Racism." USA Today, July 23, 2020. https://www.usatoday.com/story/opinion/2020/07/23/racism-eugenics-margaret-sanger-deserves-no-honors-column/5480192002/.

"Heritage Foundation Releases 2023 Index of U.S. Military Strength, Gives U.S. Military First-Ever 'weak' Overall Rating." The Heritage Foundation. Accessed May 19, 2023. https://www.heritage.org/press/heritage-foundation-releases-2023-index-us-military-strength-gives-us-military-first-ever/.

"How Much Does the U.S. Contribute to the UN?" Council on Foreign Relations. Accessed July 4, 2023. https://www.cfr.org/article/funding-unit-

Bibliography

ed-nations-what-impact-do-us-contributions-have-un-agencies-and-programs#/.

Howse, Brannon. *Grave influence: 21 Radicals and Their Worldviews that Rule America from the Grave*. Collierville, TN: Worldview Weekend Pub., 2009.

JC, "Jamie Foxx Calls Barack Obama 'Our Lord and Saviour.'" Praise 104.1, July 2, 2019. https://praisedc.com/1323603/jamie-foxx-calls-barack-obama-our-lord-and-saviour/.

Jones, Jeffrey M. "U.S. Political Party Preferences Shifted Greatly during 2021." Gallup.com, September 21, 2022. https://news.gallup.com/poll/388781/political-party-preferences-shifted-greatly-during-2021.aspx.

"Kim Davis, Kentucky Clerk, Held in Contempt and Ordered to Jail." NBCNews.com, September 3, 2015. https://www.nbcnews.com/news/us-news/kentucky-clerk-kim-davis-held-contempt-court-n421126/.

"Kofi Annan's Legacy of Failure." The Heritage Foundation. Accessed October 27, 2023. https://www.heritage.org/report/kofi-annans-legacy-failure/.

Koop, Avery. "Mapped: The Most Dangerous Cities in the U.S." Visual Capitalist, August 30, 2023. https://www.visualcapitalist.com/most-dangerous-cities-in-the-us/.

Kyros, Author: Katie. "Baltimore Back 'open for Business' despite Destruction." fox43.com, May 5, 2015. https://www.fox43.com/article/news/local/contests/baltimore-back-open-for-business-despite-destruction/521-643cf52b-9be6-4d07-8a66-0fdc56fd7248/.

Lauren Hall and Catlin Nchako. "A Closer Look at Who Benefits from Snap: State-by-State Fact Sheets." Center on Budget and Policy Priorities. Accessed May 30, 2023. https://www.cbpp.org/research/food-assistance/a-closer-look-at-who-benefits-from-snap-state-by-state-fact-sheets/.

Lee, MJ, Betsy Klein, and Kevin Liptak. "Biden Signs into Law Same-Sex Marriage Bill, 10 Years after His Famous Sunday Show Answer on the Issue | CNN Politics." CNN, December 13, 2022. https://www.cnn.com/2022/12/13/politics/white-house-same-sex-marriage-signing-ceremony/index.html.

LGBTQ studies. Accessed October 27, 2023. https://www.colorado.edu/lgbtq/.

"Log into Facebook." Facebook. Accessed May 31, 2023. https://www.facebook.com/notes/3281898858572186/.

March 2022 Medicaid and Chip Enrollment Snapshot. Accessed May 30, 2023. https://www.medicaid.gov/medicaid/national-medicaid-chip-program-information/downloads/march-2022-medicaid-chip-enrollment-trend-snapshot.pdf.

Marriage and Civil Union - Jefferson Center. Accessed August 24, 2023. https://www.jcmh.org/wp-content/uploads/Civil-Unions-and-Marriages-1-1.pdf.

Mayer, Marissa. "How a Car Accident Reignited Kelsey Grammer's Faith & Saved Him from Addiction." Pureflix, August 10, 2023. https://www.pureflix.com/insider/kelsey-grammers-faith-addiction/.

"Neighborhoodscout's Most Dangerous Cities – 2023." NeighborhoodScout, September 5, 2023. https://www.neighborhoodscout.com/blog/top-100dangerous/.

"NET Interest Will Total $10.5 Trillion over the next Decade." Committee for a Responsible Federal Budget. Accessed May 19, 2023. https://www.crfb.org/blogs/net-interest-will-total-105-trillion-over-next-decade/.

Ostrow, Ashira. "Minority Interests, Majority Politics: A Comment on Richard Collins' "Telluride's Tale of Eminent Domain, Home Rule, and Retroactivity." Scholarly Commons at Hofstra Law, 2009. https://scholarlycommons.law.hofstra.edu/cgi/viewcontent.cgi?referer=&httpsredir=1&article=1176&context=faculty_scholarship/.

Parenthood, Planned. "Campaigns." Planned Parenthood. Accessed May 26, 2023. https://www.plannedparenthood.org/about-us/newsroom/campaigns#/.

Parenthood, Planned. "The Maggie Awards Recognize Contributions Made by the Media and Arts That Enhance the Public's Understanding of Reproductive Rights and Health Care Issues." Planned Parenthood. Accessed May 26, 2023. https://www.plannedparenthood.org/about-us/newsroom/campaigns/ppfa-margaret-sanger-award-winners#/.

"Peace through Strength." Ronald Reagan. Accessed October 27, 2023. https://www.reaganlibrary.gov/permanent-exhibits/peace-through-strength/.

"Platform." Libertarian Party, June 1, 2022. https://www.lp.org/platform/.

Bibliography

"Pope Says He Won't Judge Gay Priests." POLITICO. Accessed August 18, 2023. https://www.politico.com/story/2013/07/pope-francis-gay-priests-094854/.

"Power to the People Plan." My WordPress. Accessed October 27, 2023. https://jillstein.org/power-to-the-people-plan/.

"President Obama Welcomes Gay Marriage Ruling." BBC News. Accessed May 22, 2023. https://www.bbc.com/news/av/world-us-canada-33287079/.

Pruitt-Young, Sharon. "Carl Nassib's Experience Coming out Is Very Different from NFL Players before Him." NPR, June 23, 2021. https://www.npr.org/2021/06/22/1009180945/carl-nassibs-experience-coming-out-is-very-different-from-nfl-players-before-him/.

Republican Governors Associationstated on April 29, Donald Trumpstated on September 27, Glenn Grothmanstated on April 30, Wisconsin Freedom Alliancestated on April 25, Brad Schimelstated on March 12, Tony Eversstated on March 10, Lowell Holtzstated on March 26, et al. "Politifact - Republican Governors Association Says Mayor Tom Barrett's Policies Drove up Unemployment 27 Percent in Milwaukee." @politifact. Accessed October 27, 2023. https://www.politifact.com/factchecks/2012/apr/11/republican-governors-association/republican-governors-association-says-mayor-tom-ba/.

Robinson, Bryan. "Christian Athletes: Pointing Others to Jesus through Sports." 316Tees, January 17, 2022. https://www.316tees.com/blogs/316/christian-athletes#/.

Same sex marriage states [updated May 2023]. Accessed August 24, 2023. https://worldpopulationreview.com/state-rankings/same-sex-marriage-states/.

"Sexually Transmitted Infections (STIs)." World Health Organization. Accessed May 23, 2023. https://www.who.int/news-room/fact-sheets/detail/sexually-transmitted-infections-(stis)/.

Solimeo, Luiz Sérgio. "Pope Francis: 'If I See the Gospel in a Sociological Way Only, Yes, I Am a Communist, and So Too Is Jesus.'" The American TFP, December 19, 2022. https://www.tfp.org/pope-francis-if-i-see-the-gospel-in-a-sociological-way-only-yes-i-am-a-communist-and-so-too-is-jesus/.

Sports, USA TODAY. "Michelle Obama: Michael Sam Is an 'Inspiration to All.'" The Indianapolis Star, February 10, 2014. https://www.indystar.com/story/sports/2014/02/10/michelle-obama-openly-gay-football-player-michael-sam-is-inspiration/5364653/.

"State Family Planning Funding Restrictions." Guttmacher Institute, May 4, 2023. https://www.guttmacher.org/state-policy/explore/state-family-planning-funding-restrictions/.

"Tax Rates - 1984 to Present." Tax Rates - 1984 to Present. Accessed October 27, 2023. https://city.milwaukee.gov/assessor/data/TaxRates1984to-Presen725/.

Taylor, Danielle. "Same-Sex Couples Are More Likely to Adopt or Foster Children." Census.gov, October 8, 2021. https://www.census.gov/library/stories/2020/09/fifteen-percent-of-same-sex-couples-have-children-in-their-household.html.

Tea party. Accessed May 24, 2023. https://teaparty.org/about-us/.

"The 0th Article of the US Constitution." National Constitution Center – constitutioncenter.org. Accessed May 19, 2023. https://constitutioncenter.org/the-constitution/preamble/.

"The Pledge of Allegiance - the U.S. Constitution Online." The Pledge of Allegiance - The U.S. Constitution Online - USConstitution.net. Accessed May 19, 2023. https://usconstitution.net/pledge.html.

The Straight Way of Grace Ministry, INC. "Women in Islam." The Straight Way of Grace Ministry, INC. Accessed October 27, 2023. https://www.thestraightway.org/usamas-teaching/frequently-asked-questions-and-answers/pages/women-in-islam/.

Torres, Alec. "Cuomo: Pro-Lifers Not Welcome in New York Remark Was 'Distorted.'" National Review, October 10, 2017. https://www.nationalreview.com/corner/cuomo-pro-lifers-not-welcome-new-york-remark-was-distorted-alec-torres/.

Treasury, U.S. Department Of The. "Debt to the Penny." U.S. Treasury Fiscal Data. Accessed May 17, 2023. https://fiscaldata.treasury.gov/datasets/debt-to-the-penny/debt-to-the-penny/.

Tumin, Remy. "Same-Sex Couple Households in U.S. Surpass One Million." The New York Times, December 2, 2022. https://www.nytimes.com/2022/12/02/us/same-sex-households-census.html.

Bibliography

"What Is the Employer Mandate?" healthinsurance.org, February 27, 2023. https://www.healthinsurance.org/glossary/employer-mandate/.

"Where Do Abortion Rights Stand in the World in 2023?" Focus 2030. Accessed August 4, 2023. https://focus2030.org/Where-do-abortion-rights-stand-in-the-world-in-2023/.

"Will Graham Devotion: 4 Ways to Spot False Teaching." Billy Graham Evangelistic Association, May 5, 2023. http://www.billygraham.org/story/will-graham-devotion-4-ways-to-spot-false/.

Willems, Devin. "Furries in Wisconsin Schools? Districts Respond to Alleged 'Furry Protocols.'" WFRV Local 5 - Green Bay, Appleton, April 27, 2022. https://www.wearegreenbay.com/news/local-news/furries-in-wisconsin-schools-districts-respond-to-alleged-furry-protocols/.

Wilson, Craig. "'Feminine Mystique' at 50: Timelessly Revolutionary." USA Today, February 12, 2013. https://www.usatoday.com/story/life/books/2013/02/11/betty-friedan-feminine-mystique-50th-anniversary/1899371/.

"Woke Definition & Meaning." Merriam-Webster. Accessed June 1, 2023. https://www.merriam-webster.com/dictionary/woke/.

Worland, Justin. "John Kerry Says U.S. Should Help Address Climate Damages." Time, October 28, 2022. https://time.com/6225834/john-kerry-loss-and-damage-climate-interview/.

"World Religion Day 2023: History and Significance." cnbctv18.com, January 15, 2023. https://www.cnbctv18.com/world/world-religion-day-2023-history-and-significance-15661981.htm.

Zeigler, Cyd, and Jim Buzinski. "These 61 Current NFL Players, 13 Owners and 9 Head Coaches Support Gay and Bi Athletes." Outsports, October 27, 2022. https://www.outsports.com/2022/10/27/23425352/nfl-gay-bi-players-straight-support-lgbt-rk-russell/.

www.ingramcontent.com/pod-product-compliance
Lightning Source LLC
Chambersburg PA
CBHW052130070526
44585CB00017B/1775